PRAISE FOR *DARK BEYOND DARKNESS*

"Jim Blight and janet Lang have created a tour de force, a cri de coeur, a ringing call to action to jolt an apathetic, if not hostile, audience." —**Mark Garrison**, former U.S. deputy ambassador in Moscow; founding director of the Center for Foreign Policy Development, Brown University

"I'm no historian, but I've reached the age where some of my life's experiences have become history—the Cuban missile crisis of 1962 a case in point. As an eight-year-old in Florida's Orange Country that fall, I, like most of my peers, was buffered from much of the anxiety associated with the crisis. Tacitly, we all knew something was up. We practiced our nuclear war drills daily. We crowded quietly in our cloakrooms while hating the Soviets for cutting into our recess time. We were relieved for all the wrong reasons when the principal's voice crackled the all clear over the intercom. We were not frightened.

"The threat wasn't quite real for me until the night my father, a Marine who saw combat in Korea, exploded after the evening news. He screamed at no one in particular: why couldn't, why wouldn't, why hadn't the most powerful military on the planet already obliterated this very real threat in our neighborhood? We could goddamn be there tomorrow, he said." I then became frightened.

"Dad's earnest but naïve solution, I suspect, was not the minority opinion. *Dark Beyond Darkness* illuminates how complicated the situation in 1962 was and how incredibly lucky the world was to have escaped Armageddon so narrowly. This is not hyperbole. Today, especially, we need to recognize that political platitudes and simplistic reactions to complex situations jeopardize all life on this planet. After reading *Dark Beyond Darkness*, I'm still frightened."

—**James Mercer** teaches mass media and English in Nebraska public high schools since the 1970s; author of poems, essays, and short fiction

"This book builds in intensity, from the first shocking page to the last sober reflection. The sensory material about the impact of the U.S. low-level flights over Cuba is perfect, brilliant. These are true war sounds. It's great to have this dimension in the book. (I'm going to use *Dark Beyond Darkness* in my Indiana University course, 'The Bomb in American Life.') Reading this book in the age of Trump is truly horrifying: the IMAX version of the most dangerous moment in recorded history." —**Edward T. Linenthal**, Indiana University, former editor-in-chief, The Journal of American History.

"Before, during, and following the Cuban missile crisis, the U.S. government, and even leading U.S. scholars of the missile crisis, focused on the crisis as if its core cause (Cuba) did not matter at all beyond serving as a parking lot for missiles. They misunderstood the origins, unfolding, and outcome of the crisis. The task of this passionate, learned, and provocative book is to get us into the minds of those who nearly destroyed our planet to make it more likely that we will not do so now." —**Jorge I. Domínguez**, professor of government, Harvard University

"In this remarkable book two of our foremost scholars of the Cuban missile crisis distill thirty years of research into a penetrating and moving reassessment of the crisis—and an impassioned plea for the abolition of nuclear weapons. It was mostly luck that prevented an unfathomable catastrophe in the fall of 1962, they convincingly argue; can we really count on being so fortunate the next time around?" —**Fredrik Logevall**, professor of international affairs and history, Harvard University; author of the Pulitzer Prize-winning *Embers of War: The Fall of an Empire and the Making of America's Vietnam*

"*Dark Beyond Darkness* is a cry from the heart and from the head. James Blight and janet Lang, leading scholars of the Cuban missile crisis, have written a wake-up call on the dangers of nuclear weapons for citizens of the 21st century. Revisiting the U.S.-Cuban-Soviet stand-off over missiles in Cuba, they document how lucky the world was to escape a nuclear holocaust. No book could be more relevant in a time when the Trump administration prefers military might over diplomacy, and rogue countries like North Korea possess nuclear weapons. Read it, absorb the lessons of history, and act." —**Ambassador Derek Shearer**, Chevalier Professor of Diplomacy; director, McKinnon Center for Global Affairs, Occidental College, Los Angeles

"Jim Blight and janet Lang place Cuba at the center of the Cuban missile crisis in this chilling wake-up call about our complacency with nuclear weapons." —**Bruce Riedel**, adviser to four U.S. presidents, a senior fellow at the Brookings Institution, and director of the Brookings Intelligence Project

"Read this book! Then go outside and soak up the bright sunshine, or the cleansing rain. Inhale deeply the still breathable air. Look at the fields and forests, brimming with life. Notice the clarity of the water you drink. After that, pass the book on to others, so that they too can head out into the fresh air where they will notice and appreciate that they are not withering away from radiation. Those readers living inland will not take for granted our productive, relatively uncontaminated land. Those living near an ocean can note with gratitude that, standing on the shore they aren't staring at fetid fish flesh and green slime. We should never forget: after a nuclear war our babies will die first, then the small children, and finally the elders, whose ballyhooed wisdom alas did not include sufficient attention to the abolition of nuclear weapons. When your number comes up, and you are being vaporized instantly, or dying slowly of radiation poisoning and starvation, few if any will hear your screams of agony.

"Remember that the bomb shelters that have been built for our leaders are not for us. But even those in the shelters will be doomed, once their supplies run out, and they emerge to observe the hideous catastrophe for which they are in part responsible.

"*Dark Beyond Darkness* is scary—really scary—because the scenario at its core—the Cuban missile crisis—is real! It will fill you with gratitude for the world in which we live, and with the conviction to prevent its destruction." —**Sonya Stejskal** teaches world civilization and modern Chinese history at the University of Nebraska at Omaha, fifteen miles from the headquarters of the U.S. Strategic Command (StratCom)

"An immensely valuable book that will be of interest to historians of the Cold War and to ordinary readers who yearn to know how the world managed—just—to escape a nuclear extinction, and why, even decades after that close-call, complacency is not an option." —**Steve Wasserman**, former editor, *Los Angeles Times* Book Review

"In the histories of the current and the past centuries, superpower conflicts have led to deaths mostly in small countries. Only once did one of those conflicts reach world-historical ranks, namely, the missile crisis because its victims would have included those living in big countries. That is why it is remembered—and promptly forgotten. This groundbreaking book addresses the challenge of understanding those in small countries—those who in 1962, and still today, have been on the dark edge of annihilation by nuclear or conventional means." —**Rafael Hernandez**, founder and editor of the magazine *Temas* (*Themes*), published in Havana, Cuba

"Once again, the threat of nuclear war crowds the front pages, and once again James Blight and janet Lang have crafted another indispensable book proving that the lessons of the Cuban missile crisis may hold the key to our current survival—if only we learn them. Using history, psychology and their gifted imaginations, they force us to recognize how precarious is a world with nuclear weapons, and how stunningly lucky we have been to avoid catastrophe. *Dark Beyond Darkness: The Cuban Missile Crisis as History, Warning and Catalyst* is as encouraging as it is terrifying. It encourages us to rid the world of nuclear weapons, and terrifies us with an unforgettable understanding of what happens if we don't." —**Phil Alden Robinson**, screenwriter and director, whose credits include "Field of Dreams," "Sneakers," "Freedom Song," "Band of Brothers," and "The Sum of All Fears"; currently developing a miniseries based on *The Armageddon Letters*, by Blight and Lang

"The authors of this remarkable book do two rare things for the reader: they entertain in this genuinely funny book about Armageddon (!), while they inform deeply. The authors know more about the missile crisis than anyone, having researched it for thirty years, and here make the case in new ways for its pivotal importance in the history of humankind. Blight and Lang gracefully weave together a fabric of scholarship, literature, and memory to provide not merely the facts of this haunting episode, but the broader meaning of nuclear annihilation—which is what was at stake in 1962. They draw on cultural artifacts—everything from Lord Byron to Cormac McCarthy—to brace and explore the meaning of the nuclear peril. And that is a peril, they convincingly remind us, which remains with us today and demands new attention. Their conclusion is powerful: they challenge millennials to recognize the danger and act to abolish nuclear weapons. *Dark Beyond Darkness* should be atop every citizen's reading list." —**John Tirman**, executive director and principal research scientist, Center for International Studies of the Massachusetts Institute of Technology; author of *The Deaths of Others: The Fate of Civilians in America's Wars*

DARK BEYOND DARKNESS

DARK BEYOND DARKNESS

The Cuban Missile Crisis as History, Warning, and Catalyst

James G. Blight and janet M. Lang

Foreword by Matthew Heys

ROWMAN & LITTLEFIELD
Lanham • Boulder • New York • London

Cover, Artwork, Photo Credit

Jacket Artwork and Design: Chloe Batch
Artwork for each of the four parts of the book: Chloe Batch
Authors' picture: Photo-booth sequence by Trevor Hunsberger

Permissions to Reprint

Passages in chapters 1 and 8 are expansions of pieces that originally appeared in *Truthdig*.
Truthdig (www.truthdig.com) grants, in perpetuity, the rights to use the ideas and text developed for Truthdig for the pieces:
The Scream and the Cuban Missile Crisis:
http://www.truthdig.com/arts_culture/item/scream_and_the_cuban_missile_crisis_still_echo_20150501 (posted 1 May 2015)
and
The Goldsboro Incident:
http://www.truthdig.com/report/item/the_goldsboro_incident_how_the_world_might_have_ended_20150623 (posted 23 June 2015)

The epigraph for Part I:
"In a Dark Time," copyright © 1960 by Beatrice Roethke, Administratrix of the Estate of Theodore Roethke; from COLLECTED POEMS by Theodore Reothke. Used by permission of Doubleday, an imprint of the Knopf Doubleday Publishing Group, a division of Penguin Random House LLC. All rights reserved.

Mary Oliver's poem, "The Uses of Sorrow," reprinted in chapter 9.
"The Uses Of Sorrow" *from Thirst* by Mary Oliver, published by Beacon Press, Boston Copyright © 2014 by Mary Oliver, used herewith by permission of the Charlotte Sheedy Literary Agency, Inc.

Quotation from Carl Richards, "the Sketch Guy," along with the accompanying artwork originally appeared in *The New York Times* on March 10, 2014. It is reprinted in chapter 11 with permission of Mr. Richards.

Published by Rowman & Littlefield
A wholly owned subsidiary of The Rowman & Littlefield Publishing Group, Inc.
4501 Forbes Boulevard, Suite 200, Lanham, Maryland 20706
www.rowman.com

Unit A, Whitacre Mews, 26–34 Stannary Street, London SE11 4AB

British Library Cataloguing in Publication Information Available

Library of Congress Cataloging-in-Publication Data

Names: Blight, James G., author. | Lang, janet M., author.
Title: Dark beyond darkness : the Cuban missile crisis as history, warning, and catalyst / James G. Blight and janet M. Lang.
Other titles: Cuban Missile Crisis as history, warning, and catalyst
Description: Lanham, MD : Rowman & Littlefield, [2017] | Includes bibliographical references and index.
Identifiers: LCCN 2017031418 (print) | LCCN 2017049510 (ebook) | ISBN 9781538102008 (Electronic) | ISBN 9781538101995 (cloth : alk. paper)
Subjects: LCSH: Cuban Missile Crisis, 1962. | Nuclear disarmament. | Nuclear warfare—Prevention. | Cuban Missile Crisis, 1962—Influence. | Nuclear crisis control—Case studies.
Classification: LCC E841 (ebook) | LCC E841 .B568 2017 (print) | DDC 972.9106/4—dc23
LC record available at https://lccn.loc.gov/2017031418

∞ ™ The paper used in this publication meets the minimum requirements of American National Standard for Information Sciences—Permanence of Paper for Printed Library Materials, ANSI/NISO Z39.48-1992.

Printed in the United States of America

To "Maximum" Bob McNamara
Friend, teacher, co-author, co-conspirator
June 9, 1916–July 6, 2009
In Memoriam

When he woke in the woods in the dark and the cold of the night he'd reach out to touch the child sleeping beside him. Nights dark beyond darkness the days more gray each one than what had gone before. Like the onset of some cold glaucoma dimming away the world. His hand rose and fell softly with each precious breath. He pushed away the plastic tarpaulin and raised himself in the stinking robes and blankets and looked toward the east for any light but there was none.

—Cormac McCarthy, *The Road* (2006, 3)*

*Cormac McCarthy, *The Road* (New York: Vintage, 2006).

CONTENTS

PART III: DARKEST

PART IV: THE DARKNESS DEFINED AND DEFIED (Nuclear Abolition via the *Black Saturday Manifesto*)

FOREWORD

For those willing to take the risk of opening a book that is hard to put down and harder to forget, *Dark Beyond Darkness* unfolds like a dark mystery where a dangerous artifact of a forgotten kingdom is unearthed by a generation unprepared to cope with it. We begin thinking we are walking familiar terrain. Cuba. Castro. Kennedy—reason triumphing over brinksmanship at the eleventh hour of the thirteenth day. It's the stuff of an ominous movie trailer, but for a film we think is a sequel to a well-worn story. Then nothing is as it seems.

Dark Beyond Darkness is a story about political and strategic miscalculation, to be sure, but it is also and more importantly a story about *the history of the history* of the world's brush with destruction in 1962. It is a story about our refusal to confront in the 21st century what we should have learned in the 20th. It sobers the imagination to realize we are as far removed now from 1962 as those who lived through that eventful October were from Queen Victoria or the Wright Brothers, yet even now more than a half-century later we have barely a functional literacy in the variables that were truly at play. In *Dark Beyond Darkness* those variables are not "hints," they aren't curious detours in the fossil record of the nuclear arms race; they are still with us, still present, still unaddressed at the highest levels of power and unknown in public discourse. Throughout *Dark Beyond Darkness*, almost nothing we think we know turns out to be true. Every time we wait for the airbag to deploy and cushion us with the realization that a particular claim is speculative, or unsupported by the primary source record, or shrouded by government redaction, it remains stubbornly coiled up inside the steering wheel of undeniable fact. We read on. We watch the accident unfold. We see no lessons learned from it.

Written in a style and structured in a way that will appeal to experts and lay readers young and old, and skillfully blending everything from modern literature to accessibly framed primary source intelligence documents and oral histories from participants, *Dark Beyond Darkness* is the text we want our students to carry with them—not just in their backpacks, but in their brains, and not in the spirit of some hackneyed hope that the children of the future address the mistakes of the past. Far from it, *Dark Beyond Darkness* is the book we want to see them arguing about and applying now. It is a powerful work that sits at the intersection of historical scholarship and moral responsibility.

Matthew Heys
2017 Gilder-Lehrman Institute American History Teacher of the Year for Nebraska.
Millard South and Millard West High School, and the University of Nebraska
Omaha, Nebraska
July 17, 2017

AUTHORS' NOTE

10/27/62
Because Luck is Insufficient

On *Black Saturday—October 27, 1962*—leaders in the U.S., Russia, and Cuba came close to blowing up the world. They and we escaped, in good measure, because of luck.

This book is written as an act of resistance—a data-based cry of the heart—to the widely accepted idea that we can live forever with nuclear weapons without another Cuban missile crisis–like event, but this time, one in which our luck runs out and we destroy ourselves irreversibly.

We invite you to join us for a journey into human history's heart of darkness. The *history* gets progressively darker, and the *warning* becomes increasingly dire, chapter by chapter, until the end of chapter 9, where we merge the risk of slower, disastrous climate change with the risk of nuclear Armageddon. In chapters 10 and 11, we summarize our argument, showing why nothing less than the abolition of nuclear weapons will suffice. We are far from the first authors to argue for abolition, but by embedding the argument for abolition in the history of the Cuban missile crisis, we have tried to give the call for nuclear abolition human faces, names, and fears that we hope resonate with your own fears, once you know the facts.

In chapter 12, we reveal how the Cuban missile crisis might serve as a *catalyst* for moving toward the abolition of nuclear weapons. Here is the headline:

10/27/62
Because Luck is Insufficient

We hope that by the time you encounter this tagline again in chapter 12 and the Epilogue, you can begin to use it as a candle to find your way out of this *Dark Beyond Darkness*.

PROLOGUE

ARMAGEDDON IN RETROSPECT

On the Road with Papa & The Boy

[Boy] Are we going to die?
[Papa] Sometime. Not now.
And we're still going south.
Yes.
So we'll be warm.
Yes.
Okay.
Okay what?
Nothing. Just okay.

—Cormac McCarthy, *The Road* (2006)[1]

You are about to watch the 2009 post-apocalyptic movie, *The Road*, a film by John Hillcoat, adapted from the 2006 Pulitzer Prize-winning novel by the American writer Cormac McCarthy.[2] The film has two principal characters, a father and his son, who wander the East Coast of the United States following a catastrophic nuclear war. Although the book and film have tender moments between Papa & The Boy, the film and book are overwhelmingly grim, frightening, and very sad—sad because life on planet earth will not survive, nothing grows, and the only living creatures are a few people who have either found stashes of canned food or have engaged in cannibalism, or both. Papa & The Boy, who repudiate cannibalism, live in constant fear of being captured and eaten. They inhabit a living hell that is trending toward nothingness.

You have watched the movie. You are moved by the events it portrays and the destroyed world in which the characters are forced to eke out their pitiful existence. The movie ends, the credits roll. But instead of putting your coat on and heading out into the lobby of the theater, you are sucked, like dust into a vacuum cleaner, into the world you have just encountered vicariously in *The Road*. You scream, you protest, but the unthinkable is happening. You are forced to join Papa & The Boy on the road to nowhere, trying to avoid cannibals and stay alive without resorting to cannibalism. Somehow or other, you have not just *gone* to a horror movie, you have begun to *inhabit* that horror movie. The virtual has become literal. Everything you depend on in your daily life is gone: no family, no cell phone, no Internet, no TV or radio, no infrastructure, no medical assistance or drugs, no cars, no renewable food supplies, no friends, no schools, no books, no nothing—nothing but fear and hunger and cold. You are living like a wild animal. You will not live for long. And when you are dead, there will be no record that you ever existed.

This is the mindset for reading this book: *begin with the endpoint, with what we all want to avoid, which is nuclear Armageddon.*[3]

OCTOBER 1962

"A Graveyard Smash"

We invite you to time travel and space travel with us. It is October 1962, and we are on the Caribbean island of Cuba. The Russians try to sneak nuclear missiles into their new ally, Cuba. But the U.S. discovers the missiles as they are being assembled and orders the Russians to remove them, or else! The Russians are defiant and tell the U.S. to mind its own business. The outraged and fiery Cubans prepare for war with the Americans, who have assembled a huge attack and invasion force near the island. The stage is set for the *Cuban missile crisis.*[4]

Ironically, the number one pop song in America the week of October 16, 1962, two weeks before Halloween, is a novelty song by Bobby Pickett and the CryptKickers. The song is a parody called "Monster Mash," sung and spoken by Pickett in a voice that is a near perfect impersonation of Boris Karloff, who played Frankenstein's monster in several films. The fictional monster, like actual nuclear weapons, was created by human ingenuity but has the power to destroy those who created it. The dance, called "the monster mash," according to the faux Karloff/Frankenstein narrator of the song, "is a graveyard smash." It's very funny, a ghoulish delight, perfect for the run-up to Halloween.[5] But the graveyard being unwittingly contemplated just prior to Halloween by the U.S., Russia, and Cuba is the entirety of planet earth. It is the un-funniest prospect imaginable.

On the afternoon of October 16, 1962, the New York Yankees beat the San Francisco Giants 1–0 to win their twentieth World Series. The night before, the U.S. president John F. Kennedy cleared out time on his schedule so he could watch the game. The next day, he forgets about the game entirely.[6] By the time the game is ending, around 6:00 p.m. Eastern time, Kennedy has discussed with his advisers whether to authorize an air attack against the Russian nuclear installations in Cuba. He decides to delay the decision until the following day. Kennedy and his advisers did not know what we now know, which is that a U.S. air attack on the Russian missile sites, and a follow-up invasion of the island, would likely have escalated to global nuclear Armageddon. Hundreds of millions of people would have perished around the world. It would have been the end of human civilization as it had evolved to that moment.

ARMAGEDDON IN RETROSPECT

During the last weekend of October 1962, the end of the world as we know it was actually underway. It began in the minds and calculations of Cuban and Russian leaders *in Havana.* That the beginning did not lead to the end was due mostly to luck.

7,500,000 Martyrs?

Armageddon—the last battle, as described in the biblical book of Revelation, chapter 16, verse 16—began the only way it could begin: leaders, citizens, and allies on the island of Cuba began to ask, not how do we avoid Armageddon, but since Armageddon is inevitable and imminent, how can we do the honorable thing—how can we ensure that our sacrifice is not for nothing, and that our destruction is redeemed by our martyrdom?

Cuban leaders were willing to pay this price for the total destruction of their enemy, the United States of America. Psychologically, many in Cuba began to imagine the post-Armageddon world that they themselves would never see. World socialism would triumph. World capitalism would perish. And "Cubita" ("Little Cuba") would live forever in history as the country that sacrificed its 7.5 million inhabitants for the great cause of socialism. That we regard this aspiration and expectation as delusional and horrifying now, more than a half-century after the crisis, does not render it any less real and compelling to those who experienced it in real time.

How Lucky Can You Get?

We now know that the principal reason the psychologically vivid Armageddon imagined by the inhabitants of Cuba did not morph into the physical destruction of human society was *plain dumb luck!* Not *only* luck was involved. The three leaders—Fidel Castro, John F. Kennedy, and Nikita Khrushchev—were, at the last minute, resourceful in reversing the downward spiral toward the apocalypse that they had unwittingly initiated. But they were more lucky than clever. Kennedy and Khrushchev were mostly clueless about how close nuclear war actually was. Neither knew that the Cubans and Russians in Cuba had already begun to seek their martyrdom rather than trying to prevent a war they felt was not in their power to avoid.

Kennedy was under tremendous pressure to attack Cuba by air and invade by sea. If Kennedy had ordered that attack, Russian commanders in Cuba would have retaliated with short- and medium-range nuclear weapons; with Cuba destroyed, Khrushchev would have been under irresistible pressure to invade West Berlin. Had West Berlin been seized, World War III would have commenced.

The War that Didn't Quite Happen

The CIA believed that Russian nuclear warheads never reached the island. They were wrong. By late October 1962, there were 162 nuclear warheads on the island, which in the event of war would have been installed in short-range and medium-range missiles and aimed at U.S. targets. Much of the U.S. invasion force would have been nuked in their transport ships at sea. U.S. Marines who had escaped detection would have been incinerated at their landing areas on the beaches of the north coast of Cuba. The U.S. Naval Base at

Guantanamo Bay, in eastern Cuba, would have been nuked just after the first U.S. bombs exploded on the beaches of Cuba, instantly killing the U.S. troops stationed there. Any use of nuclear weapons by Russian-Cuban forces in Cuba would likely have elicited a nuclear response from the U.S. on Cuba that would have fulfilled the prophecy of Armageddon with which the Cubans had been living. Any U.S. nuclear attack on Cuba would likely have been met with a Russian nuclear response, probably in Europe, where the Russians were dominant, just as the Americans were dominant in the Caribbean. The nuclear war in Europe, as devastating as it would have been, would only have been preliminary to all-out nuclear war between the U.S. and Russia, completely devastating both countries and the world.

IMAGINE THAT . . .

How to Take Personal Possession of the Cuban Missile Crisis

We invite you to personalize the closest call to Armageddon with an analogy. Imagine that you are walking home from school or work through a familiar and usually empty intersection, as you and a friend text each other furiously, back and forth. Suddenly, you hear the roar of a plane overhead, so you look up. As you are looking up, you find yourself staring at the headlights of a bus bearing down on you with its horn blaring and brakes screaming. You leap out of the way, just before the bus would have crushed you. On the sidewalk, you respond to those asking if you need help that you are fine, that you just have a few scratches.

But you are not fine, not even close to fine. You begin shaking as you continue your walk home. You begin fighting back tears. You begin to see the afterimage of the headlights of the bus getting larger and larger until they seem so close you can touch them, and you imagine that you can smell the burning brakes and tires skidding on the street. For several weeks, you avoid that intersection altogether. Gradually, as time passes, the effect of what seems in retrospect like a very near death experience wears off. You go back to texting while you walk. But you never walk across an intersection again without at least giving a quick peek left and right, just in case. For you could be dead. In fact, you would be dead, if it hadn't been for that noisy airplane that caused you to look up and, incidentally, to see the bus that was just about to kill you.

This is the psychology of the catastrophic near miss. Maybe you narrowly escaped a head-on car accident. Maybe your oncologist told you that the tumor you feared was malignant and inoperable, and thus fatal, is in fact benign and manageable. Maybe you fell to the floor and, just before passing out, concluded that you were having a fatal heart attack, when in reality your fainting spell turns out to be caused by having skipped breakfast. Maybe you open an email from someone with whom you are in love, convinced that after an argument the night before this is it, that the relationship is over and you will never be happy again, whereas the email actually contains your lover's apology and pledge of everlasting love and devotion. And so on. In the immediate aftermath of such events, we find it impossible to contain our emotions. Having the bejesus scared out of us, only to discover that all is well, can even lead to resolutions never to pass that way again (figuratively speaking): to drive more carefully, to take better care of ourselves, to never skip breakfast again, or to resolve to never say a discouraging word to a lover again.

These psychological reactions to a catastrophic near miss resemble the feeling shared by Kennedy and Khrushchev after what seemed to them like a nearly miraculous escape from Armageddon. Just as you would have been (say) cautious about your texting venues after your near collision with the bus, the two leaders emerged from the crisis determined to move toward nuclear abolition, as part of a strategy to begin to tamp down the Cold War. But JFK was murdered in Dallas on November 22, 1963, and Khrushchev was ousted in a coup on October 15, 1964. Those who replaced them had virtually no responsibility in the Cuban missile crisis, and thus did not learn from it the abolition imperative or the reasons behind it, as Kennedy and Khrushchev had. This was the greatest missed opportunity of the nuclear age, the disastrous side effect of an assassin's bullets and a political coup.

THE TRUTH ABOUT OCTOBER 1962

Stranger, Scarier, More Dangerous, and Much Weirder Than Fiction

The claims we make in this book may be new to you. We refer to propositions such as: the world as your parents or grandparents knew it in October 1962 nearly ended in a spasm of nuclear Armageddon; that an outcome none of the leaders in the three involved countries wanted nearly happened anyway; and that this very near brush with Armageddon more than a half-century ago holds lessons for us now in the early 21st century. You may be inclined to think "Oh, come on, authors, get real. That's ridiculous."

Sorry, but it's the truth, as we will demonstrate throughout this book.[7]

When we began our research on the crisis more than thirty years ago, our findings about the Cuban missile crisis at first seemed really weird even to us. We offer you the same advice we had to give ourselves nearly every day as our research unfolded, and as the facts seemed eventually to point overwhelmingly to the truth of the claims in the previous paragraph: reexamine your reasoning about just how misinformed and misguided leaders can be about one another. The unthinkable came within a hair's breadth of occurring due to the toxic intermingling in the crisis of human fallibility and the availability of nuclear weapons. We can't fix human fallibility. This is why we must move as swiftly and safely as possible to a world with zero nuclear weapons. Otherwise (sooner or later) it is *The Road*, for real.

PART I

DARK

In a dark time, the eye begins to see.

—Theodore Roethke, "In a Dark Time" (1961)[1]

In the dark days of the U.S.-Russian Cold War, each side believed that the other sought world domination, and that the enemy might actually risk catastrophic nuclear war to achieve its ambition. Each was wrong about the other. Each was blind to the fear of annihilation that drove both sides in the Cold War. The fear-driven confrontation reached its darkest hour in the October 1962 Cuban missile crisis, in which the Russians put nuclear missiles in Cuba, the U.S. threatened war if they were not removed, and the Russians dug in their heels. The world was gripped by fear and trembling, as Washington and Moscow moved their pieces on the Cold War chessboard. The Cuban and the Russian forces in Cuba prepared for Armageddon, in which they believed Cuba would be totally destroyed. Unbelievably, neither Washington nor Moscow understood the mood in Cuba. The forces on the island acted provocatively, believing they had nothing to lose. Nuclear war was barely avoided. The world was very lucky.

Unfortunately, the history of the crisis was for many years written by American writers as if it were a geopolitical "Super Bowl," with winners, losers, and players who merely watched from the sidelines. The following three chapters provide brief but authoritative accounts of:

- *What almost happened: Armageddon (chapter 1)*
- *What didn't happen: a U.S. victory/Russian defeat (chapter 2)*
- *What actually happened: a very, very close call to the end of the world as it was known in October 1962 (chapter 3)*

1

SHIT (ALMOST) HAPPENED IN OCTOBER 1962

The Struggle to Avoid Armageddon Involves the Struggle of Memory Against Forgetting[1]

Quaking with angst—I felt the great scream in nature.

—Edvard Munch, on the night he first imagined *The Scream* (1892)[2]

And the most terrifying question of all may be just how much horror the human mind can stand and still maintain a wakeful, staring, unrelenting sanity.

—Stephen King, *Pet Sematary* (1983)[3]

ARMAGEDDON DEADENED

Can a Painting of a Screaming Face Be Worth 119 Million USD? (Answer: "Yes")

On May 2, 2012, Edvard Munch's famous painting *The Scream* was auctioned by Sotheby's in New York for $119,922,500. According to Sotheby's, the sale "marked a new world record" for the price of a work of art sold at an auction.[4]

$119 million and change for a picture of the distorted face of a screaming individual. Why? Was it Munch's capacity to convey terror on canvas—was it because this work of art is the scariest thing ever painted? Or was it perhaps because Edvard Munch is regarded as the greatest artist of all time—better than Michelangelo, better than Picasso, than Van Gogh, than Vermeer, better than *anybody*, thus warranting the more than $119 million investment to acquire a piece of his work? Or: was it because Munch's personal backstory is as bizarre perhaps as the image in *The Scream*? You may think: Who knows? Maybe he went mad as he was painting it. Or did Munch go completely off the rails and murder someone while he was painting the image? Might the victim in fact have been the very person whose face is distorted in the painting? Did any of these or similarly sensational connections between the painting and the painter greatly increase the value of a painting, for reasons that have nothing to do with whatever might be the intrinsic worth of the art?

The answer to all of the above is "no." *The Scream* fetched such an astronomically high price primarily because you, and we, and a high proportion of the people on this planet, have probably seen more images of Munch's *The Scream* than of any other image that began as a serious work of art. *The Scream* has become one of the most recognizable images of Western pop culture, along with images of Elvis, Marilyn Monroe, Homer Simpson, SpongeBob, Lady Di, and other former or present celebrities, either actual or virtual. However this happened, you are unlikely to encounter anyone anytime soon who is unfamiliar with the image. Go ahead: try to find someone above the age of, say, twelve, who has never seen an image of *The Scream*.

One way to determine how embedded an image is in pop culture is to estimate what we call its "merch rating." That's "merch" for "merchandise": how many people are wearing the image, are drinking coffee from a mug with the image on it, are giving their children cuddly dolls with the image on them, and so on? The merch rating of *The Scream* is huge, more or less correlated with the sky-high price paid for it in the Sotheby's auction. The image is firmly ensconced in the zone of sugar-coated pop culture, cohabiting space with Disney, the Muppets, and Marvel Comics. One can purchase *Scream* underwear, compression pants, socks, stuffed toys, and much more. A quick cruise on the web yields all manner of fanciful adaptations of people with *Scream*-ish faces: from Barack Obama to Santa Claus to Che Guevara to Mickey Mouse, from Mona Lisa to Barbie, and many more.[5]

ARMAGEDDON REALIZED

Can a Painting of a Screaming Face Represent the End of the World? (Answer: "Yes")

Years ago, we decided to adopt *The Scream* as a pictorial shorthand for conveying to our students the horror we believe everyone should feel when recalling the Cuban missile crisis.[6] The major powers—Cuba's U.S. enemy and its Russian ally—*both* ignored Cuba's concerns. Instead, they played the chess game of superpower geopolitics as if Cuba was only a bit player, and together they inadvertently convinced Cuba's leaders that Cuba was doomed and that its doom might be redeemed by an all-out Russian nuclear attack on the U.S., an act that, if it had happened, would have killed a significant portion of the roughly 190 million citizens of the U.S. (in 1962). Looking back, we should also let out a metaphorical scream, no matter where we live. Not only would the United States of America have been destroyed but human civilization is unlikely to have survived such a Russian attack and the predictable and devastating U.S. response. Our fellow human beings nearly blew up the world in October 1962, even though such an outcome was no one's objective and was in no one's interest.

The Scream seemed to us to come closer than any other image to conveying something of what it must have felt like to have the fate of the earth on one's shoulders at the moment of nuclear truth. *The Scream* is without words; it is beyond words, just as the sense of impending Armageddon was beyond any words uttered by leaders during the crescendo of the crisis on the last weekend of October 1962. So we adopted *The Scream* as a kind of anti-mascot, a symbol to make you shake in your boots and keep a light on in the room when you consider both the potential horror of the Cuban missile crisis and the threat of nuclear extinction we still face now in the 21st century. You want horror? we asked ourselves. Okay, we'll show you horror, in this single image of raw, unvarnished horror: *The Scream*. At last we had found a way to inject something elemental, something beyond mere words like *apocalypse* or *Armageddon*—something that addresses more directly than is possible in prose the emotional reality that accompanied an up-close and personal confrontation with Armageddon.

But we were wrong, dead wrong. We soon discovered that we had doubled the trouble we were having bringing our students' understanding of the Cuban missile crisis into line with what we, and our colleagues, had discovered about the crisis. Hardly any of our students thought *The Scream* was frightful. Instead, they told us they thought it was cute, funny, weirdly cool—anything but scary. *Ach!!*

Cute, funny, and cool was, to put it mildly, not what Munch intended. The artist was a withdrawn, somewhat morbid, obsessive individual. The available evidence suggests that in *The Scream* (all four versions of it), the artist meant to convey some portion of the cosmic angst and horror he felt during a particularly terrifying experience. *The Scream* was never meant to be ironical, or funny, or any of the other variations that are partly responsible for its high merch rating. Munch wasn't kidding. He meant for the painting to convey pure horror, the kind of horror Stephen King seeks to produce in his novels: primitive, preverbal, preternatural fright.

On January 22, 1892, Munch recorded in his journal a horrifying experience. In 1895, he turned his journal entry into a poem, which he hand lettered onto the frame beneath one of the four basic versions of *The Scream*:

I was walking along the road with two friends
The Sun was setting—the Sky turned blood-red.
And I felt a wave of Sadness—I paused
tired to Death—Above the blue-black
Fjord and City Blood and Flaming tongues hovered
My friends walked on—I stayed
behind—quaking with Angst—I
felt the great Scream in Nature.[7]

Together with the painting, we find this apocalyptic ode fully the terrifying equal of representations of Armageddon in our own time, such as Bob Dylan's song "A Hard Rain's A-Gonna Fall" (1963), the TV film *The Day After* (1983), Cormac McCarthy's *The Road* (2006), and many songs deriving from the heavy-metal tradition of the past thirty or so years. Munch's painting and poem represent his attempt to render visually and verbally the end of everything—Armageddon. We are sure that Edvard Munch would have screamed if he had known that his allegory of the apocalypse was to become a preferred pattern on spandex pants.

ARMAGEDDON KITSCHIFIED

How Much Horror Can the Human Mind Stand? (Answer: "Not Enough")

Milan Kundera famously wrote in *The Book of Laughter and Forgetting* (1980): "The struggle of man against power is the struggle of memory against forgetting."[8] Kundera, a Czech refugee writing in Paris, intended to counter communist propaganda, the heroic stories of how so much Communist Party-mandated human suffering is actually all to the good in advancing the interests of an abstraction called "the people."

What is forgotten? Chiefly, it is the cruelty and the suffering: the mindless cruelty of war machines and their consenting human tools, together with the unspeakably despondent cries of loss and suffering from the victims. Instead, memories are *kitschified*. Some believe that Kundera's concept of *kitsch* is vague and obscure. But in a passage of crystalline clarity in his most famous novel, *The Unbearable Lightness of Being*, he defines it this way:

> The fact that until recently the word "shit" appeared in print as s—has nothing to do with moral considerations. You can't claim that shit is immoral, after all! The objection to shit is a metaphysical one. The daily defecation session is daily proof of the unacceptability of Creation. . . . The aesthetic ideal of the categorical agreement with being is a world in which shit is denied and everyone acts as though it did not exist. This aesthetic ideal is called kitsch. . . . Kitsch is the absolute denial of shit, in both the literal and the figurative senses of the word; kitsch excludes everything from its purview which is essentially unacceptable in human existence.[9]

The shit of historical reality becomes the doo-doo of contemporary fantasy. History is transformed into a variant of reality TV. Reenactors of the Battle of Gettysburg mistake the kitsch in which they are involved for the actual Battle of Gettysburg. The most frequent viewers of the History Channel give the channel its nickname, "the Hitler Channel." Obsessed with the panorama of Nazi parades and Hitler's sweating, screaming gyrations, they conveniently ignore the incalculable suffering inflicted by the Nazis, in the face of which a better response than watching films of Hitler and the Luftwaffe would be a meditative, silent remembrance of the victims of Hitler and his cronies along with taking a vow of tolerance toward those we call "others."

Modern metaphors of this struggle of memory of mass slaughter against forgetting are often the place-names of the locales where the tragedies occurred. These include Hiroshima and Nagasaki, Auschwitz, My Lai, the Somme, the Cambodian Killing Fields, Halabja, Rwanda, and all too many other locales. Those who embrace the transformation of such physical spaces into metaphors for human cruelty mean to inspire revulsion at the acts of cruelty; and empathy with the victims. It's about remembering a portion of the past accurately, concretely, in ways that engage not only the intellect but also the emotions. It's about inducing outrage.

But outrage is not enough. The hope is that outrage will fuel an infusion of energy. Those who remember have the responsibility to do something, however modest, to share the greater meaning of their experience, often stated simply as "Never again!" Never again shall nuclear weapons be aimed at defenseless populations (Hiroshima and Nagasaki in August 1945); never again shall genocide against an entire people be permitted (Auschwitz, 1940–1945, Cambodian Killing Fields, 1975–1979); never again shall defenseless civilians be slaughtered at close range by those prosecuting a war (My Lai, March 1968); never again shall soldiers be sent by their commanders to meaningless mass slaughter simply because a war plan calls for it (the Somme, July–November 1916); never again shall chemical weapons be used against helpless civilians as a tool of terror and intimidation (Halabja, March 1988); never again shall a majority ethnic group slaughter a minority ethnic group (Rwanda, 1994). Only one of these exhortations has, so far, been inviolate: nuclear weapons have not been used since the August 1945 bombing of two Japanese cities by the U.S. Army Air Force.

The struggle of memory against forgetting is also a critical component in the struggle to prevent nuclear Armageddon. The supreme nuclear danger of the October 1962 Cuban missile crisis has been largely forgotten, even though it was easily the closest brush in recorded history with Armageddon—an all-out nuclear war that would likely have ultimately left behind, in the telling phrase of Jonathan Schell, "a republic of insects and grass," if that.[10]

The kitschification of Munch's art and the amnesia regarding what almost happened in October 1962 are connected. The Cuban missile crisis was scary as hell to the leaders who (barely) engineered the great escape of October 1962. It should be scary to us as well. But mostly it's not, because most of us never think about it, except during anniversaries of the event divisible by at least ten without remainder, and in such pop culture icons as the TV series *Mad Men* and the popular fantasy movie *X-Men: First Class*, and in video games containing "Cuban missile crisis" elements, with commandos swooping around Cuba, offing bad guys and defusing nukes. As Munch's *Scream* is now gauzy and campy, the missile crisis is now a game.[11]

THE OCTOBER 1962 REALITY HORROR PICTURE SHOW

When the Shit Came "That Close" *to Hitting the Fan*

Picture the following image in your mind's eye as you read this book. It is a thumb and forefinger brought so near to each other that they almost, but not quite, touch. As the thumb and forefinger nearly touch, a voice says, "That close. We came *that close* to nuclear war in the Cuban missile crisis." Significant decision-makers in the Cuban missile crisis, including Fidel Castro and the American Defense Secretary Robert McNamara, used this image when trying to convey how close the world was to nuclear annihilation in October 1962. As they spoke these or similar words in our presence, the pupils in their eyes dilated, their voices cracked, heavy with barely managed emotion. That was their psychological reality of that moment. In their minds, in their premonitions, the shit was about to hit the fan.[12]

The struggle to recover the memory of what actually happened, and what was actually about to happen, in the Cuban missile crisis requires us to confront two of its most powerful myths: first, that since "nothing" happened, we should pay little attention to it; and second, that what people like us claim *might* have happened, indeed was *about* to happen, strikes many as too outlandish, too ridiculous, to ever happen. Really, they ask: How can we believe that otherwise rational leaders were about to instigate a nuclear war that probably would have constituted a nuclear Armageddon? Such an outcome is in no one's interest. So they wouldn't have done it. For these reasons, with each passing year, the risk of a nuclear catastrophe in October 1962 seems increasingly remote. Nothing happened. Nothing was about to happen. End of story.

This grotesque underestimation of the danger in the Cuban missile crisis may be an honest mistake, caused overwhelmingly by focusing on Moscow and Washington to the exclusion of Havana. The event has come down through more than a half-century of history as the moment when the world's two biggest bullies stared each other down in a schoolyard called Cuba. These Big Guys were the United States and Russia, the nuclear superpowers, who tested each other's resolve but had not the slightest intention of starting a war—something that each understood about the other even in the early stages of the crisis. Havana and in fact all of Cuba is regarded as little more than a jungle-covered parking lot for Russian missiles. The Russians parked them for a while; then under U.S. pressure, they unparked them and returned them to Russia from whence they came. Havana had a non-speaking, walk-on role in the drama. Since the crisis, most historians have followed suit, ignoring what the Cubans said at the time, and ever since, about the event.

This is an example of what the American philosopher William James referred to as "a certain blindness in human beings, the blindness with which we all are afflicted in regard to the feelings of people different from ourselves."[13] The historical record of the Cold War suggests that it is almost impossible for great and powerful countries to empathize with—to put themselves in the shoes of—smaller, weaker countries, which have no global capabilities, and which are by comparison with the great powers poor, weak, and insignificant. John F. Kennedy, Nikita Khrushchev, and their subordinates ignored the Cubans in the event, and most historians have ignored them in retrospect, even now, when a great deal has been revealed about what was happening on the island of Cuba as those on the island prepared for what they believed would be Armageddon.

Here is the highlight film of what Washington and Moscow *missed* about Cuba between April 1961 (the failed Bay of Pigs invasion of Cuba) and October 1962 (the missile crisis). As you read it, you might repeat to yourself occasionally: "How in the world did Moscow and Washington miss all this?"

Such was the bubble of arrogance and ignorance shared by Washington and Moscow, that neither noticed that immediately after the failed invasion of CIA-backed Cuban exiles in April 1961, Fidel Castro and others in the Cuban leadership began speaking and writing about the imminence of Armageddon. Concluding that Washington was determined to destroy their revolution, Fidel and his associates began preparing the Cuban people for the final battle. Their position never wavered. It went like this: the U.S. will destroy us; we will resist, we will not cave in, no matter what; we will make the U.S. pay as big a price as possible, effectively martyring Cuba for socialism. Repeat: for the *eighteen months* prior to the U.S. discovery of the missiles, the Cuban leaders and the Cuban people prepared for their total destruction at the hands of the Americans.

So try to imagine the surprise of the Cuban leadership when Moscow offered to put nukes into Cuba. Khrushchev told them he wanted to save Cuba, to protect Cuba. But the Cubans believed that far from saving Cuba, Russian nuclear weapons in Cuba would be discovered by the Americans, who would be furious at the Russian deception, following which the long-expected massive attack by Washington on Cuba would commence. Fidel and his associates believed the attacks would begin with massive bombing of the nuclear weapons sites before proceeding to other targets on the island, culminating in a full-scale invasion of the island. As Fidel et al. saw it, Russian nukes in Cuba did nothing but increase the speed and enthusiasm with which the Kennedy administration would launch its expected attack on the island. The nukes made Cuba an even more appealing target for a U.S. attack than it was before the nukes arrived.

Khrushchev rejected the Cubans' point of view. He said, in effect, "No, no, you young, ignorant allies, we Russians will protect you with these weapons, which we will install without the Americans finding out until they are ready to fire, after which they dare not move against Cuba." The Cubans laughed. Not find out? More than once they pointed out to their new Soviet big brothers that Cuba was a mere ninety miles south of Key West, Florida. They urged Khrushchev to install the weapons publicly and announce to the world that the deployment was for Cuban defense and that those who object should mind their own business. The deployment, as the Cubans saw it, was legal and entirely normal. The Russians rejected their plea for transparency, informing the Cubans in various condescending statements that they were naïve and that the Russians knew better. Alas, the Cubans got it right.

To the Cubans, the most interesting feature of becoming the world's most rapidly proliferated nuclear state in history was this: when the Americans attacked, the possibility existed of using the attack as the signal that Moscow should launch a nuclear attack at the U.S., using both the Russian nuclear missiles and airplanes on the island and those based elsewhere. Washington never picked this up, even though the Cubans discussed it frequently in public. Maybe that's not so odd given that U.S.-Cuban relations at that point had ceased to exist and that Fidel Castro's government had kicked the Americans off the island.

But the inability of the *Russians* to pick up this message from their Cuban ally is truly remarkable. They were, in effect, placing their nuclear missiles in an environment and among people who expected to be destroyed and who yearned to redeem their martyrdom with a Soviet nuclear strike against the U.S. In retrospect, we can say the Cubans were incredibly naïve, that they were a bunch of young, hot-headed guerrilla fighters who did not understand the realities of the nuclear age. They had no idea that a Russian attack of hundreds of nuclear weapons aimed at the U.S. could also lead, via U.S. retaliation, to the annihilation of the Russians and perhaps everyone else on the planet as well. They didn't understand that the only way to martyr Cuba might be to also martyr Russia, which was something the Russians thought was lunacy, which it clearly was since Cuban martyrdom would have had no purpose. The socialist world as well as capitalist world would have been destroyed, rendering "martyrdom" pointless. So, yes, it is absolutely true that the Cubans didn't understand what they were getting into when they accepted the Russian missiles. But the incapacity of Washington and especially Moscow to credit anything the Cubans said or did with regard to the nukes is stunning and decisive in making the crisis so dangerous.[14]

As Washington and Moscow went sleepwalking toward the nuclear brink, Havana embraced what they believed was its inevitable fate: obliteration. When, inspired by the Cubans, the Russians shot down the U-2 on the morning of Saturday, October 27, the war nearly began. Kennedy's hotheads wanted to bomb Cuba immediately. Khrushchev's hotheads, sensing that the Americans might act, wanted to preempt by attacking West Berlin. The hawks in both camps were barely beaten back. The Cuban gunners continued to fire at every U.S. low-level plane overflying the island but failed to bring any of them down. If they had shot down one or more of the U.S. reconnaissance planes, an attack on Cuba would have been likely, a Russian response would likely have been forthcoming on the island, and that response would probably have included, among other actions, nuking the U.S. base at Guantanamo Bay. Armageddon would have followed in short order.

Once again, picture this: we came "*that close*" to nuclear war in the Cuban missile crisis.

BACK TO MUNCH

Let's Get Our Shit Together, Shall We?

Several recent short films suggest ways in which our Cuban missile crisis anti-mascot, Munch's *Scream* image, can still profoundly disturb us, disorient us. It may even lead us, perhaps, to experience some of the terror Munch says he felt the night in 1892 when he was first visited by the terror he would render as *The Scream*, along with its accompanying poem. A roughly one-minute film produced in 2012 has a voice-over from Munch's account of the night when the *Scream* first appeared to him. (It was used as an ad by Sotheby's prior to their sale of the painting.) It is slick and highly commercial, but it works its dark magic in spite of the fact that it is an invitation to bid on the painting, or (for those lacking 119 million USD or so in spare change) at least watch the May 2, 2012, Sotheby's auction live online.[15]

The Romanian animator and filmmaker Sebastian Cosor has lately led a kind of "back to Munch" movement. Three examples of his creative revisioning of Munch for our time are: a three-minute-plus film that uses Pink Floyd's

"The Great Gig in the Sky" as a ghostly audio backdrop, as two animated figures walk and talk about fear of death as they cross a bridge over a fjord. They pass, without noticing (or barely noticing), a disturbing, writhing Munchian *Scream*-like creature.[16] Cosor has also produced a spooky, disturbing two-minute film in which the figures cross a bridge over a frozen fjord. They also pass the disturbing, writhing *Scream*-like creature, who is wearing, believe it or not, a Santa Claus hat.[17] There is also a shortened version of Cosor's original animated feature, without the dialogue, but with an additional programmed vocal "Scream to Us."[18] We think of this as the silent movie version (with music, but without dialogue) of Cosor's "talkie." All three versions effectively make their viewers uncomfortable.

FROM A SCREAM TO THE ABOLITION IMPERATIVE

Write a "Pre-Mortem" of Armageddon (and Keep Rewriting It)

Let's combine the missile crisis and Munch's *Scream*. In metaphorical terms: Were Kennedy's and Khrushchev's mouths wide open in unutterable terror, like Munch's screamer? (Fidel's would have been wide open in anger at having been ignored, set up for destruction, and denied Cuba's chance for socialist immortality by a nuclear attack on the U.S., authorized by Khrushchev.) Still metaphorically: Were the arms of leaders in Washington and Moscow writhing as if to the unearthly vocals of Clare Torry on Pink Floyd's "The Great Gig in the Sky?" Were their eyes figuratively bulging out at the very real prospect of Armageddon? Did they feel themselves chained to a runaway train whose destination was doomsday? Did they feel the "great scream" felt by Munch? The answer, respecting the limits of metaphor and the differing circumstances and eras, is *absolutely yes!* Munch felt his world exploding and ending at least twice: first, in November 1883, when he had the transformative experience of the blood-red sky by the Oslo fjord; and again, on January 22, 1892, when he composed his poem to accompany *The Scream*. Kennedy, Khrushchev, and Castro felt that the world, as they knew it, might be about to disappear in a convulsion of nuclear war by the last weekend of October 1962.

Having just read the previous paragraph, do you feel a deep, metaphorical, Munchian "*Scream*" coming on? Are you able to put yourself in the shoes of Kennedy and Khrushchev and Castro on the last weekend of October 1962?

No, probably not yet. Ask yourself: Why not? What is missing? What would it take to shock you into a more vivid awareness of the fragility of a world with thousands of nuclear weapons and governments full of fallible human beings in charge of the nukes? Do you feel like pitching in and doing what you can to try to abolish nuclear weapons? Not yet? That's okay. We've only begun bringing you up to speed on the Cuban missile crisis and its implications for the 21st century. The more you know *and feel* about October 1962, and the more you know *and feel* about our current nuclear predicament, the more likely you are to be on the same page as Munch in November 1883, and on January 22, 1892, and also with leaders in Washington, Havana, and Moscow by October 26–27, 1962. That's when you will realize the appropriateness of something as extreme as screaming in response to the reality faced in 1962 and today.

We urge you now to undertake a thought experiment. It involves writing what the Nobel Prize-winning Princeton psychologist Daniel Kahneman calls a "pre-mortem."[19] Imagine that the currently unimaginable has occurred, or partially occurred. There has been a "small" nuclear war, millions are dead or missing, a few cities have been destroyed, but an all-out global conflagration has somehow been avoided. With the devastation still everywhere visible, with *The Road* the apt description of large swaths of the planet, you are called into the White House or Kremlin or another headquarters relevant to the conflict and asked to explain, in two hundred words or less (about half a page), what went wrong, why it went wrong, and what can be done in the future to avoid another such event. In other words, you are to imagine being asked to do a *post*-mortem of the war, in a *pre*-mortem context—that is, now, today, before any such war has occurred.

We urge you to do this periodically, as you read this book. The more you know about the Cuban missile crisis and our current nuclear predicament, the richer will be your ruminations as to how such a war might happen and the more useful will be your ideas about what needs to be done to prevent it. Your pre-mortem will likely be suffused with regret at letting a nuclear war actually happen—some "retrospective" variant of the abolition imperative: "I wish, oh how I wish, we had abolished nuclear weapons before this happened."

First you scream. Then you act. Good luck!

2

THE BULLSHIT

Bad Guys Threaten; Good Guys Stand Firm; Good Guys Win; Bad Guys Lose; the Little Guy Doesn't Matter; JFK's Moxie Prevails

[JFK's] combination of toughness and restraint, of will, nerve, and wisdom, [was] so brilliantly controlled, so matchlessly calibrated, that [it] dazzled the world.

—Arthur Schlesinger Jr., *A Thousand Days: John F. Kennedy in the White House* (1965)[1]

. . . bullshit is a greater enemy of the truth than lies are.

—Harry G. Frankfurt, *On Bullshit* (2005)[2]

The VERY *IDEA* OF BULLSHIT

The Liberation Philosophy of Harry G. Frankfurt

Let's talk about bullshit. Not your bullshit or our bullshit, but the *idea* of bullshit. The ability to distinguish bullshit from the truth will be helpful in distinguishing between two events: (1) the *bullshit* Cuban missile crisis that never happened but many believe happened; and (2) the *true* Cuban missile crisis that happened but with which too few are familiar.

In 2005, an eminent philosopher summoned the courage to give the proper label to a phenomenon with which we are all familiar, and that most of us refer to when speaking or writing privately—but a name we typically shy away from when speaking or writing publicly. In that year, the Princeton philosopher Harry G. Frankfurt published his best-selling book *On Bullshit*, liberating the rest of us in the English-speaking world to follow suit.[3] We are grateful to Frankfurt because "bullshit" is, in our view, the best way to describe the event so many people have written about that they mistakenly call "the Cuban missile crisis."

As Frankfurt points out, the term *bullshit* is often used simply as a derogatory term, a way to denigrate and delegitimize a view with which we happen for some reason to disagree. For example, we recently overheard the following exchange between two young people while we were all waiting in line to order pizza:

FIRST STUDENT: Soy milk sucks!
SECOND STUDENT: No way—that is total bullshit!

Calling something "bullshit" in this sense is the spoken equivalent of sticking your tongue out or giving "the finger" to someone.

But this is not what Frankfurt is about, and it has nothing to do with why we apply the term to the collection of myths that make up the common understanding of the Cuban missile crisis. Frankfurt is quite precise about what he means by "bullshit." He points out that if one individual seeks to tell the truth, and another means to tell a lie, they both share an important characteristic: both are concerned about the truth. One tries to represent it accurately, the other inaccurately. But both begin with a shared idea of what constitutes the truth.

Bullshitters, writes Frankfurt, are not concerned about whether their statements are true or false. Instead, they are concerned about whether the tales they tell serve their ulterior motives. Their bottom line is neither truth nor falsehood but effectiveness in convincing another of what is being said or written. Frankfurt writes: "The bullshitter . . . does not reject the authority of the truth, as the liar does, and oppose himself to it. He pays no attention to it at all. By virtue of this, bullshit is a greater enemy of the truth than lies are." Repeat, "Bullshit is a greater enemy of the truth than lies are."[4]

THE BULLSHIT, OCTOBER 1962

The Glorious Victorious Cuban Missile Crisis that Never Happened

Here, compacted into one paragraph, is our 260-word variant of the bullshit most have been led to believe about the Cuban missile crisis:

> *In October 1962, unprovoked and out of the blue, the Soviet Union (the bad guys, the aggressors) precipitated a crisis with the U.S. (the good guys, the victims) by attempting to install nuclear missiles in Cuba (a "parking lot" for the missiles), ninety miles from the shores of the U.S. Luckily, U.S. intelligence discovered this provocative plan before its completion—in fact, before any nuclear warheads had arrived in Cuba, rendering their delivery vehicles, missiles, planes, and boats—useless. And, so, with fearless, finely calibrated coercion, President John F. Kennedy compelled Nikita Khrushchev to back down and remove the missiles. Kennedy stood strong; he stood tall; he did not compromise; and in just thirteen days, he secured an unequivocal victory for the U.S. over the Soviet Union. Since Kennedy's forces had overwhelming local military superiority in the Western hemisphere, and global superiority in deliverable nuclear warheads all over the world, the crisis was not as dangerous as some made it out to be. Khrushchev had no choice. He had to capitulate or risk being destroyed and he knew it, which is why he "blinked" and Kennedy didn't. Kennedy and Khrushchev rightly ignored the ranting of Cuban leader Fidel Castro since his views were irrelevant to both the deployment and removal of the missiles. October 1962 was Kennedy's finest hour, Khrushchev's worst humiliation, and Castro's introduction into the high-stakes game that was the Cold War, as played by the Big Boys from Washington and Moscow, a game in which a small country like Cuba was merely a bit player.*

Now you've met the enemy: the collection of bullshit in the above paragraph. *Everything in that paragraph is dead wrong.*[5]

In what follows, we'll provide some context for understanding how this myth got started and what has sustained it over the more than half-century since the Cuban missile crisis.

A WINNER AND A LOSER

The Super Bowl of the Cold War

An event viewed as decisive, as a turning point, or a watershed can make or break the reputations of the principal participants. When verifiable facts about the Great Event are few—as was the case with the Cuban missile crisis in the 1960s, due to lack of access to the relevant documentation—the ground is fertile for the growth of myths and legends: heroes and villains, good guys and bad guys, winners and losers.

Americans like their foreign policy myths to mimic their sporting events, especially football games. Perhaps it was inevitable, therefore, that the retrospective fascination with the Cuban missile crisis has been spun into a dominant narrative that frames the crisis as the Super Bowl of the Cold War. The contest pitted the home team against the visitors—the Americans versus the Russians—for all the marbles. Our guys were good; their guys were bad. Our team held the line. Just when it looked bleakest, our guys pulled a rabbit out of a hat. We won. They lost. There were many heroes on our team, but our quarterback, our play-caller and field general, was the MVP—the Most Valuable Player—of the game. Our MVP's name was John Fitzgerald Kennedy.

Graham Allison, a political scientist at Harvard's Kennedy School of Government, spent much of the latter 1960s interviewing members of the Kennedy administration about the crisis. His 1971 book reporting his findings is *Essence of Decision: Explaining the Cuban Missile Crisis*.[6] He summarized his results concisely: "For thirteen days in October 1962, the U.S. and the Soviet Union stood 'eyeball to eyeball,' each with the power of mutual annihilation in hand. The U.S. was firm but forbearing. The Soviet Union looked hard, blinked twice, and then withdrew without humiliation."[7] In Allison's view, the Cuban missile crisis was a hell of a game, with the outcome in doubt until the last minute. JFK had forced Khrushchev to "blink twice"—first, on October 24th when Khrushchev ordered Russian ships on their way to Cuba to halt, and then reverse course, rather than risk a military confrontation at sea; and then, on October 27th, when Khrushchev gave the order to begin dismantling the missiles in Cuba and begin shipping them back to the Soviet Union. The USA won; the USSR lost. What could be clearer than that?[8]

Moreover, the victor not only won but won graciously. At the conclusion of the now famous thirteen days, JFK thanked Khrushchev for his constructive contribution to peace on earth, and Khrushchev reciprocated. This was in the spirit of the conclusion to the 2015 Super Bowl, when Richard Sherman, the outspoken and often arrogant star cornerback of the losing Seattle Seahawks, shook hands with Tom Brady, the quarterback of the victorious New England Patriots. Allison gives Kennedy and Khrushchev credit for a similar degree of good sportsmanship at the end of their bitterly contested struggle over the missiles in Cuba. In October 1962, it was all about winning and losing, not about arrogance and humiliation.

Graham Allison's *Essence of Decision* would eventually become far and away the best-selling academic book ever written on the crisis. Despite its often highly academic style and its focus on abstract "models" through which the crisis can be framed, it has sold almost five hundred thousand copies since its publication. The book sold so well, so consistently (roughly ten thousand copies per year), that a second edition, by Allison and Philip Zelikow, did not appear until 1999. The 1999 edition frames the crisis in precisely the same way as the first edition. In the twenty-eight years since the publication of the first edition, many new facts had come to light. But according to Allison and Zelikow, the basic storyline had not changed one bit. Somebody won: Kennedy. Somebody lost: Khrushchev. Somebody was still irrelevant: Cuban leader Fidel Castro.[9]

JFK HAD THE MOXIE

The Dominant Myth, 1962–1990

If, during the quarter-century or so after the Cuban missile crisis, one had been asked to provide a very brief explanation for what happened (and what didn't happen) in the Cuban missile crisis, two words would have been sufficient: "Kennedy's *moxie*." Here is the dictionary definition of *moxie*: *to face difficulty with courage; aggressive energy; nerve, vigor, guts, backbone.*" That is what most people believed about Kennedy. That is what we were taught as students when we began to study the crisis in the 1980s. Volumes were dedicated to proving the moxie hypothesis. Indeed, most still believe the moxie hypothesis, long after the paradigm should have shifted in light of new information.

But mythology is difficult to supplant, especially (as we have discovered) when the key player in the myth is John F. Kennedy, the 35th president of the United States, whose posthumous presence in Western culture has much in common with Elvis Presley. Like Elvis, JFK died tragically young, in the prime of his life. Like Elvis, JFK was good looking, rich—a rock star, in other words, in everything other than his chosen occupation. Many still go to Elvis's museum-like home, Graceland in Memphis in an attempt to recapture the magic of "the King" of rock 'n roll. Likewise fans of the departed 35th president of the United States flock to various Kennedy-related locales, especially the John F. Kennedy Presidential Library and Museum in Boston, in an effort to relive the glory of the Kennedy-era "Camelot."[10]

Of course, rock stars are entertainers, while U.S. presidents bear the awesome burden of responsibility for protecting their constituents, including avoiding a catastrophic nuclear war. And even diehard football fans must admit that a crisis that threatens to explode into an all-out nuclear war that destroys human civilization is not *exactly* like a football game. But from the early 1960s through the 1980s, a narrative developed that was consistent with the Super Bowl template but which spoke to some of the specific issues and events associated with the Cuban missile crisis.

THE COURT HISTORIANS

The Origins of the Moxie Hypothesis

The absence of relevant documentation did not prevent scholars and former U.S. officials from assigning blame and giving credit for what happened in the Cuban missile crisis. On the contrary, a torrent of books, magazine pieces, memoirs, and interviews came forth in great profusion after the crisis. In the document-free zone of the 1960s and 1970s, there arose two, equally U.S.-centric, ideologically driven, document-thin, often shrill narratives. The dominant view, sometimes called the Camelot narrative, portrayed JFK as a courageous, steely nerved warrior who stared down Khrushchev at what Kennedy's National Security Adviser McGeorge Bundy, called "the moment of thermonuclear truth."[11] JFK was a hero because he stood firm and forced Khrushchev to remove the missiles in Cuba without a war. JFK and his men showed the Soviet communists that the U.S. meant business. Kennedy had more *moxie* than Khrushchev—more toughness, determination, and courage.

This view was infused with triumphalism. It was all about how Kennedy "won" this decisive Cold War encounter with the Russians. The dominance of this view was due to several features of the American political scene following Kennedy's assassination on November 22, 1963. Most importantly, there was the overwhelming grief felt by most Americans regarding JFK's assassination in Dallas.

To those who did not live through those surreal days, it must seem like a stretch to claim that 180 million people grieved for a president they had never met, and who nearly half of the voting public had rejected in the 1960 presidential election, less than three years before. But grieve they did, and Kennedy's reputation grew accordingly with the passage of time. JFK's posthumous popularity skyrocketed, far beyond his popularity when he was president. Even many of those who had opposed Kennedy while he was in office now tended to regard him as a martyr worthy of the highest respect. For those who had supported Kennedy, posthumous respect began to ooze over the edge of admiration into outright adoration and veneration. Some cynics suggested shortly after JFK's death that his assassination was a terrific posthumous career move, in the sense that the martyred president, viewed in the rearview mirrors of his avid supporters, seemed to have morphed from a highly controversial president into a great president. Kennedy is still regarded by the American public as one of the greatest presidents, a view that is not shared by many influential historians.

The campaign to establish JFK's posthumous secular "sainthood" included the publication of three influential books, all written with insider knowledge of the Kennedy White House. These books were effusive about Kennedy's steely determination in the Cuban missile crisis, JFK's "finest hour," when he faced down the Russians and provided the U.S. with one of its few clear-cut "victories" over the Soviet Union.

The first of these to appear, in 1965, was *A Thousand Days: John F. Kennedy in the White House*, by Harvard historian and Kennedy White House aide Arthur Schlesinger Jr. Although he was not personally involved in the administration's deliberations during the crisis, he had an office in the White House and good access to JFK and everyone advising the president during the crisis. Once he had his facts in hand, Schlesinger found himself in awe of Kennedy's "combination of toughness and restraint, of will, nerve, and wisdom, so brilliantly controlled, so matchlessly calibrated, that [it] dazzled the world."[12] It certainly dazzled Schlesinger and his huge readership. The book won the Pulitzer Prize and the National Book Award and became a global best seller. Schlesinger's prose, filled with remembered White House conversations with JFK and with Schlesinger's soaring phrase making, quickly became the template against which future accounts of JFK and the missile crisis would inevitably be compared.

Schlesinger's book was complemented the same year (1965) by another JFK biography, by his chief of staff and principal speechwriter, Theodore Sorensen. The biography, called simply *Kennedy*, was, like *A Thousand Days*, long and adoring and well stocked with recollected conversations with JFK.[13] Whereas Schlesinger's praise of his former boss is delivered in the brilliant, learned flourishes of an eminent historian, part of the charm of Sorensen's memoir is the straightforward, transparent *awe* in which he held his subject. Here is Sorensen's JFK on the morning of October 28, 1962, upon hearing the news that Khrushchev had agreed to withdraw the missiles from Cuba in exchange for a U.S. pledge not to attack and invade the island:

> John F. Kennedy entered and we all stood up. He had, as Harold MacMillan would later say, earned his place in history by this act alone. He had engaged in a personal as well as a national contest for world leadership and he had won. He had reassured those nations fearing we would use too much strength and those fearing we would use none at all. The hard lessons of the first Cuban crisis (the Bay of Pigs fiasco) were applied in his steady handling of the second with a carefully measured combination of defense, diplomacy and dialogue.[14]

One can almost hear the drums beating, the horns blaring, and perhaps a choir reaching a crescendo as Kennedy appears, elegant (as always) and modest (as always), in Sorensen's telling.

In recounting JFK in the missile crisis, however, Sorensen the minimalist wordsmith ultimately felt compelled to resort to a literary comparison to make his point. After the meeting on October 28th, Sorensen reports that he went back to his office and grabbed a copy of Kennedy's 1956 Pulitzer Prize-winning book, *Profiles in Courage*, off his shelf and read a passage aloud from it to his secretary, Gloria Sitrin. It is from Edmund Burke's eulogy for British parliamentarian Charles James Fox: "He may live long. He may do much. But here is the summit. He can never exceed what he does this day."[15]

Schlesinger's and Sorensen's books were influential, but it was a third book from the Kennedy inner circle that locked into public consciousness the "JFK had the moxie" understanding of what happened in October 1962. In 1969, JFK's brother Robert Kennedy, the attorney general during JFK's presidency, posthumously published *Thirteen Days: A Memoir of the Cuban Missile Crisis*.[16] It is a short book that packs a big punch—a dramatic cliffhanger, with the fate of the earth in the balance. JFK is portrayed as calm, clever, and even philosophical, as the U.S. and Soviet Union seem headed for a nuclear showdown.

Thirteen Days humanized our image of JFK during the Cuban missile crisis without making him appear less tough and heroic than he appeared in the portrayals by Schlesinger and Sorensen. The message was that while of course JFK had the moxie to force Khrushchev to back down, Kennedy was a president who knew that a peaceful outcome was not guaranteed. Indeed, due to the outrageous and irresponsible behavior of Khrushchev and the Soviets, the risk of nuclear war could not be excluded, if for some reason Khrushchev refused to back down—if he was determined to go to war over the missiles in

Cuba. Here are RFK's reflections on JFK on October 24, 1962, as the Soviet ships are approaching the quarantine line around Cuba. The ships have a submarine escort. The U.S. Navy warships have been ordered to stop and search any Soviet ships approaching the line. War at sea may be imminent.

> Was the world on the brink of a holocaust? Was it our error? A mistake? Was there something further that should have been done? Or not done? His hand went up to his face and covered his mouth. He opened and closed his fist. His face seemed drawn, his eyes pained, almost gray. We stared at each other across the table. For a few fleeting seconds, it was almost as though no one else was there and he was no longer the president.
>
> Inexplicably, I thought of when he was a child and almost died; when he lost his child; when we learned that our oldest brother had been killed; of personal times of strain and hurt.[17]

The drama is irresistible: the two Kennedy brothers, with Armageddon imminent, toughing it out together and, against the odds, emerging victorious, without a war, forcing Khrushchev to remove the missiles. Conclusion: Team Kennedy victorious! *Thirteen Days* was drafted just as Robert Kennedy entered the race for the Democratic nomination for president. It was drafted as an unorthodox but compelling campaign memoir. It's not terribly subtle subtext goes something like this: yes, the candidate is only forty-two years old (in 1967, when the book was drafted); yes, he has been known in some circles for his youthful hot temper and brutal arm-twisting; but in addition, this is the man who was by the president's side, playing an indispensible role, helping to save the country and the world from nuclear Armageddon.[18]

MOXIE? . . . SCHMOXIE?

A Note on the Anti-Camelot Revisionist Bullshit

Parallel to the heroic "JFK had the moxie" narrative, another view evolved, the anti-Camelot narrative, which portrayed JFK as a reckless, immature, disorganized president who needlessly and dangerously brought America and the world to the brink of Armageddon, principally to prove he was tougher than Khrushchev. For example, the British historian and activist E. P. Thompson accused JFK and his government of having initiated "Kennedy's dance of death during the Cuban missile crisis" by challenging Khrushchev over the missile deployment in Cuba.[19] At the same time, as he praised Khrushchev for his "pragmatism" in agreeing to Kennedy's terms, Thompson declared Khrushchev to be "the philosopher king of nuclear deterrence."[20] JFK's moxie? . . . schmoxie! these writers assert. They claim we've confused moxie with recklessness, having relied for too long on the unsubstantiated and thoroughly biased views of people close to JFK.

In the U.S., the best-known advocate of the anti-Camelot view is the MIT linguist Noam Chomsky, who has issued anti-Kennedy screeds from the early 1960s right down to the present. In October 2012, for example, on the 50th anniversary of the crisis, Chomsky wrote that JFK was the biggest part of the problem—the heightened threat of nuclear war—during the crisis, not part of the solution. Like E. P. Thompson, Chomsky wrote, "In 1962, war was avoided by Khrushchev's willingness to accept Kennedy's hegemonic demands. But we can hardly count on such sanity forever."[21] Because of Kennedy's alleged aggressiveness, according to Chomsky, "it's a near miracle" that nuclear war was avoided.

But Chomsky too is trapped inside a myth he has helped to promote. While his anti-establishment rhetoric may have been convincing to some a half-century ago, the facts have starkly contradicted Chomsky's anti-Camelot sermonizing. We now know that JFK was cautious after the missiles were discovered, and he did exhibit a unique kind of moxie during the crisis—the courage to engage in what we call "heroic *in*-action." Terribly concerned by the palpable danger of events and conscious of how much he did not know, he repeatedly and effectively resisted the recommendations of his advisers who wanted him to take much more forceful military action than he was willing to order. An anti-Kennedy ideologue like Chomsky finds facts like these inconvenient. To Chomsky and his fellow travelers, JFK's decision-making in the crisis suggests that Kennedy irresponsibly behaved as if he were in a football game. This is bullshit, and we have known it is bullshit for more than twenty-five years.[22]

Revisionists like Thompson and Chomsky made little headway with those not already inclined to believe, for whatever reasons, the worst about Kennedy. It was for many years impossible to adjudicate the debate between the Camelot and anti-Camelot factions on the basis of the evidence because no one in the West could state with any confidence how dangerous the crisis actually was—how close to nuclear war the world may have come in October 1962. To answer that question, U.S. documents along with information from Soviet and Cuban sources were required. That is pretty much where matters stood in 1985 when we began our study of the Cuban missile crisis.

KHRUSHCHEV "BLINKED"

A Defining Moment in the Dominant Myth

Let's go back to October 24, 1962, around 10:00 a.m. EDT, when the U.S. blockade of Cuba goes into effect. U.S. Navy vessels have orders to stop and search Soviet ships bound for Cuba and turn them back if their cargoes are associated with "offensive" weapons in Cuba. (The term "offensive" weapons was, in the code of the early 1960s, equivalent to "nuclear.") Several Soviet ships are reported approaching the "quarantine" line, as the blockade has been rechristened by the Kennedy State Department (because a blockade is considered to be an act of war, and Kennedy did not want to start a war). The Soviet freighters had also, according to naval intelligence, picked up a submarine escort, presumably to repel any U.S. attempts to board the Soviet vessels. When given the information about the submarine escort, JFK is reported to have said, "Now it can go either way."[23] CBS newsman Charles Collingwood would say the following Sunday, October 28, that on the 24th, "there was some speculation whether that hour would be remembered as the day World War III began."[24]

What was about to happen? Would war between the nuclear superpowers break out at sea? If it did, could it be contained there, or would it spread with deadly logic and great speed to engage all the nuclear forces belonging to Washington and Moscow? Was no one in charge of this crisis anymore? Was Armageddon about to become inevitable because of some imminent incident hundreds of miles from Cuba on the open seas? Americans who were tuned to CBS News could listen to the soothing timbre of Walter Cronkite's voice describe what he saw on a big board, at which a young reporter from Texas named Dan Rather moved cardboard ships around on a symbolic Atlantic Ocean. Finally, it seemed that the Soviet ships and the U.S. ships being moved by Rather were almost close enough to touch one another.

The main vehicle by which the members of the millennial generation have become familiar with the Cuban missile crisis is the 2000 Kevin Costner movie *Thirteen Days*. The film adheres very closely to the Camelot myth, as if nothing significant had been learned about the crisis since October 1962. The film was billed as a "docu-drama," which was approximately half right: it has close to zero "docu" but a good deal of drama. It bears no resemblance to a documentary, and its portrayal of the Cuban missile crisis is often fanciful, and occasionally ridiculous. The central character in the film, in fact, is not JFK, but Kenneth O'Donnell, JFK's appointments secretary, who had almost nothing to do with the crisis. The O'Donnell character, played by Costner, is in almost every scene, sometimes giving Kennedy sage advice on how to respond to Khrushchev. (In the event, O'Donnell participated in no such discussions.)[25]

The film is, however, quite dramatic. Perhaps the most dramatic moment in *Thirteen Days* is the moment when "Khrushchev blinks"—the turning point in the crisis when Khrushchev realizes that he is outgunned, is playing a losing hand—pick your metaphor—and that it is time to capitulate. Khrushchev's alleged "capitulation" occurs when he orders the Russian ships bound for Cuba to, first, stop dead in the water, and second, to turn around and head back to Russia. At that point, Secretary of State Dean Rusk says that having gone "eyeball to eyeball" with JFK, "Khrushchev blinked," a metaphor from a game played by children in his native Georgia, in which they stare at each other until one of them blinks. If you blink first, you lose. In interviews after the crisis, several of the participants, including Rusk, recalled such a moment, including Rusk's use of the "blinked" metaphor for what had just happened.[26]

WE WIN, THEY LOSE

Khrushchev Blinks in the Movie Thirteen Days

What is indisputable is this: (1) Russian ships were heading for a showdown at the quarantine line, several hundred miles east and north of Cuba; and (2) at some point, some of the ships stopped, turned and reversed course; and (3) JFK and his advisers were greatly relieved to have avoided a military confrontation at sea. But the way the film treats this moment illustrates the way *Thirteen Days* takes the dominant Camelot myth of the crisis and embellishes it on the big screen—a larger-than-life mythic moment, accompanied by the kind of cathartic emotion that we expect of our mythic moments.

Here is how it unfolds. JFK and his advisers are sitting or standing or pacing in a room that seems too small to be presidential. There is much meaningful staring, jaw-clenching, and furrowed brows. The anxiety is thick enough to cut with a knife. The source of their anxiety? The Russians ships, presumably carrying cargoes connected to the missile deployment in Cuba, are steaming toward the U.S. Navy's blockade (or "quarantine") line. JFK has authorized the navy to stop the ships and search them. The big worry is that they will not stop but will continue onward, forcing the Americans to either capitulate and let the Russian ships pass through the blockade or fire across their bows in an effort to make them stop. If they still do not stop, JFK is wondering, then what? Then the war begins at sea, perhaps by sinking a Russian ship. After that? One of the submarines in the escort of the Russian ships perhaps fires on a U.S. destroyer and sinks the U.S. ship. At this point, the clamoring for continued retaliation, and further escalation toward the nuclear level, will become thunderous in both Washington and Moscow. It is suddenly quite possible that the world could be blown up because one Russian ship refused to stop and submit to a U.S. search. The threat of nuclear war has suddenly moved perceptibly from the realm of hypothetical war games to a terrifyingly real and ambiguous situation.

At this point, Secretary of Defense Robert McNamara is heard to say that a report has just come in. The message: Russian ships are stopping just short of the blockade line. The room becomes totally quiet. The silence is broken when Kennedy asks what the hell is going on. The camera returns to McNamara who, while not speaking, is now grinning from ear to ear. Phones are ringing off their hooks. In a flash, everyone not already standing leaps to his feet and slaps the back of whomever is nearest to him. This is followed by embraces all round. It is, as the director's instructions indicate, a "ruckus." Secretary of State Dean Rusk says to nobody in particular: "We just went eyeball to eyeball and the other guy just blinked." This statement is destined to become one of the most famous and misrepresented remarks made during the entire Cuban missile crisis.

The celebration is so loud and chaotic that when CIA Director John McCone returns to the room with the latest intelligence report, his voice is completely drowned out by the hubbub.[27] Add a few chest bumps, fist bumps, high-fives, and cries of "dude, dude!" and we could be watching a bunch of guys in suits in an executive suite at a football stadium, celebrating their team scoring a touchdown.

What's wrong with this scene? Why shouldn't we permit the filmmakers some license to bring some excitement to the screen? Consider only one feature of the weirdness of portraying the Cuban missile crisis as a faux football game—*the psychology of the moment*. In the event, JFK was mortified by the possibility of a nuclear war breaking out at sea. When the Russian ships stopped and reversed course, nuclear danger eased, but only momentarily.

Nothing else changed. The work on the missile sites in Cuba continued unabated, twenty-four hours a day. No one knew whether the nuclear warheads had already reached Cuba (they had!). But the frantic work to make the missiles operational suggested that at least some of the warheads might already be in Cuba, ready to mate with the missiles. Furthermore, Kennedy was just beginning to understand the frightening implications of managing a crisis in the nuclear age. U.S. missiles were being readied to fire; B-52 bombers carrying nuclear weapons were in the air twenty-four hours a day, circling the

Russian perimeter, ready to attack if the order came from the president. Horrible "what-ifs" began to swirl in JFK's mind: What if war breaks out and I am unable to control my own forces? What if Khrushchev is unable to control his? What if Khrushchev's hawks are as crazy as my hawks, all of them recommending forceful military action that could lead to the end of the world?

So instead of the football game celebration in *Thirteen Days*, the episode represented in shorthand as "Khrushchev blinked" served to reinforce to Kennedy (and to Khrushchev) that the course of this crisis, and the future of their societies and the entire world, was hanging by a very slender thread. Things seemed not only to be getting out of control. They seemed to have become surreal, almost *crazy*! Causes seemed to have come unstuck from effects. JFK didn't expect Khrushchev to put missiles into Cuba, but he did. He expected Khrushchev to try to punch through the quarantine line, but he didn't. What should he expect next? The real message for Kennedy (and Khrushchev) of the confrontation at the quarantine line was this: Washington and Moscow are being sucked into a spiral of events that are increasingly beyond the control of the White House and Kremlin. It won't be long before events will careen out of control and into a war that will be in no one's interest, that will have no winner, only losers. It's time to get the hell out of this situation.

But how? How, JFK asked himself, can we get the missiles out of Cuba, which is a political necessity, without provoking a war? Can we find a resolution in which we both back *off* but no one has to be seen as backing *down*? At the moment of the famous Rusk comment about blinking, there was no celebrating, no backslapping, no shouting, no triumphalism. As Rusk remembered, instead, there was only the profound silence of leaders who were exhausted, confused, and fearful that they might be incapable of finding an exit ramp from the crisis before nuclear war broke out.[28]

And this is why the crisis as it is portrayed in *Thirteen Days* is bullshit: it's not about what happened or didn't happen. It's about burnishing the myth of a Super Bowl Cuban missile crisis, and the famous victory of the Americans over the Russians.

WATCH OUT, HERE COMES THE EVIDENCE, 1985–1993

The Cubans and Russians Start to Open Up

In every respect but one, each of these bullshit narratives—Camelot and anti-Camelot—was the inverse of the other: regarding the identity of good guys and bad guys, who was the hero and who was the goat, who caused the crisis and who resolved it short of war, and so on. But in each narrative there are two, and only two, real players, and they are the nuclear superpowers, the U.S. and the Soviet Union. Implicitly for Cuba, there is no *there* there. Cuba exists, of course, but only as a parking lot for Soviet nuclear weapons. It's as if Cuban history, politics, governance, culture—everything recognizably Cuban—had nothing to do with the Cuban missile crisis. Fidel Castro's reputation as one of the great talkers of the 20th century was by 1962 already well established. But Fidel's voice was inaudible to Western scholars of the crisis in the quarter-century following October 1962, in spite of the fact that Fidel's views were readily available since the Bay of Pigs invasion eighteen months before the Cuban missile crisis.

By the mid-1980s, however, a steady trickle of declassified documents began to flow from U.S. archives, obtained under the Freedom of Information Act. Some of the new information suggested that the crisis must have been quite dangerous—that the global nuclear doomsday machine might have come close to exploding. Here, for example, are a few items that emerged from U.S. documents in the late 1980s. For the first and only time, the lids were removed from the ballistic missile silos in the Dakotas and Montana; these missiles were fully armed and aimed at the Soviet Union and its allies. More than 150,000 U.S. troops were poised to invade Cuba at two points, east and west of Havana. A massive U.S. air attack was prepared that would involve more than 1,200 bombing missions on day one alone. The U.S. expected heavy casualties—between twenty-five thousand and fifty thousand during the first week of fighting, assuming that nuclear weapons were *not* used, either by the Americans or the Russians.[29]

Much of the discussion of nuclear danger in the crisis revolved around whether or not Russian warheads had arrived in Cuba before the missile sites were discovered and the island blockaded by the U.S. Navy. The CIA believed at the time that the warheads had not arrived; they believed that the Soviet ship carrying the warheads was the *Poltava.* That ship had reversed course in the Atlantic and returned to the Soviet Union rather than risk a confrontation at sea. Obviously a U.S. air strike and invasion of Cuba would have been vastly more dangerous if Soviet nuclear warheads had been present and the commanders had authority to launch them. But without the availability of authoritative Russian and Cuban sources, it was impossible to determine the presence or absence of fully armed Soviet nuclear weapons on the island during the crisis. We had nothing concrete with which to confirm or deny the CIA's estimate at the time that the nuclear warheads had *not* reached Cuba.

Still, it seemed to us that a crisis with so many moving parts, a crisis with the fate of the world potentially at stake, was worth probing further if we could learn Russian and Cuban views of the crisis, particularly on the key issue of how dangerous it was. We pressed on, encouraged by two new developments: the relative openness of Moscow under Mikhail Gorbachev (called *glasnost*); and the desire of the Cubans to tell their side of the story in a setting that included senior American and Russian participants in the crisis. Eventually, intense Russian and Cuban interest in the crisis overwhelmed their Cold War habits of secrecy and deception. We held conferences in the U.S. and Russia. In November 1990, we were preparing for our next meeting, on the Caribbean island of Antigua, in early January 1991. At the conclusion of the Antigua meeting, we would decide whether it would be worth the time, expense, and political consequences to try to move to a conference in Havana that following year, in which Fidel Castro could be expected to participate. The big questions for us were: (1) Would we be invited to Havana after the Antigua meeting for a lengthy face-to-face encounter with Fidel Castro; and (2) If our senior people, led by Robert McNamara, were invited to Havana, would they accept the invitation? They were and they did. The epochal Havana Conference, in which Fidel participated for all four days, occurred in January 1992 one year after the Antigua conference.[30]

3

THE TRUTH

Big Guys Ignore Little Guy; Feeling Doomed, Little Guy Throws Caution to the Wind, Starts Shooting, and Asks Big Friend to Nuke the U.S.; Armageddon Nearly Occurs

ALEKSANDER ALEKSEEV: Fidel, do you mean to say [to Khrushchev] that we should be the first to strike a nuclear blow against the enemy?
FIDEL CASTRO . . . under certain circumstances, we should forestall them without waiting . . . [for] the first nuclear blow from their side. If they attack Cuba, we should wipe them off the face of the earth.

—Conversation between Cuban leader Fidel Castro and Soviet ambassador to Cuba Aleksander Alekseev, in a bunker beneath the Soviet embassy, Havana, Cuba, sometime between 2:00 a.m. and 7:00 a.m., October 27, 1962 EDT[1]

The truth can be really powerful stuff. You're not expecting it.

—Kurt Vonnegut, *A Man without a Country* (2005)[2]

THE TRUTH, OCTOBER 1962

The Cuban, *Cuban Missile Crisis, When the World Nearly Ended*

Here, in one paragraph, is our variant of the truth about what made the Cuban missile crisis the most dangerous crisis in recorded history:

> *The crisis did not come out of the blue and last thirteen days. U.S. blindness toward Cuba only made it seem that way. The crisis began eighteen months earlier, after the failed April 1961 Bay of Pigs invasion, with the Cubans' fears of an imminent full-scale U.S. invasion. They asked the Russians for defensive weapons. The Russians began providing them, and the superpower sleepwalk toward Armageddon began. The U.S. was not a victim of the deployment; its threats to Cuba were an important cause of it. U.S. intelligence assessments were atrocious: they did not predict the deployment; they did not even confirm it until the missiles in Cuba were almost ready to fire; and their conclusion that warheads for the weapons probably never reached Cuba was dead wrong. In all, 162 nuclear warheads were shipped, delivered, stored, and made ready to fire by Soviet technicians in Cuba. While JFK courageously and ingeniously resisted the many hawks in his administration urging him toward war, Kennedy had no plan when the missiles were discovered and was shocked at the deployment. Nobody won. Nobody lost. Nobody "blinked." Once Kennedy and Khrushchev realized they were losing control of the crisis, they worked feverishly, collaboratively, and effectively to terminate it. But Moscow's and Washington's dismissal of the Cuban perspective, leading to Cuban outrage and provocative behavior, sent the crisis to within a hair's breadth of nuclear war. Far from being a "bit player," Cuba became the hinge of the world. Believing they were irrevocably doomed by an imminent U.S. nuclear attack on the island, Fidel Castro wrote to Khrushchev urging him to launch an all-out nuclear attack on the U.S. ASAP, once the Americans began invading the island. The Cubans, and their Russian comrades in Cuba, prepared to nuke the U.S. Guantanamo Bay naval base and to use their short-range nuclear weapons against the invading U.S. forces. Had these been carried out, a U.S. nuclear response would likely have followed, and Armageddon would have commenced then and there.*

Every claim in this summary statement is backed by voluminous and authoritative declassified documentation, oral testimony from top-ranking leaders during the crisis, and by the careful analyses of scholars from many disciplines. What it says happened, happened!

Have another look at this statement. Notice that the basic truth of the Cuban missile crisis has two parts: the part that happened, and the part that didn't happen. The part that happened is the *actual* history: three leaders, three sets of perceptions, lots of mistaken judgments by all of them, decisions made based on assumptions that were either wrong or irrelevant, and so on. That's what happened. The part that didn't happen is the *virtual* history, the end of the world, as our forebears knew it, in 1962. Compare your own daily life, your sense of personal, familial, and national history and the future you expect, with the bleak, lifeless planet confronted by Papa & The Boy in Cormac McCarthy's *The Road*. However you may judge your life and prospects at the moment, they are substantially more comfortable and promising than those of the living hell Papa & The Boy inhabit. If the Cuban missile crisis had exploded into nuclear war, the world afterward would have closely resembled that living hell.

The bullshit version of the Cuban missile crisis represents only a partial history of what actually happened. It is partial because it typically omits, as insignificant, events that occurred on the island of Cuba, and focuses almost entirely on events in Washington and Moscow.[3] Kennedy did this. Khrushchev did that. U.S. troops moved from A to B. Soviet forces moved from C to D. And so on. The history of the Cuban missile crisis told in the movie *Thirteen Days* is like this. It is true that both before the movie appeared in 2000 and after, some fine historians have departed from the Washington-Moscow exclusivity and have begun to make use of the data our project has been generating since the 1980s, and generated additional data themselves.[4] But for various reasons, they and we have failed to break through and change public perceptions of the crisis. As a consequence, discussion of the contemporary nuclear threat has not moved to where it needs to be: focused on abolishing nuclear weapons from this planet.

What is chiefly omitted from the bullshit version of October 1962 is what we sometimes call the *Cuban*, Cuban missile crisis: the physical and psychological reality faced during the crisis by everyone *in Cuba*, including the more than forty-three thousand Russians who were, with Cuban collaboration, preparing for war with the U.S. In Cuba, the crisis was not a chess match or any other kind of game, nor was it a test of wills between the superpowers. In Cuba, the crisis was experienced as preparation for the last battle, for Armageddon, an event that Cuban leaders and their constituents had been anticipating for a year and a half, ever since they had foiled the CIA-backed invasion of Cuban exiles at the Bay of Pigs, on Cuba's southern coast, in April 1961. This meant preparing to fight to the death. It meant carrying the fight to the Americans in every way possible, even though Cuba had no chance of surviving an all-out war with the U.S. Above all, it meant adhering to a code of conduct with deep roots in Cuban history (a history grasped neither by Washington nor Moscow): no surrender; no compromise; no negotiations. It meant dying honorably. It meant taking as many of the enemy down with you as possible.[5]

Notice that the *Cuban* Cuban missile crisis requires no imagination whatever to conjure up Armageddon. The Cubans, and the Russians on the island, imagine it for us. They thought their fates were sealed: all of Cuba was about to disappear; therefore, the way to convert the imminent meaningless slaughter of Cubans and Cuba, along with their Russian comrades on the island, to the glorious martyrdom of the Cuban nation was to nuke the United States the moment the anticipated U.S. attack on Cuba had begun. Kennedy be damned and Khrushchev be damned. Cuba was going under and so, those in Cuba fervently hoped and planned, was the United States of America.

THE LETTER, OCTOBER 27, 1962

A ". . . harsh and terrible solution"

By the fall of 1990, we had been researching the Cuban missile crisis for roughly five years. Many scholars of the crisis told us we had set out on a fool's errand. It was now more than a quarter-century after the crisis—long enough, they argued, for most of the relevant facts to be known and fitted into the history of U.S. foreign policy. But the received wisdom was lopsidedly U.S.-centric. For a quarter-century after the crisis, Western scholars had virtually no access to Russian or Cuban sources—either documents or senior officials responsible for making their governments' key decisions during the crisis. In addition, almost all of the relevant U.S. documentation was still classified as well.[6]

On the afternoon of November 23, 1990, while we were working on the logistical details of a conference on the crisis on the Caribbean island of Antigua (scheduled for January 3–7, 1991), a paper bombshell arrived unbidden from Havana. Our assistant, David Lewis, came dashing into our office and handed us his quick, Spanish-to-English translation of a letter, published earlier that day in Cuba, from Fidel Castro to Nikita Khrushchev dated October 27, 1962. Cuban diplomats in Washington, DC faxed it to us. The cover note asked rhetorically, "No es interesante?" ("Isn't this interesting?")[7]

Many people of a certain age can tell you in great detail and with confidence exactly where they were and what they were doing when they learned that JFK had been assassinated in Dallas on November 22, 1963. Psychologists call this sort of memory *eidetic;* memory so vivid, often involving all the senses, that one's recollection may seem to be almost as acute as real-time experience. An eidetic memory approximates total, multisensory recall.[8] In remembering when they first learned of JFK's death, for example, many find themselves fighting back tears, more than a half-century after the death of someone they never met and whom they may not have thought of in many years. Many decades from now, people who watched the events of 9/11 unfold on television will doubtless recall the events of that day with a vividness that will surprise them, each time the subject arises, especially each September 11th when the media will be filled with images of the tragedy.

In recalling our first glimpse of Fidel's letter, we remember that it was about 4:00 p.m.; we were sitting at a folding table on the upper floor of Brown

University's Center for Foreign Policy Development, where we had moved our Cuban missile crisis project earlier that year from Harvard's Kennedy School of Government. We were drinking Constant Comment tea and eating popcorn as we assembled materials for the Antigua conference. We remember asking—several times—if our assistant, David Lewis, was sure about the translation. He was.[9] That was the moment, for us, when almost everything we had previously believed about the Cuban missile crisis began to break apart and melt away, like a glacier unable to retain its integrity in the heat of the changed climate.

Now, telling you that we have eidetic memories of our first exposure to Fidel's letter will only get us so far. *Telling* you about it may not be terribly interesting to you, though it is of course to us. So here is what we suggest, by way of *showing* you what we felt like.

What follows is the complete text of Fidel Castro's "Armageddon letter" to Nikita Khrushchev during the Cuban missile crisis, which we first saw on November 23, 1990. We urge you not to read the text of the letter until you repeat to yourself, several times, the headline of the received view of the crisis:

> *Nothing* that happened on the island of Cuba—*nothing* involving the Cubans and Russians on the island—had any significance for the cause, evolution, level of nuclear danger, or resolution of the Cuban missile crisis!

Now read the letter, along with the contextual material we have added (indented, italicized, and with the identifier ***J&j,*** to help you get inside Fidel's mindset. Then you'll know what he knew or thought he knew as he was writing this desperate letter to Khrushchev:

HELLO NIKITA; GOODBYE WORLD

Fidel Castro to Nikita Khrushchev, October 27, 1962

[7:00 a.m. Saturday, October 27, Havana, Cuba]
Dear Comrade Khrushchev:

From an analysis of the situation and the reports in our possession, I consider that the aggression is almost imminent within the next 24 to 72 hours.

[J&j: The Americans are preparing for a massive attack on Cuba. Hundreds of attack planes are massed in Florida and preparing to attack. The plan is to attack Cuba, once the command is given, with 1,200 bombing runs on the first day alone. It will be a huge air attack. In addition, tens of thousands of fully armed troops are loading onto amphibious vessels in south Florida and heading toward Cuba. The landing is scheduled to occur near the city of Mariel, west of Havana, following which the U.S. troops will fight their way east toward Havana. As it happens, many of the Russian nuclear warheads are stored just south of Mariel, near the town of Bejucal, in a hillside bunker, guarded by a Russian special intelligence unit of the KGB.][10]

There are two possible variants: the first and likeliest one is an attack against certain targets with the limited objective of destroying them; the second, less probable although possible, is invasion. I understand that this variant would call for a large number of forces and it is, in addition, the most repulsive form of aggression, which might inhibit them.

[J&j: The U.S. airstrike against Soviet missile sites is coming. The invasion of Cuba will follow in order for the Americans to certify the removal of all Soviet nuclear weapons and to remove the revolutionary government and replace it with a government of Cuban exiles living in Miami, who will be willing to rule Cuba in a way that is consistent with Washington's desires.]

You can rest assured that we will firmly and resolutely resist attack, whatever it may be.

The morale of the Cuban people is extremely high and the aggressor will be confronted heroically.

[J&j: We anticipate our total destruction. We have been waiting for this moment ever since the failed, CIA-backed invasion of Cuba by 1,300 Cuban exiles in April 1961. There is nothing we can do to stop the Americans from destroying Cuba, other than surrender, which is unthinkable. We are prepared to disappear beneath the Caribbean Sea. But Comrade Nikita, do not worry about us. We 7.5 million Cubans are doomed only in the physical sense. We are ready to die honorably for Cuba, martyrs in the fight against imperialism.]

At this time I want to convey to you briefly my personal opinion.

If the second variant is implemented and the imperialists invade Cuba with the goal of occupying it, the danger that that aggressive policy poses for humanity is so great that following that event the Soviet Union must never allow the circumstances in which the imperialists could launch the first nuclear strike against it.

> ***[J&j:*** *At the first sign that the invasion of our island has begun, I urge you to launch an all-out nuclear attack on the U.S. Never again will the world have to tolerate aggression by the world's biggest bully. Cuba will be honored to have provided the occasion for the total destruction of the U.S.]*

I tell you this because I believe the imperialists' aggressiveness is extremely dangerous and if they actually carry out the brutal act of invading Cuba in violation of international law and morality, that would be the moment to eliminate such danger forever through an act of clear legitimate defense, however harsh and terrible the solution would be, for there is no other.

> ***[J&j:*** *Of course, ordering the destruction of the U.S. requires a momentous decision by you and your colleagues. But Uncle Sam is totally out of control—a monster trampling whole nations like ours underfoot without fear of retribution in kind. They have been warned. It is time to act.]*

It has influenced my opinion to see how this aggressive policy is developing, how the imperialists, disregarding world public opinion and ignoring principles of the law, are blockading the seas, violating our airspace and preparing an invasion, while at the same time frustrating every possibility for talks, even though they are aware of the seriousness of the problem.

> ***[J&j:*** *We will continue to try to destroy the U.S. planes now overflying our island on an hourly basis. Their violation of our sovereignty is humiliating to us. And each plane might be the first plane to begin the bombing attack on our people.]*

You have been and continue to be a tireless defender of peace and I realize how bitter these hours must be, when the outcome of your superhuman efforts is so seriously threatened. However, up to the last moment we will maintain the hope that peace will be safeguarded and we are willing to contribute to this as much as we can. But at the same time we are ready to calmly confront a situation which we view as quite real and quite close.

[J&j: You have the awesome responsibility to destroy the U.S. when their invasion commences. We Cuban comrades also have had an awesome responsibility that we have understood ever since the Bay of Pigs invasion in April 1961: to prepare our people to be martyred for our just and glorious cause. They are prepared. We are all prepared. We are now living our last minutes, perhaps hours, in calm equanimity, proud to provide you with a just cause for the annihilation of the U.S., the leader of the entire imperialist world.]

Once more I convey to you the infinite gratitude and recognition of our people to the Soviet people who have been so generous and fraternal with us, as well as our profound gratitude and admiration for you, and wish you success in the huge task and serious responsibilities ahead of you.

[J&j: Please remember us, remember Cuba, when it comes time to write the history of the moment when righteous representatives of the oppressed resisted the Great Imperialist Entity, just before it was destroyed once and forever!]

Fraternally,
Fidel Castro

THE CLARIFICATION, JANUARY 5, 1991

"We should wipe them off the face of the earth"

Less than two months after we first saw the letter, we participated in our Antigua conference, where Felix Kovaliev, head of the Russian Foreign Ministry Archives, added a chilling coda to Fidel's Armageddon letter. The letter,

Kovaliev told the conference, was written in a bunker beneath the Soviet embassy in Havana. Fidel and the Russian ambassador, Aleksander Alekseev, had worked on it together through the early morning hours of October 27, 1962. Two days after Fidel's letter was sent to Khrushchev, on October 29, Alekseev sent a cable to Khrushchev in an effort to clarify what he, Alekseev, thought might be some ambiguity in Fidel's own letter.

Alekseev's account provides a rare window on a leader struggling, in the fog of a deep and confusing crisis, with the catastrophic options he is facing, as Cuba prepares for Armageddon. Fidel wants to tell Khrushchev what is on his mind—martyrdom, and the necessity of Khrushchev's participation by ordering the destruction of the U.S. At the same time, Fidel wanted to come across to Khrushchev as fully rational, in control of his emotions. He wants to appear *logical*, as Alekseev later told us. He doesn't want to alarm Khrushchev, but only to inform him of the situation the Cubans, and the Russians in Cuba, are facing.

We invite you to vicariously join Fidel and Alekseev, in the wee hours of the morning of October 27, 1962, as Fidel struggles to find a way to avoid alarming Khrushchev, while asking him to nuke the U.S. in the event of an invasion he believes is both inevitable and imminent. As usual, Alekseev is chain-smoking cigarettes while Fidel, also as usual, puffs on one cigar after another. Both are eating sausages and drinking strong Cuban coffee to stay alert. The air circulation is negligible. It is almost impossible to see through the smoke from one side of the small room to the other. A nonsmoking visitor would have felt suffocated, but Fidel and his friend, "Alejandro," are energized by the pollution they are generating. Both are aware that they are approaching awful and awesome decisions.[11]

Here is the relevant portion of Alekseev's cable, exactly as it appears in the official English translation from the Russian Foreign Ministry Archives:

> On the 27th of October, at 2:00 AM Cuban time, [Cuban President Osvaldo] Dorticós called me at my apartment and said that Fidel Castro had already left to see me for an important conversation. Fidel stayed at my place until 7:00 AM Cuban time. Explaining the critical nature of the moment, he dictated and dictated again the letter sent to you. Fidel sometimes dictated, and sometimes made drafts by himself until he reached the final version. I asked him directly, "Do you mean to say that we should be the first ones to strike a nuclear blow against the enemy?" "No," answered Castro; "I do not want to say this directly. But, under certain circumstances, we should forestall them without waiting to experience ourselves the perfidy of the imperialists and the first nuclear blow

> from their side. *If they attack Cuba, we should wipe them off the face of the earth!*" He was positive that an attack was inevitable, and he said there were only five chances in a hundred that it would not happen.[12]

Both Fidel and Alekseev told us years later that they felt that the U.S. war against Cuba might begin at any moment. Thus, Fidel felt it was urgent to get the proper message to Moscow as soon as possible. As one of Fidel's colleagues, Jorge Risquet, said at the Antigua conference, "Fidel might not have had the time to send it later; it's not easy to write a letter amid radioactive rubble."[13]

Our initial reaction to Fidel's letter and Alekseev's "clarification" was rather schizoid. *Intellectually*, Fidel's letter, as clarified by Alekseev, seemed perfectly clear. On the last weekend of October 1962, Fidel had told Khrushchev what he thought was about to happen: a massive airstrike and an invasion of Cuba. Next, he had asked Khrushchev to respond to the expected U.S. attack and invasion by nuking the U.S, totally destroying it, killing its roughly 185 million inhabitants. But *emotionally*, we found it difficult to come to grips with the implications of what Fidel's letter seemed to imply. What in the world would it be like, we wondered, to make such a request? What would drive a leader to urge his powerful ally to assist in the martyrdom of one's entire country?

We saw two options: (1) Fidel had during the missile crisis become suicidal, or possibly already had suicidal tendencies that became manifest only as the crisis seemed to be careening toward all-out war; or (2) there must be some vast piece of the Cuban missile crisis that we knew nothing about—some information that would help us, if we understood it, to stand vicariously in Fidel's shoes during the crisis and conclude, as he had, that the least-worst option for Cuba was to ask his Soviet ally to destroy the U.S. in a nuclear attack, just as Cuba was being totally destroyed. It seemed on the face of it quite unlikely that Fidel had been in the grip of some presumed suicidal demons. After all, although everything about Fidel's reign in Cuba was controversial, he had by 1991 ruled Cuba creatively and forcefully for thirty-two years, in the face of tremendous U.S. hostility. How does someone who is suicidal do that? He doesn't. So, we thought, we must be missing something—something big.

Of course, we didn't know what we didn't know. But we thought it had to be connected to events on the island of Cuba, where Fidel spent the entire crisis and which the CIA during the crisis and American scholars ever since saw basically as a jungle-covered parking lot for Russian missiles. Theodore Sorensen, JFK's chief of staff and speechwriter, once told us unapologetically that he thought then, and still thought (in 1990), that Fidel and the Cubans were "bit players" who were basically irrelevant to the crisis. [More than a decade later, Ted would revise his view and join us in Havana for a discussion with Castro.]

Fidel Castro, we would learn later, decided to publish his missile crisis correspondence with Khrushchev at this time in part to insert his own, and Cuba's, point of view into the dialogues at our Antigua conference. Fidel's letter was the most discussed element of a discussion that was disorienting for the Americans. None of us, whether scholars or close associates of JFK like Robert McNamara and Arthur Schlesinger Jr., had ever before participated in an extensive discussion of the events of October 1962 from the Cuban point of view, let alone with senior Cuban officials and scholars. We learned a lot. For the first time we found ourselves discussing formerly unresearchable subjects like Cuban troop movements and Cuban intelligence assessments of the U.S. threat to the island. But we heard nothing that helped us understand Fidel's Armageddon letter to Khrushchev. We couldn't empathize. We could not yet *inhabit* the history that Cubans lived in October 1962. We could not yet stand in Fidel's shoes and write the letter he had written. The next step would be taking our team to Havana and cross-questioning Fidel as he attempted to contextualize his own letter. That conference convened one year after the Antigua discussions, meeting from January 9–12, 1992, at the National Conference Center in Havana, Cuba.

THE REFLECTION, JANUARY 9, 1992

"We took it for granted that we were going to disappear"

At the Havana conference, our Cuban and Russian colleagues continued to fill in details of the "*Cuban* Cuban missile crisis": the crisis as it appeared from the island to the 7.5 million Cubans and forty-three thousand Russians who were preparing to defend Cuba against all odds, to the last man, woman, and child on the island. We were getting closer to an appreciation of the situation in Cuba before, during, and after the Cuban missile crisis.

In the following short "highlight film" of a few things we learned at the conference, and following the conference, we switch to the *present tense*, because this was how we heard it at the time, in January 1992. The Cubans and Russians who were on the island during the crisis spoke with a degree of emotion and conviction that was very powerful. It was obvious that most of the people in the conference room—the Cubans and Russians—were sharing a common montage of eidetic memories of an unforgettable moment in their lives.

The CIA is wrong. There are more than forty-three thousand Soviet troops in Cuba rather than the roughly five thousand the CIA estimated. The Soviet nuclear warheads *have* arrived, and the Soviet forces in Cuba *are* preparing to use them in an effort to repel the U.S. invasion. In addition, Soviet forces are actively preparing to attack the U.S. naval base at Guantanamo Bay with, as we learned later, short-range tactical nuclear weapons.[14] Like the U.S., the Soviet Union is also operating at a very high level of military alert, just short of readiness for nuclear war. At roughly the same time Fidel sends his Armageddon letter to Khrushchev, Soviet forces in Cuba are ordered to change into their Soviet uniforms in order to honor their country by dying in their own uniforms. (They have previously tried to disguise themselves as Cubans.)[15]

The Cubans are on a war footing. A quarter of a million troops are pledged to fight, as Fidel writes during the crisis, to "the last man, woman and child on this island capable of holding a weapon."[16] In the east of Cuba, Defense Minster Raul Castro will lead a Cuban guerrilla force and, along with Soviet forces in the region, take the fight to the invading Americans, initially by destroying the base at Guantanamo. In central Cuba, including Havana, Fidel himself will assume command. While the nuclear forces in Cuba remain under Soviet control, all Soviet and Cuban forces on the island assume (wrongly) that the war will go nuclear almost immediately, when the Americans nuke the Cuban beaches and the Soviets reply in kind. In the west, Ernesto ("Che") Guevara is prepared to retreat with his forces into the caves of the tobacco-growing region of Pinar del Rio and, as the U.S. is settling into its occupation of Havana, his forces, along with a Soviet contingent equipped with Soviet tactical nuclear weapons, will attack whatever is left of Havana and destroy it, killing all of the occupying force.[17]

By the last weekend of October 1962, tiny Cuba has become the hinge of the world. The hinge can give way at any moment that any commander decides, for any reason, to start shooting. Once the shooting starts in earnest, a catastrophic nuclear convulsion will likely follow, an eventuality that is embraced by Castro and by most Cubans and Soviets in Cuba, but which strikes terror into Kennedy and Khrushchev, who struggle mightily to control the Frankenstein's monster they have created.

Under these conditions, Fidel Castro asks Nikita Khrushchev to nuke the U.S. when the expected invasion commences. "If the invasion had taken place in the situation that had been created," Fidel tells the January 1992 conference participants, "nuclear war would have been the result. Everybody here was simply resigned to the fate that we would be forced to pay the price, that we would disappear."[18] He recalls being utterly convinced that the Cuban people preferred martyrdom to simply being destroyed meaninglessly by the overwhelming U.S. attack and invasion, which Fidel believes is inevitable and, by October 27, 1962, imminent. The fuse of Armageddon, according to Fidel's understanding, could be lit at any moment on the final weekend of October 1962. Just as Cuba is to be wiped off the face of the earth, the U.S. should also be totally and irrevocably destroyed. Fidel's letter to Khrushchev is written as the last will and testament of the Cuban nation, as imagined by their leader.

We would later learn from Nikita Khrushchev's son and biographer, Sergei Khrushchev, what his father told him about how he had reacted to Fidel's Armageddon letter. Khrushchev and the Soviet leadership receive the letter at a moment when Khrushchev and Kennedy are struggling to defuse the crisis short of war. Khrushchev explodes: "*What? Is he proposing that we start a nuclear war? That we launch missiles from Cuba?*" An aide confirms this. "*That is insane. We deployed missiles there to prevent an attack on the island, to save Cuba and defend socialism. And now not only is he preparing to die himself, he wants to drag us with him.*"[19] Kennedy never learned about this Armageddon letter from Fidel to Khrushchev. But if he had known about it, he would undoubtedly have shared Khrushchev's view: Fidel is not just a loose cannon; he is a certifiably suicidal lunatic.

THE TRUTH IS SCARIER THAN THE BULLSHIT

But we now know that Fidel was far from insane, far from suicidal. He was rational, given that he had concluded that Cuba's destruction was inevitable (an impression that the Americans were trying to convey but without sufficiently thinking through the implications of such a strategy). If Fidel's letter had been the raving of a crazy man, the relevance of the crisis would simply be the common-sense injunction to try to keep crazy people from becoming leaders of countries. But in October 1962, rational leaders, making decisions each believed were in their country's interests, unwittingly went sleepwalking together toward the nuclear abyss, dragging the whole world with them. The Cuban missile crisis is scary and perennially relevant not because Fidel Castro was crazy, but because he was *not* crazy![20] Something like it could happen again, in our 21st century world, with its nearly fifteen thousand nuclear weapons.

That's no bullshit. That's the truth. As the great American novelist Kurt Vonnegut wrote: "The truth can be really powerful stuff. You're not expecting it."[21] You are here today, reading these words, because three leaders got lucky in October 1962. Ask yourself how it feels when you consider that the planet you inhabit today was saved from total destruction in October 1962 principally by luck. Let the idea sink in. Will you bet we'll get that lucky next time?

Don't. For more than half a century, we've been told that the Cuban missile crisis was a great victory because the Russians blinked and the Americans didn't (while the Cubans didn't matter). But that is total bullshit.

If we continue to subscribe to the bullshit version of the Cuban missile crisis, we will likely pay insufficient attention to its Great Lesson—that the event was not a victory of any kind, for anybody. It was instead a colossal failure by rational leaders to steer clear of the abyss of nuclear Armageddon. They deceived themselves, as they discovered when it was almost too late to avoid catastrophe. This is the history that leads to the warning: the next time the world finds itself staring into the nuclear abyss and war breaks out, the lucky ones will likely be those who die quickly. The living will envy the dead. Their nasty, brutish, and short existence will resemble that of Papa & The Boy in *The Road*. Moving swiftly and safely to nuclear abolition is the way to save Papa & The Boy, and the rest of us.

PART II
DARKER

You want it darker.

—Leonard Cohen, (2016)[1]

At the peak of danger in the Cuban missile crisis, prospects for avoiding Armageddon looked very dark. U.S. and Russian leaders seemed unable to find an exit ramp from their downward spiral toward nuclear war. But the Cubans, and Russian forces in Cuba, faced a darker, apocalyptic certainty, well beyond the darkness of anxiety and uncertainty felt in Washington and Moscow. The Cubans prepared for what they were convinced was their inevitable, total annihilation. They had concluded that the U.S. meant to crush the Revolution; a U.S. air attack and invasion was imminent; and there was nothing they could do to prevent it. Thus did the Cuban leadership inform the Russians of their willingness to martyr the Cuban nation of 7.5 million in exchange for the total destruction of the U.S. in a Russian nuclear attack.

Part II provides a three-part immersion in the Cuban mindset of martyrdom:

- *An introduction to "habitable history," a method for conducting accurate history, fortified with plausible conjectures as to what the main characters in the crisis were thinking and feeling in real time (chapter 4)*
- *The education of JFK's Secretary of Defense, Robert McNamara, derived from his extraordinary dialogues in Havana, thirty years after the crisis, with Cuban leader Fidel Castro, who explained to McNamara in detail why he asked the Russians to nuke the U.S. (chapter 5)*
- *A psychological journey into the mind and circumstances of Fidel Castro, at the height of the crisis, as he prepared his people for a U.S. nuclear attack that would destroy Cuba (chapter 6)*

4

HABITABLE HISTORY

How Hilary Mantel's Wolf Hall *Became the Template for a "WABAC" Machine for the Cuban Missile Crisis*

Habitable: suitable or good enough to live in.

—Oxford English Dictionary[1]

An imaginative writer . . . has a responsibility to get the history right. . . . That's the absolute foundation of what I do. I begin to imagine at the point where the facts run out. But, like a historian, I'm working on the great marshy ground of interpretation.

—Hilary Mantel, in an interview with Jeffrey Brown, *PBS NewsHour,* April 3, 2015[2]

LEARNING FROM MR. PEABODY AND SHERMAN

Building an Armageddon WABAC Machine from Scratch

How, we wondered, can we reach out and connect with people like yourself in ways that put you in touch, at best imperfectly and retrospectively, but with some nontrivial fraction of the psychological reality of the Cuban missile crisis as it was experienced by leaders in real time, moving forward, uncertain of the outcome, not knowing if they would find a peaceful way out?

How do we do this as scholars who lack that single rarest and most valuable quality: *being there, then*—like former Defense Secretary Robert S. McNamara, our focus in chapter 5, or like Fidel Castro, the central player in chapter 6? How do we build an Armageddon space/time machine for the Cuban missile crisis that is engaging to all of us, but especially to the young emerging digerati of this 21st century? How do we make the ancient history of more than a half-century ago come alive today? How do we prevent the scariest event in recorded history from becoming just another dusty story, full of dates on which this, that, or the other thing happened?

In a desperate moment that combined wishful thinking, outright fantasy, and a bit of gallows humor, we found ourselves wishing we could call on two animated heroes from the Saturday morning cartoons of our long-gone youth: Mr. Peabody, the creature with the body of a beagle, the brain of an Einstein, and a finishing school accent, and his adopted boy, Sherman.[3]

All the plots revolved around a time machine Peabody built for Sherman as a birthday present. They called their machine the WABAC (pronounced "Way Back"). At the beginning of each show, Peabody would instruct his boy to "set the WABAC machine, Sherman" for the moment and locale in time to which they were about to time/space travel. Over our dinner table, we took turns bombarding one another with instructions like: "Set the WABAC machine for Havana, Cuba, October 26 to 27, 1962, Sherman. We're going to shadow Fidel Castro as he makes his final preparation for Armageddon." But, unable to summon Peabody, Sherman, and the WABAC, what, we wondered, might constitute *a literary WABAC machine* that would permit us, in the 21st century, to time/space travel vicariously to that moment of maximum peril, such that real empathy is possible with the leaders who, in those extraordinary circumstances, carried the fate of the world on their shoulders?

Are you sitting down? We think it advisable to read the next sentence sitting down. We will attempt to transport you vicariously to the moment of supreme nuclear truth by adapting a technique used recently by an author to achieve a similar transport to the court of England's King Henry VIII—the monarch who kept marrying and ditching his wives (killing two of them outright) in his doomed pursuit of a viable male heir to his throne. Really. Read on.

HILARY MANTEL'S MAGIC

Learning to "Slide Inside" the Protagonists in the Cuban Missile Crisis

Enter Hilary Mantel—Dame Hilary Mantel—the author of two recent landmark historical novels about Thomas Cromwell, *consigliere*, "fixer," to King Henry VIII, each a winner of Great Britain's most prestigious literary award, the Man Booker Prize: *Wolf Hall* (2009) and *Bring Up the Bodies* (2012).[4] In awarding her the 2012 prize, the Man Booker committee wrote that the two books together represent "one of the greatest achievements of modern literature."[5] In addition, two fine adaptations of the books appeared in early 2015, one each by the BBC and the Royal Shakespeare Company.[6]

We read Mantel's *Wolf Hall* at a critical moment for us. We were impressed by reviews from specialists in Tudor history commending Mantel for having mastered the scholarly literature; and we were personally astonished by the power of her gift for communicating the immediacy and contingency of lives lived forward, without knowledge of the future. Mantel came to her history of Cromwell's England having spent half a lifetime developing her skill at empathetic historical fiction. In 2009, when *Wolf Hall* was published, we read her book after half a lifetime of immersion in the history of the October 1962 Cuban missile crisis, the Biggest Bang in recorded history that almost, but didn't quite, happen.

We were searching for a way to make the nuclear danger of the crisis more vivid and real than we or anyone else had done before, while sticking to the rules of good history as Mantel has done: not falsifying the record, inventing neither characters nor situations, and by what Mantel calls "sliding inside" the individuals through whose prisms all the action occurs. Mantel is usually classified as an author of historical fiction—that is, a writer of tales that never really happened. But this is misleading. She is a learned historian who chooses, as she puts it, "to imagine when the facts run out." We call this *habitable history*: real history, and really compelling. In Mantel's Cromwell books, we happily follow her as she inhabits the life, mind, and times of Thomas Cromwell.

"SO NOW GET UP!"

Hilary Mantel Takes Her WABAC Machine to Young Cromwell, Putney, 1500

Wolf Hall opens in Putney, in southwest London, in the year 1500, with fifteen year-old Thomas Cromwell hearing Walter, his father, shouting "*So now get up!*"[7] It is the first sentence in the book. The boy Thomas is in the midst of a terrible beating by his brutal alcoholic father. Thomas is cheek down on the cobblestones bruised, bleeding, vomiting, and nearly unconscious. In some instinctual way, he manages in that moment to consider his options, which reduce to two: he can crawl away from his father and, as he has done countless times in the past, nurse his wounds and try to avoid his father as long as possible before the next violent episode. Or, he can slip away this time, nurse his wounds, and, as soon as he is able, leave home and Putney forever and take his chances on the open road, bound eventually for whatever fate awaits him "across the narrow sea," on the European continent.[8]

Hilary Mantel spent more than five years of immersion in the history of the Tudor period before she wrote "*So now get up!*" That's a lot of reading, note taking, querying the academic experts on the events and personalities of the period, arranging and rearranging ideas for how to organize the as-yet-unwritten first draft of an eventual book.

Mantel has spoken eloquently of that moment when, after years of research, the beginning and the essence of *Wolf Hall* became manifest to her—the moment when she felt herself beginning to inhabit the person of Thomas Cromwell:

> *I remember when I began Wolf Hall, and I had no idea when I sat down to write how the book was going to sound or, really, what viewpoint the story was coming from. But I had a voice in my head. I had a voice saying, "So now get up!" And when I listened to that, the voice was above my head. Then a picture formed, and the picture was a sideways angled view of a boot, it was a close-up, it was the stitching of the boot, it was a knot in the twine of the stitching. And the cobbles—when you feel the cobbles under your cheekbone—and then you can't see anything because there's blood in your eyes. And so the way I described it at one point was: in a simple twist of being, I was inside Thomas Cromwell's body. He's a fifteen-year-old boy, lying on the cobblestones with a sense that death is imminent.*
>
> *And then, all the [major] decisions about the novel have been taken:*

- *Where is this story coming from? Well, from behind his eyes.*
- *No question of who's in charge of the narrative, because he is.*

- *No question of what tense to use because—when is this happening? It's happening now.*

> *So in that act of sliding inside another character's body—or a person's body, you should say if they're a real person—that is the mediation, and that trick—the sliding inside—has to be repeated again and again and again. I find the transition is instant, or it will never occur.*[9]

What does Hilary Mantel mean when she says she slides into the body of Thomas Cromwell? Mantel's relationship to Cromwell on the cobblestones (and subsequently) seems to lie somewhere between the merely figurative and fully physical. It feels vividly real to her. If it didn't feel this way, according to Mantel, then as a writer she would have no chance of conveying convincingly Thomas Cromwell's life and world to her readers. Of course, we do not actually *become* Cromwell. But instead, we *inhabit* him. It's as if we visit Cromwell from the inside out. His world is our world, for the length of our visit.

Moreover, Mantel seems to us in earnest when she says that the important decisions shaping the novel were taken once she hears those four words—"So now get up!"—in their particular physical and psychological context. This command is, in fact, the grain of sand in which it is possible to see the world of Cromwell unfold over the 942 pages that follow in the two novels—the way the world shapes him and the way he eventually shapes the world of Tudor England. The boy who survives his brutal beating will also survive, and eventually thrive, all over the European continent, as a soldier, merchant, banker, linguist, and, eventually, the second most powerful man in England after his boss, Henry VIII. He is confident, tough, smart, crafty, calculating, and intensely ambitious. Mantel the historian has nailed her man.[10]

Mantel introduces us to a man who, in addition, is funny, compassionate, heartbroken at the deaths of his wife and daughters due to the "sweating sickness," and a man who uses his lower-class background to his advantage, as an exotic semisavage, who just happens to know how to cook, how to fix a jury, how to kill a man in a multiplicity of ways with all manner of weapons, who puts in eighteen-hour days working while the grandees amuse themselves in chasing after foxes, or each other. We spend the entirety of both novels thoroughly embedded in the ruminations of a deeply ironical intelligence. We want to be in the company of this remarkable man; thanks to Hilary Mantel's gift of supreme empathy, we want to inhabit him.

Bring Up the Bodies concludes thirty-six years after Cromwell's father shouts at him, "so now get up!" It is the evening of May 19, 1536. The queen,

Anne Boleyn, has just been beheaded, an act ordered by Henry VIII, and organized, justified, and implemented at Cromwell's orders. Cromwell has played the only merciful card in his hand and argued successfully to Henry that Anne should die painlessly, decapitated by an expert swordsman from Calais. It is late at night, as we come in on Cromwell, who has just finished going over the late queen's debts.

> *His next task is somehow to reconcile the king and the Lady Mary, to save Henry from killing his own daughter; and before that, to stop Mary's friends from killing him [i.e., Cromwell]. He has helped them to their new world, the world without Anne Boleyn, and now they will think they can do without Cromwell too. They have eaten his banquet and now they will want to sweep him out with the rushes and the bones. But this was his table: he runs on the top of it, among the broken meats. Let them try to pull him down. They will find him armored, they will find him entrenched, they will find him stuck like a limpet to the future.*[11]

We know how it will end for Cromwell: on the chopping block four years later, as Henry VIII becomes increasingly unstable, vindictive, and desperate. But the hallucination of presence created by Hilary Mantel is so convincing that our foreknowledge of Cromwell's demise doesn't much matter. It's as if we are with Cromwell, in his space and time and situation, rushing headlong into the darkly uncertain future. He got up when he was fifteen, and he has now gotten up again at fifty. We expect to be oddly surprised at the ending, when it comes, just as we have been surprised by the death of Anne Boleyn. Surprised, and saddened.

HABITABLE HISTORY AND THE LESSONS OF THE PAST

Dame Hilary has set the bar high for habitable history. Its requirements are easily identified but implemented only with considerable difficulty. The WABAC machine that results in habitable history—with readers inhabiting the main characters in a realistic, data-driven way—has two principal requirements: (1) the primary material must be history, not fantasy. The stuff it contains happened, or is believed by credible witnesses to have happened, and the reflections such happenings induce in the characters are credibly delivered to the reader. And (2) the principal character, or characters, must be thoroughly inhabitable—knowable, believably complex—a creature from a place and time other than where and when we reside, one who is recognizably from there and then, but whom we can to a significant degree understand and appreciate here and now.

Habitable history must therefore reflect two kinds of historical reality: what really happened, as far as we can tell from documents and oral testimony; and how what really happened looked and felt to those to whom it was happening. The magic of the habitable history of Hilary Mantel's Cromwell books is that we are both there, then, and not there, not then. Or, put even more cryptically but with fewer negative formulations: in Hilary Mantel's books, you can be 16th century Thomas Cromwell, and at the same time you can be 21st century yourself. We are aware that this seems to violate the laws of physics. But *inhabiting history is a psychological act, not a physical act.* So we urge you not to worry about the physics of time and space travel. Habitable history is tough to pull off. But when it works, you can be sure that you are not only enjoying the ride back in *time* but also back into *history.* Our chapters on Robert McNamara and Fidel Castro—chapters 5 and 6—are as strongly reality-based as we know how to make them. They contain signs, pointers, and hints of the lessons that we, as fellow human beings, should draw from their histories and apply to our present and future.

5

BE ROBERT S. McNAMARA

Bringing the Abolition Message Home, With (and Without) "Maximum Bob"

Whoever is educated by anxiety is educated by possibility . . . So when such a person graduates from the school of possibility, he knows better than a child knows his ABC's that perdition and annihilation live next door to every man.

—Søren Kierkegaard, *The Concept of Anxiety* (1844)[1]

I was there; I have had direct experience in trying to handle a nuclear crisis with the fate of the earth on the line; I know—I am not guessing or speculating, I know—that we were just plain lucky in October 1962, and without that luck most of you would never have been born because the world would have been destroyed instantly or made unlivable. And something like it could happen today, tonight, next year. It will happen at some point. That is why we must abolish nuclear weapons as soon as possible.

—Robert S. McNamara, in a lecture at Brown University, April 27, 2005[2]

"MAXIMUM BOB"

The Hair-Raising Message of Bob McNamara

Our essential partner in the enterprise of discovering the hidden history of the Cuban missile crisis was Robert S. McNamara, secretary of defense to presidents Kennedy and Johnson. One of our nicknames for Bob

McNamara, with whom we collaborated for more than twenty years, was "Maximum Bob," after a character in an Elmore Leonard crime novel (also called *Maximum Bob*).[3] The nickname was fitting. Everything about Bob's approach to the Cuban missile crisis was "maximum": the intensity, the take-no-prisoners demeanor, and the messianic zeal with which he delivered his message.

Alone among top American officials who advised President Kennedy during the crisis, McNamara emerged from his experience of the Great Escape of October 1962 with a "calling," in the old-fashioned sense of a vocation that seems to have sought him out rather than the other way around. He was incapable of discussing the events of October 1962 dispassionately. He refused to participate in discussions of issues like "how probable was nuclear war in the Cuban missile crisis?" on the grounds that he couldn't care less what the probability was, and in any case no one will ever know what the probability was anyway.

To Bob McNamara, the salient fact about the crisis was that nuclear war was *possible*. In his opinion, if it was *possible* that the world could have been destroyed as a result of the crisis—if the catastrophe would have been infinite in scope, as he believed it clearly would have if nuclear war had broken out—then the conversation should in his view move immediately to the ways and means for abolishing the nuclear weapons that could have destroyed human civilization in October 1962. Otherwise, according to Bob, the human race, particularly leaders of nuclear-armed nations, must live with the responsibility of protecting their constituents and fellow citizens from catastrophe, knowing all the while that leaders who were charged with that responsibility in October 1962 nearly blew it, even though none sought doomsday, no one was crazy, all were rational. To Bob McNamara, in light of the near miss of the Cuban missile crisis, the acceptance of living with nuclear weapons is, to use one of his favorite phrases, "*absolutely insane!*"[4]

A singular attribute of McNamara was this: when the topic of the Cuban missile crisis arose, he spoke and acted almost as if he had actually experienced Armageddon. His demeanor was that of a man who had been to the deepest level of hell and had returned to tell his tale and issue forth with a dire warning that is nicely summarized by two lines in an old spiritual, "Mary Don't You Weep":

> God gave Noah the rainbow sign,
> No more water, but the fire next time.[5]

To McNamara, our demise will commence with the nuclear fire next time, and the proof lay at the heart of the Cuban missile crisis, which "should" have exploded into nuclear war but mysteriously and fortunately did not—a stroke of cosmic luck unlikely to be repeated in some future crisis. Armageddon had not *quite* occurred in the crisis. But Bob McNamara's body language when addressing the crisis suggested that he had imagined things that were previously unthinkable: the nonmetaphorical, no-kidding, I-am-not-exaggerating-for-effect end of the world as we know it. The *imagined Armageddon* he experienced was vividly horrifying. He struggled throughout the rest of his life to convey in words the horror he experienced. But he had no trouble at all explaining what that experience meant: the world—beginning with the U.S. and Russia—must abolish nuclear weapons as swiftly and safely as possible.

THIS "JEREMIAH" WAS DEFINITELY A BULLFROG

"The Bony Finger and Crazy Agenda of a Street Saint"

According to the Old Testament, the prophet Jeremiah was ordered by God to warn the people of Israel of the coming destruction of Jerusalem, their capture, and their removal to Babylon for many years. They had taken to worshiping Baal, breaking their covenant with God, and bringing God's wrath down on them. Because of his doomsday message and his fierce, unyielding demeanor, Jeremiah was immensely unpopular with his own people, who attempted unsuccessfully to murder him to shut him up. Undeterred, Jeremiah continued his solitary struggle to wake his people to their imminent danger. We all know what happened. Jeremiah may have been a pain in the neck to his people, but Jeremiah was *right!* The Israelites, deaf to Jeremiah's warnings, were carted off to suffer through their half-century-long Babylonian captivity.

Bob McNamara was the Jeremiah of the Cuban missile crisis and of the nuclear age. McNamara did not claim to have received messages from God or anyone else, but he did claim to have looked into the nuclear abyss in the crisis and to have special insight into the fragility of peace in the nuclear age, and especially about how even a master planner like himself could be faced, unexpectedly and unprepared, with a situation in which the entire world was at risk. In our minds' eyes, we can still see him, a stooped octogenarian, left shoulder drooping far below the level of the right (Bob was left-handed), wearing his tattered Burberry raincoat, carrying his ancient travel bag through some airport, on his way to some place to scare the hell out of yet another audience by connecting the dots, as he saw them, between the situational insanity of his experience in the Cuban missile crisis and the urgent necessity of moving as swiftly and safely as possible to nuclear abolition.

It is said that for every pond there can be only one bullfrog. Otherwise, a fight will ensue to determine who stays and who goes. Wherever Bob McNamara went to speak about the Cuban missile crisis, no matter what kind of audience he addressed—defense experts, teachers, retirees, military officers, students, you name it—he was the bullfrog. His volcanic personality, his amazing command of facts and figures, the quickness of his mind, even into his late eighties—meant that Bob's agenda would be *the* agenda. When we were participating with Bob McNamara in events—whether before a live audience, on TV or radio, in films, or before students in the classroom—there were moments when it seemed to us that his "Jeremiah" tendency might overwhelm the audience or interviewer or students or whomever was the object of his message. Bob seldom noticed, in the white heat of his presentation. When this happened, when we thought "Jeremiah" was beginning to turn off his audience, one of us would begin to hum, or write out (as the occasion required), "Jeremiah was a bullfrog/he was a good friend of mine"—the first two lines of the 1971 Hoyt Axton pop hit "Joy to the World" performed by the band Three Dog Night.[6] We don't believe Bob McNamara ever noticed us noticing his Jeremiah moments. But they were our self-initiated cues to intervene, lighten things up, tell a joke, or whatever it took to help Bob's medicine go down a little easier, or at the very least, to keep the audience from freaking out and bolting toward the exits.

One time at Brown University, where we were on the faculty for twenty years, Bob McNamara was getting out of control in front of an audience of mostly undergraduate students. His blazer had come off. His sleeves were rolled up. He was sweating and pounding the table as he made his points. He'd gone on far past his allotted time to speak and was showing no sign of slowing down or concluding. One of us (JGB) was on the panel with him, the other (jML) was in the first row. Following a "Jeremiah was a bullfrog" moment between the two of us, one of us (JGB) interrupted Bob, startling him into temporary, unplanned silence—saying simply, "Bob!" Loudly—and then continuing, to the audience: "The only reason we are letting Secretary McNamara speak first, and go on so long, is that this is National Secretaries Day. Normally, we'd have cut him off by now." Bob got the joke, but not right away, which made the joke even funnier. He laughed along with the audience, but about two beats behind them. He then quickly concluded and the panel moved on.[7]

Bob McNamara's demeanor, which resembled that of the original Jeremiah, intimidated some and infuriated others, who resented his self-assurance about the close proximity of the crisis to catastrophe, the necessity of abolishing nuclear weapons, and his steadfast unwillingness to consider alternative views. People of diverse political persuasions and historical sensibilities felt, as one of his former subordinates, Paul Nitze, told us, "McNamara was traumatized by the crisis and he never recovered." Nitze clearly thought McNamara had freaked out unnecessarily—that he panicked, that the crisis wasn't really as dangerous as McNamara believed. Nitze went further. "The Cuban missile crisis of lore," he told us, "was in McNamara's brain, not in the Caribbean. But because McNamara had the president's ear, instead of someone more experienced and less panicky, Kennedy let the Russians off the hook when we could have squeezed a lot more out of them."[8]

We once mentioned Nitze's comment to McNamara, that he had been "traumatized." Bob's response was: "You're damn right I was traumatized by the prospect of us blowing up the world. How could you *not* be traumatized if you think nuclear war is about to break out and you don't know how to prevent it? I don't need a psychiatrist; I need the world to abolish nuclear weapons. Then I'll be over my trauma."

Longtime *New Yorker* staff writer Roger Angell spoke for many when he wrote about his experience of seeing McNamara perform in *The Fog of War*, Errol Morris's brilliant Academy Award-winning 2004 documentary about McNamara. Angell wrote that he felt uneasy watching "old Robert McNamara . . . standing in our path with the bony finger and crazy agenda of a street saint."[9] This captures well the nuclear-age Jeremiah that McNamara became late in life. In fact, *The Fog of War* presents the best opportunity now available to see McNamara in action discussing the Cuban missile crisis.

Why not have a look, before continuing. The entire movie is available free and online. But first watch a 2:17 clip from the film of McNamara on the crisis. (The note provides the link to this video clip.)[10] Don't worry if you feel you should run for cover, to protect yourself from an assault by this eighty-five-year-old man who seems to be leaping off the screen straight at your face. We've often had that feeling when in a room with Bob!

In *The Fog of War*, McNamara is dressed semi-formally in his "official" interview outfit: blue blazer, white shirt, and blue tie. In person, Bob would usually remove his blazer even before he began to speak, anticipating the added internal combustion he planned on generating when he really got rolling. He would then roll up his sleeves, Bobby Kennedy style, all the way past his elbows, creating fewer restrictions on his left arm, which was his gesturing and pounding arm. He would lean forward, ready to come straight at you with high-volume recollections of the crisis, references to research on the crisis, and admonitions to abolish nuclear weapons before they abolish us. Nearly all such performances were accompanied by the rhythmic pounding of his left fist on the table or lectern, a feature regrettably missing from the movie, as Errol Morris did not provide Bob with anything on which to pound. Peter Osnos, founder of PublicAffairs, who published two books one of us (JGB) coauthored with McNamara, used to urge us to try to offer live audiences some "comic relief" because, he said, "Bob is the scariest man any of these people will have ever encountered."[11] Bob's response was that it was his moral responsibility as a historical witness—as a decision-maker in history's most dangerous crisis—to say what frightened him, why we today should be frightened of the nuclear threat, and what we should do about it.

BE ROBERT McNAMARA, OCTOBER 1962

Peer Into the Nuclear Abyss with Him and Be Very Afraid

Imagine you are Robert McNamara, on the last weekend of October. Slide inside McNamara and monitor what you see and feel. Of course, this will be artificial, but try it. Even an exercise as removed as this one is from the real context of October 1962 can teach us something if we let it. Climb aboard the WABAC machine, set for late at night at the Pentagon on Friday, October 26, 1962, in the office of the U.S. secretary of defense.

> *[The following scenarios are written in the* present tense. *Try to stay in the present tense—read them as if they are happening now, at this very moment, or seem about to happen, a few moments from now. They are not only happening now, you don't understand why they are happening, or what they imply about the motives of the Russians. You don't understand how leaders like yourself could have gotten into this perverse fix. But here you are: confused, scared, exhausted (you've slept on a cot for a couple of hours a night in your Pentagon office throughout the previous nine days of the crisis), and burdened with an awesome sense of personal responsibility for screwing up so badly that the thing you most want to avoid, nuclear war, may be on the verge of happening.]*

You are assaulted by many plausible paths to Armageddon. You are struggling with three doomsday scenarios, often on an hourly basis, and usually simultaneously. You know—in excruciating detail better than any other human being—how and why the U.S. nuclear forces are wired so that if any scenario begins to occur, nuclear war may break out in a spasm of hideous destruction, and the kicker is that it may not be in your power to prevent it or stop it once it is underway. If whole nations are destroyed in a matter of minutes or hours, the world as you know it will cease to exist. There will be no future for you, your children, or anyone, anywhere. In your position as secretary of defense, it is your job to prevent all that from happening, via a combination of threats and accommodation. If nuclear war breaks out, you will have failed utterly, when everything—literally everything—was on the line.

Here's what you are worried sick about:

- *The Panicky Second Lieutenant.* What if a zealous Russian second lieutenant manning a missile site in Cuba panics, becomes trigger-happy, and launches a nuke at American military or civilian targets in the U.S.? Tens of thousands, even millions, might be killed. U.S. and NATO military doctrine requires a nuclear response to a nuclear attack. But if the U.S. responds in kind, then what? Probably further escalation in a matter of minutes or hours to all-out nuclear war and, in your favorite doomsday phrase, "*the destruction of nations.*"
- *The Move Against West Berlin.* What if, in reaction to U.S. moves against Cuba, the Russians, with hundreds of thousands of troops nearby, move against West Berlin? The NATO force of just twelve thousand troops (from the U.S., UK, and France) will quickly be massively outmanned, and so forced to respond with tactical nuclear weapons, leading to probable escalation throughout Europe, then all over the world. Then what? "*The destruction of nations.*" You pound your left fist on your desk.
- *War Breaks Out at Sea.* When the U.S. Navy intercepts a Russian vessel bound for Cuba, what if the intercepted ship tries to elude U.S. attempts to stop it from continuing on to Cuba? What if the U.S. Navy is forced to sink the Russian ship? What if one or more Russian attack submarines counterattacks? What if that war at sea spreads, ultimately involving U.S. and Russian forces in Europe and elsewhere in which nuclear forces from both sides come into play? Then what? Yup: "*the destruction of nations.*"[12]

On October 26–27, you, as Secretary of Defense Robert S. McNamara, see the world begin to crack and disintegrate along a rapidly expanding array of fissures. That this catastrophe does not unfold is a colossal relief and a surprise—a surprise as incomprehensible, shocking, and unexpected as your vision that Armageddon was about to start. These two factors together—you did *not* expect a crisis threatening Armageddon and, from deep inside its most dangerous moments on October 26 to 27, 1962, you did *not* expect to escape Armageddon—these shocks lead you straightaway to the conclusion that "*We lucked out.* It was *luck* that prevented nuclear war in the Cuban missile crisis!"[13]

BE ROBERT McNAMARA, JANUARY 1992

It was More Dangerous than You Ever Imagined

Our research on the crisis over the past thirty years proves beyond reasonable doubt that Paul Nitze (who believed that the crisis was not so dangerous) was dead wrong and Bob McNamara was dead right. We now know from the archives of all three countries, and testimony of former officials, that the three doomsday scenarios Bob worried about *were* likely to occur, if the precipitating conditions he also worried about had occurred. But it turns out that McNamara did not know the half of it in October 1962. We now know that nuclear war could have commenced in many other ways as well, and under many conditions that McNamara could not foresee, simply because the U.S. government lacked the relevant information about the motives and capabilities of the Cubans and the forty-three thousand Russians manning the nukes in Cuba.

For example, the Russians on the island were ready and willing to nuke any invading U.S. force, something that McNamara never dreamed was possible. (The CIA believed at the time that no nuclear warheads had yet arrived in Cuba.) Another example: in the event of a U.S. invasion, the Russians were also ready and willing, with Cuban assistance, to nuke the U.S. base at Guantanamo Bay, in eastern Cuba, another eventuality that never appeared on McNamara's scope. If either of these scenarios had happened, a nuclear U.S. counterattack would have killed millions of Cubans and thousands of Russians on the island. Cuba would have been completely destroyed. And that would have been only the beginning—of the end of the world, as we know it.

Most of the information bearing on these scenarios has come from Russian and Cuban scholars, as well as many former high-ranking officials, at conferences we organized in the U.S., Russia, and Cuba. We were sitting next to Bob McNamara in Havana in January 1992 when he learned about the possibility of a nuclear attack on an invading U.S. force in Cuba, a force that would not have been equipped with nuclear weapons. He was speechless. His face turned pale. He couldn't believe what he had just heard. The interpreters confirmed the accuracy of the first translation. Bob was absolutely mortified.

SET YOUR WABAC MACHINE, READER

Time & Space Traveling to Havana, Cuba, January 9–12, 1992, as Maximum Bob Meets the Maximum Leader

The most important single fact ever revealed about the Cuban missile crisis, the revelation that has led to a total rethinking of its danger and relevance to the 21st century, occurred in a conference room in Havana, Cuba. Anatoly Gribkov, a Russian general you have probably never heard of, disclosed it. What the Americans had believed was impossible turned out to be not just possible, but actual. The drama was palpable.

Take a (vicarious) seat at that conference table in Havana where we were forced to imagine the previously unimaginable. Climb into the WABAC machine, set for Havana, Cuba, in early January 1992.[14]

It is now just before 3:00 p.m., January 9, 1992. We are gathered in a large conference center in Havana, Cuba, in the room typically used for meetings where Fidel Castro or others in the leadership are participating. Security is tight. All members of the three delegations—Cuban, Russian, and American—are seated and quiet, as are those in the contingent in the periphery, here to observe the proceedings. These back-benchers are a varied lot: members of the extended Kennedy family; a large force of security guards, all in dark blue business suits, many with an earphone that betrays their purpose in being present; two TV crews—one from Cuba, one from the U.S. The most peculiar, yet somehow relevant, individual among the observers is the American actor and singer Mandy Patinkin, who starred on Broadway as Ernesto ("Che") Guevara—Fidel Castro's radical, Argentine-born lieutenant and cultural icon—in the Andrew Lloyd Webber musical *Evita*.

Exactly at 3:00 p.m., Fidel Castro, known around the world (though not in Cuba) as *el Líder Máximo* ("the Maximum Leader"), enters the conference room, accompanied by his deputy for international affairs Jorge Risquet; his legendary interpreter Juana Florinda Vera García ("Juanita," who would become a good friend of ours over the years); and a bevvy of beefy, scowling bodyguards. Making his way around the large, rectangular conference table, Fidel introduces himself to each of the conferees, shaking hands with each, and offering *un abrazo* (a one-armed, side-by-side Cuban hug) to some of the Russian participants. Risquet formally introduces his boss to those at the table not previously familiar to the Cuban leader. Finally, after making his way around the table past the Russian and Cuban delegations, he arrives at the U.S. delegation. As he arrives at our side of the table, he pauses and jokes that he is delighted to welcome the delegation of "imperialists" and "aggressors," a joke that will be repeated throughout the conference by both Castro and Risquet. We laugh, but our leader, Maximum Bob McNamara, does not.

Fidel Castro pauses just as he is about to be introduced to McNamara. He knows *of* McNamara, of course. Here, standing right in front of him, is Robert McNamara, whose signature is on countless documents from the period authorizing various sorts of covert operations against Cuba. Here is the man who ran the naval blockade of Cuba during the Cuban missile crisis. Here is the man who once was poised to order an airstrike and a massive invasion of Cuba, the goal of which would have been to liquidate the Cuban Revolution and its "Maximum Leader" along with it. Castro has been fully briefed by his Cuban colleagues on McNamara's performance at previous conferences on the crisis in Moscow and on the Caribbean island of Antigua: they have emphasized McNamara's passionate intensity, his willingness to admit mistakes, but also his relentless pressure on the Cubans and Russians to reciprocate by admitting their mistakes. Castro knows that if McNamara is to remain in his seat throughout the conference and not walk out in protest, the discussion that is about to commence must not be either one-sidedly anti-American nor just a stroll down memory lane, yielding no important "additions to history," as McNamara likes to put it.

Fidel Castro is fitted out from head to foot as if ready for battle: green fatigues, highly polished combat boots, and a degree of girth through his chest that suggests he is wearing a bullet-proof vest. Bob McNamara, in contrast, is standing next to us wearing what we have come to call his "official" conference outfit: a short sleeve blue polo shirt, khaki pants, and New Balance 990 running shoes.

Bob McNamara, unable to stand the tension anymore while Fidel stares at him for what seems like a very long moment, suddenly strikes preemptively. Before Risquet can get in position to introduce Bob, McNamara turns toward Castro, and blurts out: "*Robert McNamara, sir!*" as he extends his right hand to the Cuban leader. Taken by surprise, Castro takes a step backward. He stares at McNamara full in the face, and clasps his hands over the shiny buckle on his leather military belt, priestlike, in what will become a familiar pose. After an extended moment of silence, during which one could have heard a pin drop in the large and crowded conference room, a broad smile breaks out over the Cuban leader's face, and he extends his right hand to McNamara, saying, via Juanita, his interpreter, "So, Mr. McNamara, we meet at last. Welcome to Cuba!" Applause breaks out around the room among all but the security guards, who maintain their "mannequin challenge" postures throughout.

The two of us have worked with our Cuban colleagues for three years to produce this conference. All of us on the U.S. side notice that the audio equipment is not the East German stuff used at the 1989 conference in Moscow. It is state of the art, manufactured by Sony in Japan. Someone behind us remarks on his surprise at finding examples of Asian capitalist iniquity right here in the epicenter of avowedly Socialist Cuba. The entire conference, lasting three days, is filmed and audio recorded. The interpreters are working in the three operative languages—Spanish, English, and Russian—from elevated glass booths at the back of the conference center. We can hear them loud and clear. The floor language—the language being spoken by the speaker who has the floor—is also crisp and clear.[15]

"WHATEVER REMAINS, HOWEVER IMPROBABLY, MUST BE THE TRUTH"

The Nuclear Education of Robert S. McNamara

Embedded in Gen. Anatoly Gribkov's opening presentation is the revelation that none of the Americans present even dreamed of. It is an extended, surreal moment. Gribkov is a thick-necked, humorless, prickly military man right out of Soviet central casting. He electrifies the members of the U.S. delegation with two claims: first, that the Soviets had tactical nuclear weapons, including warheads, in Cuba during the crisis; and anticipating the loss of secure communication with Moscow, Khrushchev had pre-delegated the authority to use the tactical nukes to his field commander on the island, Gen. Issa Pliyev.

What Gribkov Revealed

If You [Americans] had Invaded, We Would have Nuked Your Troops on the Beaches in Cuba!

Gen. Anatoly Gribkov. . . . I was instructed to leave for Cuba by plane, with some other admirals and generals, as a representative of Minster of Defense

Malinovsky, to check on the status of the operation . . . [I informed our forces that] the tactical nuclear forces . . . could be employed with nuclear weapons during a direct invasion by the aggressor. It was said that before arriving at a decision on employing the tactical missiles, the situation had to be very thoroughly and carefully assessed, and in case of extreme need only, then could the decision be made. That was my mission when I was sent to Cuba.

. . .

We were all ready and willing to fight to the very last man. We didn't just plan an initial resistance. We even decided that if it proved necessary—if large tracts of land were occupied—we would form guerilla units in order to continue defending the interests of revolutionary Cuba. I'm using the very words that we used in 1962. That's the way we were then. We did not have anywhere to withdraw to. No retreat was possible. Our Soviet soldiers were willing to give their all to defend Cuba.

. . .

Allow me to say . . . the world was on the brink of a nuclear holocaust.[16]

What McNamara Asked Castro

Were You Aware that the Russians were About to Initiate Nuclear War on the Beaches in Cuba?

Robert McNamara: . . . the most extraordinary statement I have heard here in Havana—at least with respect to the military aspects of the crisis—was that of General Gribkov who . . . stated that the Soviet Union anticipated the possibility of a large-scale U.S. invasion of the type that we were equipped for by October 27: . . . something on the order of 1,190 air sorties [attacks] the first day, five army divisions, three Marine divisions, 140,000 U.S. ground troops. The Soviet Union, as I understand it, to some degree anticipated that, and equipped their forces here—the 42,000 Soviet troops—with . . . tactical nuclear warheads.

. . .

My question to you, [President Castro], is this: were you aware that the Soviet forces . . . were equipped with six *Luna* launchers and nine nuclear warheads; and . . . something I could never have conceived of—that because the Soviets were concerned about the ability of the Soviet troops and the Cuban troops to repel the possible U.S. invasion using conventional arms, the Soviets authorized the field commanders in Cuba, without further consultation with the Soviet Union—which of course would have been difficult because of communications problems—to use those nuclear launchers and nuclear warheads? . . . Were you aware of it? And . . . what was your interpretation or expectation of the possible effect on Cuba? How did you think the U.S. would respond, and what might the implications have been for your nation and the world?[17]

*What **Castro** Believed*

The War Would Go Nuclear; Cuba Would Totally Disappear; We Would Go Down Fighting Honorably, as Martyrs!

Fidel Castro: Now, we started from the assumption that if there were an invasion of Cuba, nuclear war would erupt. We were certain of that. If the invasion had taken place in the situation that had been created, nuclear war would have been the result. Everybody here was simply resigned to the fate that we would be forced to pay the price—we would disappear.

. . .

You want me to give you my opinion in the event of an invasion with all the troops, with 1,190 sorties? Would I have been ready to use nuclear weapons? Yes, I would have agreed to the use of nuclear weapons. Because, in any case, we took it for granted that it would become a nuclear war anyway, and that we were going to disappear. Before having our country occupied—totally occupied—we were ready to die in the defense of our country. I would have agreed, in the event of the invasion you are talking about, with the use of tactical nuclear weapons. You've asked me to speak frankly, and in all frankness, I must say I would have had that opinion.

If Mr. McNamara, or [President] Kennedy, had been in our place, and had their country been invaded, or if their country was going to be occupied—given an enormous concentration of conventional [non-nuclear] forces—they also would have used tactical nuclear weapons.[18]

*What **McNamara** Concluded*

If the U.S. Invasion Force had Been Nuked, Cuba Would have been Destroyed in a Nuclear Counterattack, and the Entire World Would likely have been Destroyed as Well!

Robert McNamara: Some of us [in the Kennedy administration] believed there was great danger—possibly greater danger than our publics understood—in the events of October 1962. I think we've learned here [in Havana] that we greatly underestimated this danger. It was far more severe than I thought.

On Saturday night—which would have been October 27th, a beautiful, fall evening in Washington—when I was leaving the president's office at dusk to return to the Pentagon, we were walking out of the Oval Office and we conversed on the veranda. I thought then I might never live to see another Saturday night. Now, that is evidence of some apprehension. But I tell you I did not understand until the day before yesterday that I was understating the danger, rather than exaggerating it.

We have learned here in Cuba that the Soviet forces—which at that time numbered 42,000, . . . although we then believed there were less than 10,000—not only had thirty-six warheads for the missiles that were capable of striking the U.S., at a time when we weren't certain but believed there were *none* on the island; we also learned here there were six launchers, which the Soviets called *Lunas*—our designation was FROGS—six *Luna* launchers, supported by nine missiles and nine nuclear warheads, which had a capability of being fired at the invasion force. And further, we learned that the command authority to utilize those warheads had been delegated—for reasons that seemed appropriate to the Soviets—to their field commanders. The presumption is that they would have been used against the U.S. invasion force, the use of which, as many of you know, was an issue that had not been fully resolved on the 27th or the 28th.

We can only speculate how the decision would have been made [by President Kennedy] with respect to that [U.S. invasion] force had not Khrushchev announced on the 28th that the missiles would be withdrawn. But what we do not need to speculate about is what would have happened had that force been launched, as many in the U.S. government—military and civilian alike—were recommending to the president on the 27th and the 28th. We don't need to speculate about what would have happened. It would have been an absolute *disaster* for the world. Our force was not accompanied, and would not have been accompanied, by tactical nuclear warheads; but no one should believe that a U.S force could have been attacked by tactical nuclear warheads without responding with nuclear warheads. And where would it have ended? In utter disaster.[19]

In chapter 6 of Arthur Conan Doyle's *The Sign of Four*, a slightly irritated Sherlock Holmes says to his earnest but less deductively gifted colleague Dr. John Watson: "How often have I said to you that when you have eliminated the impossible whatever remains, *however improbable*, must be the truth?" Holmes believes Watson needs to carefully distinguish between what is improbable (but still possible), and what is, for whatever reason, simply impossible. What Holmes knows, and what he preaches incessantly to Watson, is how little is really *impossible*.[20]

On the final weekend of October 1962, Bob McNamara and the entire U.S. leadership believed implicitly that it was virtually *impossible* that the Russians would have deployed tactical nuclear weapons to Cuba, prepared for their use against a U.S. invasion force, and given the Russian troops in Cuba authorization to use the nukes. Why virtually impossible? Because, in these circumstances, the use of tactical nukes in Cuba would have elicited a devastating U.S. nuclear response, destroying vast areas of Cuba. To quote McNamara, "And where would it have ended? In utter disaster." As Holmes might have said: Improbable? Yes. Impossible? No. And that means that this improbable eventuality needs to be taken seriously, needs to be treated as if it could, at some point, be true.

In 1962, Bob McNamara was wrong about the presence of Russian tactical nuclear weapons in Cuba, not because his reasoning was faulty. Putting tactical nukes in Cuba was a terrible idea, virtually suicidal, when coupled with the authorization to use them against the invading Americans. He was wrong because he was unable to imagine what it *felt* like in Cuba to be looking at imminent oblivion—what it *felt* like to face a choice between guaranteed total destruction for no redeeming reason, and guaranteed total destruction, but destruction with a purpose, which was the martyrdom of Cuba for the cause of world socialism. And the main reason he was unable to imagine what it felt like in Cuba, for both Cubans and Russians on the island, was disinterest. The Americans, including McNamara and his boss, John F. Kennedy, didn't think it mattered what it felt like in Cuba to be staring at an imminent U.S. invasion, which those in Cuba assumed (wrongly, though not irrationally) would be accompanied by a U.S. nuclear attack.

After the conclusion of the Havana conference, over drinks at a post-conference gathering at the Hotel Comodoro, Bob McNamara revealed to us what he had been thinking about obsessively throughout the course of the conference, ever since he listened to Gribkov's shocking, mind-bending, opening presentation. As on most occasions, Bob spoke in the auditory equivalent of "bullet points." Here is the sequence he could not get out of his mind:

- if the U.S. had attempted to invade Cuba;
- if the U.S. invasion force had been met with nuclear fire from the Russian tactical nukes;

- if (as the plan called for) the Russians had responded by, first, nuking the U.S. base at Guantanamo, killing the (roughly) five thousand U.S. military personnel at the base, then making a move on the Western zones in Berlin; and
- if the U.S. tactical nukes were used to repel the numerically superior Russian and East German forces; and if the Russians had responded in kind . . .

That's as far as Bob would take it. Choking with imagined horror, he was unable to audibly fill in the last step for us, which might be summarized this way: *finally, the strategic nuclear forces of the U.S. and Russia, in simultaneous attempts to preempt each other, would have destroyed the world.* All of these events would have occurred in a few hours, or a day or two, at most. We thought to ourselves (though we did not say it on that occasion): "Yes, Bob, and for one brief horrible moment just before the lights went out forever, you would have realized that you were yourself in part responsible for the ultimate catastrophe."

A week later, at the National Press Club in Washington, DC, Bob McNamara voiced, to a packed newsroom, the bottom line he took away from the conference in Havana:

> *Human beings are fallible. We all make mistakes. The record of the missile crisis is replete with examples of misinformation, misjudgment, and miscalculation. Such errors are costly in conventional war. When they affect decisions relating to nuclear forces they can result in the destruction of nations. We can do little or nothing about human fallibility. To prevent the destruction of nations, we have no choice but to abolish nuclear weapons as swiftly and safely as possible.*[21]

Variants of this statement became Bob McNamara's stump speech as, after January 1992, he traveled the world speaking about the near miss of October 1962 and what it means for the future of mankind. Sherlock Holmes would have approved of Bob McNamara's conclusion: It's not good enough to make nuclear war improbable; it must be made impossible! Its possibility must be eliminated. Assertions of its possibility must be rendered "untrue!"

6

BE FIDEL CASTRO

A Leader at the Hinge of the World

The strategy of the strong confronts the strategy of the weak. . . . The strategy of the weak invites the West, which possesses unanswerable military power, to carry its strategic logic to its final conclusion, which is genocide. The weak defy us by a readiness to struggle, suffer and die on a scale that seems to us beyond the bounds of humanity.

—Townsend Hoopes, *The Limits of Intervention* (1969)[1]

We are running the risks that we have no choice but to run. . . . We know how to run those risks calmly. And we have the consolation of knowing that the aggressors in a thermonuclear war, those who unleash a thermonuclear war, will be exterminated. I think there are no ambiguities of any kind.

—Fidel Castrol, radio and television speech
to the Cuban people, October 23, 1962[2]

Set the WABAC machine, Sherman—for Havana, Cuba, October 26/27, 1962. We're going to be with Fidel Castro as he makes his final preparations for Armageddon.

—"Mr. Peabody" the brainy beagle who is (in the fantasy of the
authors of *Dark Beyond Darkness*) instructing his adopted boy,
Sherman, to prepare for space/time travel to Cuba
at the peak of danger in the Cuban missile crisis.

CUBAN MARTYRDOM

The Redemption of Cuba via the "Extermination" of the U.S.[3]

Fidel Castro and his constituents desperately need to believe that what is about to happen on October 26–27, 1962, is no mere (though terrible) tragedy, but will instead be a noble sacrifice that will transform all Cubans, and Russians on the island, from ordinary victims to heroic martyrs. Fidel and his constituents believe this will be accomplished by what Fidel calls the *extermination* of the U.S. by the Soviet Union. *Extermination* is a harsh word. It calls to mind the Nazi ovens and other examples of genocide. But Fidel does not shy away from calling a nuclear war by what he takes to be its true name and central characteristic. If a nuclear war is waged against a country, Fidel believes, that country will be destroyed utterly and completely.

Remarkably, Cuba's U.S. adversary and its Russian ally miss all of this. They are totally clueless about the dominant Cuban narrative involving their destruction and martyrdom, even though Fidel and others in the Cuban leadership have spent the previous eighteen months emphasizing, often in public, in speeches, newspaper articles and newsreels, the imminence, importance, and inevitability of Cuba's coming martyrdom.

KENNEDY LIGHTS THE FUSE!

The U.S. Makes it Official—Cuba Will be Destroyed

In a radio and television speech to the American people on the evening of Monday, October 22, 1962, President John F. Kennedy delivers the scariest speech ever given by an American president.[4] In a sober, austere manner, JFK tells his constituents the following:

- *Missiles.* The Russians have secretly and deceptively installed nuclear missiles in Cuba.
- *Threat.* The Russian weapons in Cuba can reach most of the territory of the U.S., putting ninety million Americans, half the population of the U.S., at risk from the Cuban missiles alone.
- *Nuclear War.* If any of the Russian weapons in Cuba are used against the U.S., or against any other country in the Western Hemisphere, Washington will respond with "a full retaliatory response" against the

missile sites in Cuba, as well as those in Russia itself. In short, in that case, all-out nuclear war will occur.

- *Quarantine*. At 10:00 a.m. on Wednesday, October 24th, the U.S. will initiate a naval quarantine (or blockade) of Cuba, and will stop and forcibly search all Russian ships bound for Cuba.
- *Attack and Invasion*. The quarantine is only an initial step. If the Russians refuse, under the pressure of the quarantine, to remove their nuclear missiles from Cuba, then the U.S. is prepared to remove them by force.
- *Readiness*. As the president speaks, he informs his audience the U.S. military is preparing a huge attack force in south Florida and in the Caribbean. War can be initiated in a matter of a few minutes.
- *Dire Straits*. As he concludes, JFK urges Americans to face this crisis courageously. They should, he says, be prepared for weeks or even months of confrontation. (He does not say what he and his advisers have already been discussing secretly: that this ongoing confrontation with the Russians short of war is, for the foreseeable future, the best outcome one can reasonably hope for at the moment. The worst-case scenario is so awful that they are unable, even in their secret discussions, to call it by its true name—Armageddon. Instead, they refer to it in their meetings as "general war," a euphemism for the end of the world, as we know it.)

Following the speech, terrified Americans in many parts of the country flood into supermarkets, buying canned goods to store in their bomb shelters, or basements, or wherever they believe (implausibly) they will be able to ride out and survive a nuclear war with Russia. For public bomb shelters, the U.S. government has provided, free of charge, containers holding 17.5 gallons of drinking water; that is, adequate drinking water for five people for fourteen days.[5]

But we now know that, in a nuclear war between the U.S. and Russia, those in underground shelters who survived the initial blast would discover, when they resurfaced, that virtually everything distinctly human in the world had disappeared: few people; few living things of any kind; infrastructure destroyed; no electricity, no communication possible except by word of mouth; no medical assistance; no means of transport; no means of knowing anything other than what is physically in front of you. The distinction between human beings and other animals would rapidly dissolve. Those among the living unwilling to commit suicide would envy the dead.

FOLLOWING FIDEL, PART ONE

Tracking the Evolution of the Cuban Leader's Armageddon Script[6]

No one pays closer attention to Kennedy's apocalyptic speech of October 22, 1962, than Fidel Castro and the Cuban people. The speech is broadcast on radio all over the island. Cuba is already on a war footing, its troops mobilized and ready to fight to the death. Cuba's most famous nightclub, the Tropicana, not only doesn't close but it is inundated by Cubans lined up for shows involving very tall, very underdressed Cuban women with illuminated lampshades on their heads, dreamy Latin music from famous crooners, and the main course: Afro-Cuban salsa music, to which all Cubans learn their famously world-class dance gyrations. No one goes underground. No one panics. They have done what they can do to prepare for war. Having accomplished their preparations, many Cubans conclude, why shouldn't we enjoy ourselves? Kennedy's speech does not surprise them as the Americans and much of the world are surprised by it. In Cuba, they have been waiting for Kennedy's speech for a long time—at least a year and a half.

Fidel Castro's understanding of what will happen to Cuba, to the U.S., and to the world comes to him initially in a flood of illumination in the immediate aftermath of the Bay of Pigs invasion in April 1961. But like a writer, Fidel's message to the Cuban people, in speeches and written documents, is dispensed in a series of "drafts," in which the basic storyline doesn't change but in each successive draft more details are added. Initially, neither Fidel, nor anyone else, realizes that nuclear weapons will soon be deployed in Cuba. Thus, Fidel's initial allusions to the eventual martyrdom of Cuba are necessarily vague. He has no idea how the Russians will redeem Cuba's resistance to the U.S., though he is convinced that they will find a way. When in the spring of 1962 the Russians suggest a nuclear deployment in Cuba, and Cuba agrees to it, Fidel believes the die is cast irrevocably. Everything is clear.

First Draft, April 23, 1961

The Bay of Pigs Was Only the Beginning[7]

Days after the Bay of Pigs invasion, in his speech of April 23, 1961, after rounding up the remaining CIA-backed Cuban exiles who invaded Cuba, Fidel draws a set of astonishing conclusions about the impact the defeat of the U.S.-backed brigade will have on Cuba. He will spend much of the next year and a half persuading his constituents of his breathtaking hypothesis: that Cuba is about to become the focal point of contention in an Armageddon between the U.S. and USSR. Here is Fidel's argument, which he and many Cubans find convincing:

- Aggression. *The Bay of Pigs invasion proves that the Kennedy administration means to destroy the Cuban Revolution.*
- Resistance. *Cuba, unlike the majority of Latin American countries, will not be compliant, will not cease and desist in its revolutionary activities inside Cuba and throughout Latin America.*
- Viva Cuba! *Cuba, now avowedly Socialist, will be the hub of the wheel that will crush U.S. imperialism via the intervention of Cuba's new ally, the Soviet Union.*
- Martyrdom. *Cuba must prepare for martyrdom, for Armageddon, for the final reckoning in which the Socialist community destroys, once and forever, the leading capitalist state, the United States of America.*

Fidel delivers that speech before more than a million Cubans in front of the monument to Jose Marti in central Havana. Jose Marti, poet and patriot, is the symbol of Cuba's defiant quest for independence. Fidel, in the spirit of Marti, urges the Cubans: "Have no fear; be calm! After all, the result of aggression against Cuba will be the start of a conflagration of incalculable consequences, and they will be affected too. It will no longer be a matter of them feasting on us. They will get as good as they give."[8] *Moscow and Washington either aren't listening or they discount Fidel's remarks as the ravings of an irrelevant Latin lunatic. They make a colossal mistake. The ultimate tragedy begins to unfold, as the superpowers begin sleepwalking toward Armageddon, both obsessed with each other, and both clueless about Cuba.*

Second Draft, February 4, 1962

"A Bloody Drama for America"[9]

Fastforward to early February 1962. Kennedy has announced that in several days' time, a U.S. economic embargo of Cuba will commence. Kennedy adds that Cuba might be granted relief from the U.S. sanctions if it will cease its efforts to "export the Cuban Revolution." On February 3, Cuba is expelled from the Organization of American States (OAS) for adopting a communist system, which is, according to the OAS, "incompatible with the inter-American system."

Fidel responds with the publication on February 4 of a document known as "The Second Declaration of Havana," in which a defiant Cuba responds to Kennedy's stick (the embargo) and carrot (promised relief) by promising to do everything in its power to attack U.S. interests, wherever and whenever Cuba has an opportunity to do so. Fidel quotes Jose Marti, from a letter to his friend, Manuel Mercado: "I have lived inside the monster and know its guts; and my sling is the sling of David."[10] *The document contains a statement that will become one of the Cuban Revolution's most famous exhortations: "El deter de todo revoluciónario es hacer la Revolución" ("The duty of every revolutionary is to make the Revolution").*[11] *He concludes ominously: "Even if the Yankee imperialists prepare a bloody drama for [Latin] America, they will not succeed in crushing the people's struggles, they will only arouse universal hatred against themselves. And such a drama will also mark the death of their greedy and carnivorous system." This is the dominant motif of Fidel's message to the Cubans in the eighteen months following the failed Bay of Pigs invasion: the Americans have set out to destroy us; Cuba will resist but probably it will be destroyed; but this time the Yankees will also be destroyed. How? There is only one force on earth that can successfully take on the Yankees and emerge victoriously. The new Russian ally will do its socialist duty to take the Revolution worldwide and respond to the attack on Cuba by destroying the U.S.*

Third Draft, July 26, 1962

Patria Y Muerte?![12]

Fast forward to mid-1962. Fidel continues to connect the dots. The Cubans have agreed to accept the Russian missiles and nuclear weapons, though he has pledged to the Russians not to reveal the secret. The scenario now regarded by the Cubans as most likely begins to take shape. The Soviet conventional and nuclear weapons en route to the island will bring Cuba under the Soviet nuclear "umbrella." The Cubans expect the Soviet weapons and personnel will be readily detected by the U.S., which will then escalate its preparations to attack and invade Cuba. Fidel believes these preparations are already at an advanced stage. He believes Kennedy will order a massive attack on Cuba—not using a pitiful force of Cuban exiles as he did at the Bay of Pigs, but employing the full power of the U.S. military, including U.S. nuclear weapons. But the Americans will be met with stiff resistance from the Cubans and the Soviet forces on the island, including the use of Soviet tactical nuclear weapons, which Fidel imagines (correctly) can virtually annihilate the U.S. forces involved in the initial attack. Fidel regards all of this as virtually inevitable. The endgame, however, is still a little unclear to him. He is almost certain Cuba will be destroyed, for the U.S. is the most powerful nation on earth and Kennedy (so Fidel believes, incorrectly) is obliged and utterly devoted to destroying the Cuban Revolution. Fidel hopes that if Cuba is destroyed, his Soviet patron will authorize a nuclear attack on the U.S., destroying it and rendering Cuba a martyr for socialism. Fidel has not yet discussed the endgame with the Russians. But he plans to do so, and soon.

With martyrdom—both past and future—much on his mind, Fidel travels to Santiago de Cuba in eastern Cuba on July 26, 1962, Cuban Independence Day, to explain the situation to his constituents. He tells them the U.S. attack is coming, probably soon; the attack will be massive; Cubans will resist to the death; and Cuba (and their Soviet allies) will use the occasion to destroy the United States of America. Like all his speeches given during this period, this one ends with "Patria o muerte!" ("Fatherland or death!") How many present in Santiago de Cuba, and how many in Washington and Moscow, understand the degree to which Fidel's use of "Patria o muerte" has, since Cuba and Russia sealed the deal to bring nukes to Cuba, become somewhat misleading. The exhortation has, since Fidel began using it, referred to the necessity to resist U.S. aggression to the death. But a more accurate rendition of the meaning of that phrase since the Russians began to install a nuclear arsenal in Cuba is "Patria y muerte!" ("Fatherland AND death!") Yes of course we will fight, Fidel believes, for we are Cubans, after all. But our fight will be embedded in a cause much bigger than Cuba. Our fight will be the occasion for the destruction of the U.S. Fidel is not kidding, he is not speaking metaphorically, when he predicts in his speech in Santiago de Cuba that in the coming U.S. attack, the U.S. "will be shattered."

Fourth/Final Draft, October 23, 1962

"You Do Not Fear a Glorious Death"[13]

Fast forward to October 23, 1962. At just past 8:30 p.m. Havana time, Fidel Castro arrives at a television studio in downtown Havana to deliver the official Cuban response to Kennedy's speech twenty-four hours earlier. A TV studio is not Fidel's natural element. He must sit, but his inclination is to get up on his feet, to gesticulate wildly with his long arms, neither of which is possible in the small, cramped space. Even more importantly, he thrives on the feedback of a big crowd. It spurs him to the rhetorical heights for which he is famous. He has noticed on the ride over to the studio that the streets are virtually empty—a good sign, because it means that his constituents are home or in public places where they can listen and watch his response to the Yankees' threats on radio and TV. He keeps this uppermost in his mind as he gets set up in the studio. His live audience in the studio is a collection of rather dour-looking government ministers and other officials. All of them (even the civilians) are in military uniforms.

After a perfunctory introduction, Fidel begins. At first, he squirms and seems uncomfortable with the position of the microphone. He is exhausted; he hasn't slept more than a few hours in the past few days as the crisis approached and finally erupted. But after a few minutes, Fidel warms to his task and launches into wave after wave of apocalyptic rhetoric, urging Cubans to remain calm, even serene, as the countdown proceeds toward Cuba's date with nuclear Armageddon. He is emboldened not only by his own self-reinforcing crescendo of verbal virtuosity but also because he has by this time seen reports of Khrushchev's reply to Kennedy's speech of the day before. Khrushchev has been tough and uncompromising, as Fidel understands the Soviet position, ready for a showdown with the United States of America over nuclear missiles in Cuba.

Cuba, Fidel says in many different ways, now at top volume with hands and arms punching holes in the air over the microphone, will never surrender any of its inalienable rights to the Yankees nor anyone else—regarding Soviet missiles or anything else, for that matter. His voice cracks, as it always does when he is going full tilt, in a way that surprises those new to his speeches. His phrasing is now punctuated with high-pitched squeaks. But instead of distracting listeners, Fidel's brief flights into the upper range where only countertenors can vocalize comfortably tend to focus his audience on just how difficult it is for him to say all he has to say in the time allotted for the speech—no matter that he sometimes speaks continuously for several uninterrupted hours at a time.

Now the jokes come. Kennedy says the Cuban people have been betrayed. By whom? By the leaders? By Fidel? Who are these leaders? Martians? Yes, we must be Martians, he says. He imagines people all over the island laughing at that one. He finishes with a flourish and, concludes, as usual, with "Patria o muerte." "Fatherland or death." Both the fatherland and death have never felt this close, this intense, and this significant, he thinks, as they do on this warm October evening in central Havana. But Fidel has already told his listeners that death, if that is what comes to the entire Cuban nation, will not be in vain. If "the United States continues on the path it has chosen," Fidel says, "then the United States is resolutely determined to commit suicide."[14] *The Russians, it is understood, will redeem Cuba's martyrdom by destroying the United States. Fidel's small audience of officials reacts to this apocalyptic statement oddly by breaking into uproarious laughter.*

In a concluding flourish, Fidel's rhetoric seems out of sync with his body language. Physically, he is highly agitated, even by his hyperkinetic standards. His long arms and fingers are used to frame his words the way a conductor frames the mood of the music for an audience. Yet while visibly agitated, Fidel tells the Cuban people: "We . . . face everything calmly. We are not intimidated. But we are calmed by something, and that is knowing that the aggressors will not go unpunished. We are calmed knowing that the aggressors will be exterminated. Knowing that makes us calm."[15]

A little after 10:00 p.m., Fidel concludes his hour-and-a-half-long speech. Thousands of Cubans all across the island rush into the streets carrying makeshift torches, singing the Cuban national anthem:

> *Hasten to battle, men of Bayamo,*
> *For the homeland looks proudly to you.*

You do not fear a glorious death,
Because to die for the country is to live.

To live in chains
Is to live in dishonor and ignominy.
Hear the clarion call,
Hasten, brave ones, to battle!

So it is that on the evening of October 23, 1962, Fidel tells the Cuban people, in effect, that his prophecy of April 23, 1961, a year and a half earlier, is about to be fulfilled. This is the crisis that has seemed inevitable. All that remains are the final preparations for nuclear Armageddon.

FOLLOWING FIDEL, PART TWO

Tracking the Cuban Leader's Final Preparations for Armageddon[16]

[It is Friday, October 26, 1962. President John F. Kennedy and chairman Nikita S. Khrushchev are trying to extricate themselves and their countries from a crisis that is spinning out of control. Focused almost solely on each other, they do not give the Cubans, and their leader, a second thought. Both treat Cuba as a jungle-covered parking lot for Soviet missiles, nothing more; both treat Fidel Castro as a nuisance, like lint on a sleeve. Both are about to discover, however, that Castro and the Cubans matter, and that unlike the Americans and Soviets who desperately want out of the crisis, the Cubans want to fight "to the last man, woman or child capable of holding a weapon in this territory."[17] He is not kidding, and neither are his constituents.

Fidel is unaware that Khrushchev has sent a conciliatory letter to Kennedy on October 26th, in which the Russians agree to remove the missiles in exchange for an American pledge not to invade Cuba.][18]

Fidel is in constant motion, yet outwardly calm, as he speeds around the Havana area in his Jeep—Havana being ground zero. For the first and, as Fidel believes, the last time, Cuba really matters. He thinks, and many Cubans think: "Cubita—la Bisagra del Mundo!" ("Little Cuba—the hinge of the world!")

His driver and a Russian-Spanish interpreter are with him as he inspects the trenches being dug across the north side of the island in the areas east and west of Havana. He believes the first wave of U.S. Marines will attempt a landing at one or both points, and then march on Havana. All during the morning of Friday, October

26, 1962, Fidel can be seen, gesturing from the passenger's side of the front seat of his Jeep, long arms flailing, oddly high-pitched voice shouting orders and encouragement to the Cuban and Russian troops who are preparing for war. It is a familiar sight, by now, to the Cubans, but still strange to behold: a tall barbudo (a bearded revolutionary), with professorial, black, horned-rimmed glasses, dressed in olive battle fatigues showing his rank. Modestly, for a leader with the outsized personality of Fidel, he claims only to be a major. Almost never seen without a cigar, a symbol of Cuba all over the world, he seems to know every Cuban by name, every locale by its nickname.

The Humiliation of the U.S. Overflights

He feels the troops are ready; he believes the Cuban nation is ready for the onslaught he has been expecting ever since the failed Bay of Pigs invasion of April 1961. Every hour, two U.S. low-flying, high-speed reconnaissance planes fly overhead at near supersonic velocity. At their height and speed it is almost impossible to get a stable visual fix on their location. First, they are seen but not yet heard, silent phantoms against the Caribbean sky. There follows a momentary but excruciatingly loud roar, well after the planes have passed overhead, because light travels faster than sound. The roar is followed almost instantaneously by the visual disappearance of the planes into the horizon and a long, gradually diminishing roar that fades slowly, as one's sense of hearing returns to normal. Decades later, many Cubans who experienced these overflights will find it impossible to tell their stories without physically ducking down, as if the planes were about to sever their heads from their bodies. They will recall their conviction that every plane, every time, was probably the first plane to drop the bombs and begin a war that would end with the total destruction of Cuba—bajo el Mar Caribe ("beneath the Caribbean Sea").

★ ★ ★

Optional Pause

> It is possible to experience a facsimile of the disorientation, though not the fear and anger, of the Cuban experience of the low-level U.S. overflights. Poorly made buildings are exploding from the sonic booms. Every overflight is a humiliation. Every flight is the harbinger of Armageddon. For a taste of this, we suggest that you turn up the volume on your computer, phone, or tablet and you watch a sixteen-second video twice. Notice that it is more difficult to tolerate the overflight the second time, because you know what you are in for. (The simulation is by a French stunt team; the plane is a Mirage. The man on the tarmac is wearing lead boots, which accounts for his uncanny ability to stay upright as the Mirage flies past him. The link to the video is in the note.)[19]

★ ★ ★

Fidel does not fear these planes, nor do his troops. What he and they feel is anger: the U.S. planes violate Cuban sovereignty at will. By October 26th they all share the conviction that these planes will begin to drop their bombs on Cuba. It is only, they believe, a matter of hours before the massive air attack begins accompanied by an invasion led by U.S. Marines. As he bumps along in his Jeep, Fidel reflects on how the Yankees keep finding new ways to violate Cuban sovereignty and to diminish Cuban dignitad ("dignity"). They have occupied the area adjacent to Guantanamo for more than half a century. (Fidel's government refuses to cash the yearly rent check, as a matter of principle.) They facilitate the infiltration of the gusanos ("worms," i.e., Cuban exiles on the payroll of the CIA) by the hundreds and supply them with explosives with which to terrorize the Cuban population. And now, they assert their right to fly into our airspace whenever they feel like it, the sonic booms breaking windows, terrorizing and angering the population.

Around noon, feeling that events are racing toward war, Fidel calls the Soviet ambassador, his close friend Aleksander Alekseev, and asks him to come to his command post in south central Havana, near the National Zoo. Cuban President Osvaldo Dorticós is also present. Fidel complains to Alekseev about what he believes is the overly cautious way the Soviets seem to be approaching the upcoming conflict. Fidel tells Alekseev that he cannot understand why the Soviet troops are sitting on their hands while the Americans overfly the island with impunity. Does Alekseev know—do the Russians in Moscow know—that the purpose of the Yankees' overflights is to set up the Cuban and Soviet forces for pinpoint bombing that will, according to Fidel, begin within the next twenty-four to seventy-two hours? He wants the Soviets to start shooting the planes out of the air, and he wants the Soviets to know that he is thinking seriously about ordering his Cuban troops, contrary to Soviet wishes, to begin firing on the low-flying planes that are within the range of their anti-aircraft guns. Fidel complains to Alekseev that Cuba is humiliated by the way the Soviets, at the UN, continue to deny the existence of the nuclear missiles in Cuba—as if the Soviets and Cubans had done something wrong, as if they didn't have good and sufficient reasons for wanting to protect Cuba from the aggressive North American imperialists. Alekseev records all of Fidel's complaints dutifully, as always, and promises to send them to Moscow as soon as he returns to his embassy.

"I Will Die Facing the Sun"

Jose Marti → Antonio Maceo → Fidel Castro

All afternoon Fidel moves around the area, encouraging his forces. As his Jeep carries him from one area of troop concentration to another, Fidel reflects on the situation in which he and Cuba find themselves. Suddenly, everything becomes clear: the situation, the strategy of the U.S. aggressor, the response of his Soviet ally, and his own personal role in the events that are unfolding in and around Cuba. Some lines of poetry come to him, lines that he memorized as a schoolboy in eastern Cuba. The lines are by Jose Marti, known to the Cubans as "el Apostal"—the "apostle" of Cuban independence. These lines, known to many Cubans, capture the essence of what Fidel believes must be every Cuban's dignified response to oppression:

No me entierren en lo oscuro,
A morir como un traidor;
Yo soy bueno y como bueno,
Morire de cara al sol.

[Do not bury me in darkness,
To die like a traitor;
I am good, and as a good man,
I will die facing the sun.]

Marti, Cuba's most famous patriot, was shot dead in May 1895, in the struggle against Spanish imperialism. Fidel has worshipped Marti ever since he was a child. On countless occasions, Fidel has felt that he, like Marti, is destined for a special mission in Cuba's struggle for dignity and independence. Fidel knows dozens of Marti's poems by heart, and he loves reciting them in his speeches.

But Marti is not the only Cuban patriot on his mind. He also sees a parallel between his own situation and that of another great Cuban patriot of the war against Spain, Antonio Maceo, a black general who was no poet but who was a master of guerrilla war. In March 1878, Maceo rejected overtures from the Spanish to settle on a compromise, known as the Zanjon Pact. Maceo, unlike some other Cuban advocates of independence at that time, wanted nothing to do with compromise. He stood instead for booting the Spaniards off the island once and for all. No deals. No negotiations. Take no prisoners. At a town called Baragua, in the swamps of south central Cuba, Maceo stated his position: he would fight to the death for Cuban dignity and independence. Maceo fought on, until in December 1896 he was shot and killed near Punta Brava, southwest of Havana. Since the triumph of the Cuban Revolution on January 1, 1959, "Baragua" has become synonymous with glorious inflexibility of the committed revolutionaries, who would rather die with dignity than live in what they feel is servitude and degradation.

Fidel breaks into a cold sweat as the historical analogy with Maceo hits home. He, Fidel, is Maceo for the nuclear age, a leader for whom compromise with the imperialists is alien, for whom the objective is the elimination of all imperialist influence and the restoration of dignity and independence to the Cuban people. The Soviets, as he now sees it, keep pushing him toward compromise, they keep telling him not to push the Americans too far, not to provoke them into a war. Jesus Christ in heaven, thinks this lapsed product of a Jesuit education, can't the damned Russians see that we don't have that option? The Americans have already decided to crush this revolution. I must find a way to make Khrushchev understand that our choice on this island is not to provoke the Americans or not to provoke them. The Revolution, by its very existence, provokes the Yankees. Our choice is to face our fate in a dignified way, or in a cowardly way. The Americans will never compromise because in their arrogance they do not believe it will ever be necessary for them to compromise—not with Cuba, not even with the Soviet Union. This crisis, Fidel thinks, this October crisis, is Baragua for the nuclear age. And like Antonio Maceo, Fidel will not cave in; he will not surrender to the oppressors; he and his people will go down fighting and take as many of the Yankees with them as they can. They will, in Marti's words, "die facing the sun."

From El Chico to the Malecón to the "Zoo"

Around 6:00 p.m. he rides in his Jeep to El Chico, the Soviet command post of Gen. Issa Pliyev, the Soviet field commander, which occupies a former boys reform school southwest of Havana. At El Chico, Fidel is reassured that the Soviet forces on the island are with him in spirit. He is told that all the Soviet forces have now reached combat readiness. Before resuming his inspection of his troops, Fidel makes two requests of Pliyev: to turn on the Soviet radars, so that the Soviets can target and hit the U.S. planes more accurately; and to take off their disguises and dress in the uniforms of their own country to prepare properly for the coming battle, in which many will no doubt perish. If a soldier is to perish, he should perish in his country's uniform. Soviets dying for the cause of Cuban dignity and independence ought also, as Fidel sees it, have the opportunity to "die facing the sun." Pliyev agrees to turn on the radars but refuses to order the Russians to dress in battle gear, to Fidel's amazement and disgust. (Later in the weekend, the Russians will change into their military uniforms on an order from Pliyev.)

Afterward, back again in his Jeep and on the move, Fidel stops on the Malecón, the sea wall and road that fronts the city of Havana for eight kilometers between Old Havana and the near western neighborhood of Vedado. Fidel's mind is swimming with images of the history of Cuban martyrs as he dwells momentarily on the official name of the Malecón: Avenida de Maceo—Maceo Avenue, after the great martyr himself.

Recognizing Fidel's unmistakable figure, the men and boys operating the anti-aircraft guns break into a chant: "Fidel, Khru'cho, estano con lo do" ("Fidel, Khrushchev, we are with you both"). He orders his driver to stop. Fidel asks his troops if they are ready. They are ready but are frustrated at being prevented from trying to shoot down the U.S. planes that have been flying directly over their heads all week. Fidel realizes that the time has come to change this. Inspired by these gunners, Fidel heads straight for his command post in south central Havana, near the National Zoo, in a bunker dug two hundred yards into a hillside overlooking the Almendares River. From his command post, he issues orders for Cuban anti-aircraft units to begin firing on U.S. planes overflying their positions. He thinks: this will be good for our morale, even if we don't hit anything. We all deserve the right to protect ourselves and to die with dignity as we resist the coming assault. We Cubans have the great honor of beginning this war, in which the U.S. empire will be utterly destroyed.

Fidel's Last Will and Testament for the Cuban Nation

It is now 2:00 a.m. on the morning of Saturday, October 27th. At his command post, an exhausted Fidel thinks: I have done all I can here. We are ready to fight and die in a way that will exalt our nation. What else should I do? His thoughts turn to Khrushchev. If he can only find a way to let Khrushchev know what it is like on the island, how willing Cubans and Russians in Cuba are to fight and die for the glorious cause. He decides he will write a letter to Khrushchev to encourage him, to empower him to use his nuclear forces and destroy the United States in the event of the expected U.S. invasion and occupation of the island. At 3:00 a.m., he arrives at the Soviet embassy and tells Aleksander Alekseev that they should go into the bunker underneath the embassy because the U.S. attack could begin at any moment. A groggy but sympathetic Alekseev agrees, and soon they are set up in the bunker—Fidel dictating, aides translating, writing, reading aloud, with Fidel editing and reediting the letter.

Fidel eventually becomes frustrated. He can't seem to say what is in his mind. After ten drafts, with the sun already rising in the east, Alekseev at last asks Fidel: Are you asking Comrade Khrushchev to deliver a nuclear strike on the U.S.? Fidel suddenly stops and becomes silent. Then after some moments of reflection, he resumes: No, not quite. I want to tell Khrushchev that an attack is inevitable and an invasion is highly probable. The war will go nuclear, for sure. There is not the slightest doubt about it. I want to say that the choice is yours, Comrade Nikita: you can destroy the enemy, or you can wait for the enemy to destroy you, after he destroys us. But yes, Comrade Alejandro, fundamentally I want to say to Comrade Nikita that he must be prepared to destroy the United States. If, in his judgment, Cuba must also be destroyed in the war, then so be it. Cuba is ready to martyr itself for the cause of global socialism and the destruction of America's imperial empire. Alekseev is shocked, but he dutifully assists Fidel in fine-tuning the final draft of the letter. It is not finished and sent to Moscow until almost 7:00 a.m. on the morning of the Saturday 27th.[20]

Now Fidel feels his preparations are complete. He has written to his patron what may well be the last request of a man and a nation soon to be obliterated. It is a deathbed message, urging Khrushchev to redeem Cuba's approaching destruction by transforming Cubans from victims into martyrs at this nuclear-age Baragua. Fidel is calm and pleased with the deathbed note he and Alekseev have just composed for the seven-and-a-half-million citizens of the Socialist Republic of Cuba, and the forty-three thousand Russian citizens who will die alongside them.

FOLLOWING FIDEL, PART THREE

The Russian Betrayal of Cuba[21]

It is Sunday morning, October 28. Fidel has been prowling the Havana area with the raw energy of a caged lion, making sure that all is in readiness for the air attack and invasion by the Yankees. He is more relaxed while moving, barking out orders, encouraging his forces. They feed off his energy, and vice versa. More than once on this hot and sticky morning he has caught himself thinking: well, this could be the last time I will ever see this beach, or that hill, or this friend and comrade. He recalls the briefing he received from a young Foreign Ministry official who had been assigned to study U.S. manuals of nuclear war and describe what would happen in the event of an American nuclear attack on Cuba. The briefer had said simply: "All of us, and all of Cuba, will be destroyed totally." That was all he said. Fidel remembers shaking the young man's hand and thanking him for getting to the heart of the matter. He remembers the spontaneous chant around the briefing room of "Viva Cubita!" It was a moment of great poignancy: "Long live little Cuba," a country about to be sunk by Yankee bombs beneath the surface of the Caribbean. Fidel remembers leaving the briefing in a hurry in order to hide the fact that tears were beginning to form at the corners of his eyes—tears that, in the Maximum Leader, might reduce the fighting spirit of his troops. If anything connected to little Cuba is to live after this war, Fidel thought immediately after that briefing, it will be our insistence on our dignity and our courage to pursue it to the last man, woman, and child on this island. With that, his nascent sadness is transformed into righteous anger—which he believes is the true and necessary attitude of a revolutionary.

Fidel arrives back at his Havana command post by mid-morning and is told that Carlos Franqui urgently needs to speak with him on the phone. Franqui, who fought with Fidel's 26th of July Movement in the struggle against the Batista tyranny, is the editor of Revolución, a Havana daily newspaper. Fidel takes the call. He stands totally still, without speaking for what others in the room feel is a very long time, staring straight ahead, telephone receiver in one hand, cigar in the other hand. Suddenly, in one jerky motion, he throws the entire telephone—the receiver and its cradle—against the wall, smashing it to bits, as he screams obscenities, interspersed with Khrushchev's name. He then destroys a mirror with one kick of his military boot. "Sonofabitch, bastard, asshole," he shouts over and over again. Fidel's comrades, having no idea why their commander in chief is acting this way, retreat to the part of the room furthest from Fidel's large, gesticulating body. When he finally looks up and sees the terrified looks on the faces of his aides, Fidel pulls himself together and explains quietly what Franqui has told him: the Russians have betrayed the Cubans; Khrushchev has cut a deal with Kennedy; all the nuclear missiles are to be removed in exchange for a pledge from Kennedy not to invade Cuba. Then he shouts again, louder than before: "A pledge, a fucking pledge!" Fidel explains that Franqui heard the news from a Miami radio station. Khrushchev not only did not consult with us, he did not even inform us directly. No respect from our fraternal ally!

Fidel thinks: the Russians obviously don't give a shit about Cuba. If they did they wouldn't even consider doing what they apparently have already agreed to do: withdraw the weapons from Cuba that were to guarantee Cuba's security, in exchange for—for what?—a totally useless pledge from Kennedy, who only last year authorized the invasion of Cuba at the Bay of Pigs, and whose forces are now, at this very moment, poised to turn Cuba into a radiating hill of ash. Fidel's jeep pulls up to the Soviet command post where Gen. Plieyev confirms that the Russian missiles are to be returned to the Soviet Union.

Fidel wonders: How could I have been so naive as to believe Khrushchev? That bastard lied to Kennedy about the weapons, and we told him that he would regret it—and now he understands that we were right. But why did we—why did I—believe Khrushchev would tell us the truth, would be honest and forthright with us, with me? That bastard lied to everybody.

Fidel knows he must think hard and quickly about how to explain to the Cuban people what has happened and how Cuba will respond: basically, by returning to basic Cuban values, to the fighting spirit of Jose Marti, to Antonio Maceo, to the fearlessness of David confronting Goliath, even to martyrdom if that is what it takes to preserve Cuban dignity.

WAS FIDEL CRAZY?

A Thought Experiment Comparing Fidel and the Cubans with Butch Cassidy and the Sundance Kid

We'd like to suggest the following exercise, now that you have ridden the WABAC machine to Havana during the Cuban missile crisis. Why does Fidel think Armageddon is inevitable? What propels him progressively toward a cataclysmic confrontation with the U.S.? What could he have done, short of unconditional surrender, to avoid the crisis, or at least to greatly reduce the risk of Armageddon? Put yourself in the size 12 combat boots of Fidel Castro and ask yourself what you would have done, how you would have felt, in the circumstances in which he found himself.

Was Fidel crazy, as Khrushchev believed, when he received Fidel's Armageddon letter? Consider the conclusion to the 1969 George Roy Hill film, *Butch Cassidy and the Sundance Kid*.[22] Paul Newman and Robert Redford play two bank robbers, holed up in a hut in Bolivia, surrounded by several hundred Bolivian soldiers who have orders to take them dead or alive. Bloodied and weak, the two bank robbers look at each other and smile, and then come roaring out of their hut with guns blazing. The film ends with the frame frozen on Butch and The Kid, and it gradually fades as the audience hears about ten seconds of furious gunfire. Then the credits roll.

Were Butch Cassidy and the Sundance Kid crazy? We don't think so—at least we don't think that's what the director wants us to believe. Instead, they are heroes who, much like Fidel and the Cubans in October 1962, found themselves in a situation with only two alternatives: be destroyed meaninglessly or be destroyed as you take some of your enemies down with you.[23]

Picture the island of Cuba as analogous to the hut in which Butch and The Kid are holed up. Picture the full force of the U.S. conventional and nuclear forces—the mightiest military force the world has ever seen—as something like the hundreds of Bolivian soldiers surrounding the hut. Picture Fidel and his fellow members of the Cuban leadership, convinced that a nuclear strike on Cuba is imminent and desperate to extract some justification for the "disappearance" of Cuba from the face of the earth. You are a member of that leadership. What would you do? Would you try to redeem the event you believe is about to happen by asking your big friend to do his duty and martyr your country in exchange for the total destruction of the U.S. once the destruction of Cuba has begun?

We believe one overwhelming lesson of the Cuban missile crisis is not: Don't allow crazy *people* to become leaders of nations. Instead, it is: Do not create crazy *situations* in which leaders may come to believe they have only the two options that Fidel Castro and Cuba believed they had in October 1962, especially if weapons of mass destruction are part of the equation. Keep in mind that the Cubans did not believe they were doomed for no reason. They weren't paranoid. They believed they were doomed because Washington wanted Moscow to believe a U.S. attack and invasion was imminent. Khrushchev got the message and retreated. But Fidel and the Cubans also got the same message—that a massive attack was imminent—something that Kennedy and Khrushchev overlooked. Really: Why should it matter to the two superpowers what the leaders of a little pipsqueak country like Cuba believed?

Small countries matter, and what the big countries don't know about what makes the small countries tick can result in catastrophe. The Cuban missile crisis proves it. The crisis shows what can happen in a world with thousands of nuclear weapons, controlled by fallible leaders who believe they have the best interests of their constituents in mind. Leaders will always be fallible. That's why we must get rid of the weapons—all of them—before they get rid of us in some crisis that will be as unforeseen and shocking as the crisis of October 1962.

PART III
DARKEST

I had a dream, which was not all a dream.
The bright sun was extinguish'd, and the stars
. . .
And the clouds perish'd; Darkness had no need
Of aid from them—She was the Universe.

—George Gordon, Lord Byron, "Darkness" (1816)[1]

In parts I and II, the history and the warning mentioned in this book's subtitle are closely entwined: we now know that had the Cubans been in control of the nuclear weapons on their territory, they would have used them in the event of an attack, thus unwittingly initiating a war that would have destroyed human civilization via "Armageddon-Fast." The earth would have become a dark, radiating ruin in days, or possibly weeks. The warning embedded in the history of the Cuban missile crisis is this: it nearly happened once; it can happen again.

In part III, it gets even darker, as the warning metastasizes to the many ways in which, we now know, Armageddon might begin in our 21st century:

- *Unstable hot spots around the globe where nuclear war might begin, ultimately producing "Armageddon-in-Slow-Motion" (chapter 7)*
- *The misinterpretation of nuclear accidents—"Armageddon Oops"—in which the wisdom of "accidents will happen" meets the profound truth of "Murphy's Law" (chapter 8)*
- *The dark beyond darkness, as described by the poet Lord Byron, in "Darkness," based on the climate disaster of 1816 in Europe, caused by the eruption of a single volcano in Indonesia, a small-scale prototype of the global cold and darkness that would follow a nuclear war (chapter 9)*

7

ARMAGEDDON IN SLOW MOTION

More Bullshit and Truth About Avoiding Armageddon in the 21st Century

How, then, can we fail to take the importance of factuality and reality seriously? How can we fail to care about the truth? We cannot.

—Harry G. Frankfurt, *On Truth* (2006)[1]

Take this waltz.

—Leonard Cohen, (1988)[2]

There's a scene missing . . .

—Ned Alleyn to Will Shakespeare, from the movie *Shakespeare in Love* (1999)[3]

During the Cold War, fear of nuclear war was sometimes palpable, but it was almost always the fear of instant Armageddon, the igniting of the doomsday machine constituted by the combined enormous nuclear arsenals of the U.S. and the Soviet Union. Nothing else mattered: not smaller countries with nuclear arsenals; not wars in the developing world that might involve nuclear weapons; not the long-term effects of an all-out nuclear war. Who cares about the long term if humanity is wiped out in a few minutes or hours or days? Between the all-out nuclear war and the nature of post-war life on earth, such as it might be, fell a dark shadow of disinterest, a missing scene in the darkest scenario of the nuclear age.

Here, we draw on climate science to fill in the missing scene of more limited nuclear detonations and their consequences. These findings require us to think about nuclear Armageddon in a new way. To the old-fashioned concern with blowing up the world and everything in it in thirty minutes, we must add *Armageddon in Slow Motion:* the deaths of tens of millions, possibly billions, of people worldwide over a decade or more due to starvation, disease, and consequent social upheaval and devolution of human society into we know not what forms of horror and barbarism.

Thus, the proper response to those who argue for the maintenance of the world's nuclear forces is that their argument is not just untrue—their argument is *bullshit!* It can be sustained only by the effortful disregard for the truth about the post-nuclear war climate catastrophe discovered by climate scientists in the early 1980s, and recently updated for the most prominent nuclear threats of the 21st century.

"TAKE THIS WALTZ"

The View of the Nuclear Bullshitter-in-Chief (with Bullshit Detector Included)

Not everyone accepts our policy imperative of nuclear abolition. Not by a long shot. In fact, it seems that only a few who have experience commanding and controlling the world's nuclear arsenals can foresee a world without nukes. The skeptics believe such a world is either impossible to achieve or too dangerous an alternative to the world we live in now, or both. That is the truth, as we understand it, about a view we regard as bullshit: a view that willfully disregards what we now know about the Cuban missile crisis; and a view that also ignores what climate scientists have recently discovered about the longer-term, global effects of regional nuclear wars that do not involve the massive arsenals of the U.S. and Russia.

Love (of Nuclear Weapons) is Strange, Yeah Yeah

Let's look at the views of a man we regard as the most famous and admired purveyor of nuclear bullshit, Kenneth Waltz.[4] He is widely considered to be among the most eminent scholars of his generation on the role of nuclear weapons in international politics. (Waltz died in 2013, at age eighty-eight.) Were he alive today, and were he reviewing this book, he would doubtless conclude that its authors, traumatized by their historical study of the Cuban missile crisis, had panicked and lost their composure in calling for the abolition of nuclear weapons. He is likely also to have concluded that we therefore represent a clear and present danger to the peace of the world—that peace having been maintained primarily, since 1945, by Washington's and Moscow's huge nuclear arsenals and their implied threat to blow up the world if they didn't get their way, or if they were attacked by the other superpower. Absent the global doomsday machine constructed by the nuclear superpowers during the Cold War, according to Waltz, World War III was almost guaranteed to happen. Kenneth Waltz believed that what prevented it was primarily *fear* that a crisis involving the U.S. and Russia would spiral out of control and into nuclear Armageddon. This caused Moscow and Washington to steer clear of the nuclear brink, and nuclear war.

Waltz's great virtue as a scholar of nuclear weapons was that he asserted outright what others with his beliefs often lacked the courage to say straightforwardly. His intellectual legacy is the virtual embodiment of the subtitle of the best film ever made about the nuclear threat, Stanley Kubrick's satirical 1964 masterpiece: *Dr. Strangelove Or: How I Learned to Stop Worrying and Love the Bomb.*[5]

The Viennese psychoanalyst, Sigmund Freud, divided the mind into three parts: the id (our unconscious and unvarnished basic wishes, like food, sex, shelter, and so on); the ego (our conscious, calculating mind, within which we construct the narratives of our lives, and the lives of others); and the superego (which is something like our conscience, telling us what is right and what is wrong, what ought to be done and what ought not be done).[6] Kenneth Waltz was, in this Freudian sense, the *id* of nuclear strategy, nuclear arms control, and the role of nuclear weapons in international politics. Waltz loved the bomb, and he tried to explain why we should all love it. Others in the field might say, well, Waltz goes a little too far; we don't actually *love* the bomb, even though the so-called "balance of terror" certainly has helped prevent World War III. But Waltz didn't think he went too far. To the contrary: in writing about nuclear weapons, he always seemed perplexed as to why any rational person could possibly disagree with him.

His love affair with nukes, however, requires the historical and contemporary worlds to be other than they were, and are. The facts of the Cuban missile crisis, and plausible scenarios of what will probably happen in the event of a nuclear war now or in the future, invalidate the love affair, revealing that there is nothing there to love—only the prospect of nuclear annihilation. Kenneth Waltz's actual lover—not the pacific, compliant, protective lover of his fantasies, who ensures that everyone with nukes knows better than to actually use them—turns out to be a cold-blooded killer, just waiting for the opportunity to destroy all of us when we least expect it.

The writer Joan Didion refers to this way of facing the world as "magical thinking."[7] It involves ignoring the reality and replacing it with fantasy, until such time as one of two eventualities come to pass: either the real world overwhelms and invalidates the fantasy and the magical thinker must journey psychologically back to the real world; or else, driven by anxiety, the fantasist disappears ever deeper into the magical world of his or her construction. In clinical psychology, the former is called trauma, often followed by post-traumatic stress disorder (PTSD); the latter is called psychosis, or more colloquially, insanity. Some have said that Robert McNamara was traumatized by the Cuban missile crisis, which accounts for his advocacy of nuclear abolition. We agree. But we also stress that one hardly need apologize for being traumatized by the prospect of imminent nuclear Armageddon. Any other response, in fact, seems to us ridiculously out of touch with reality. Believing in the magic of nuclear weapons won't help you avoid Armageddon, but the abolition of those nukes will.

Waltz's fantasy is "more is better." There is nothing wrong with his underlying assumption, which is that having a lot of nukes around is scary and tends to induce a certain amount of caution, at least much of the time. What is magical is ignoring the gap between *at least much of the time* and *always*; ignoring what will happen the next time fallible leaders with false assumptions and access to nukes get sucked into a crisis, screw up the way leaders screwed up in October 1962, and this time are not so lucky. Treating the prospect of Armageddon lightly, as Waltz does, is not just weird; it is irresponsible. The rhythm and blues guitar duo Mickey and Sylvia taught us in the late 1950s that "Love Is Strange."[8] But what could be stranger than to "stop worrying and love the bomb?" That is terrible advice that should be turned inside out and upside down: *we all need to learn to start worrying and abolish the bomb.*

Let's Take This Waltz and Run Him Through a Bullshit Detector

When former *Miami Herald* humorist Dave Barry wanted his readers to know that he was referring to the real world—that sometimes reality is stranger than any fiction he could concoct—he wrote reassuringly, "I am not making this up."[9] We are not making up Kenneth Waltz, or his views on nuclear weapons.

This Barry-esque story can, we believe, help you gain a better understanding of how you can be killed by a bizarre fact: Waltz's, and the entire nuclear establishment's, love for nuclear weapons.

In what follows, Waltz addresses an important question: "What does the nuclear future hold?" Following each of Waltz's five principles, which are verbatim quotes, we endeavor to decode his "nuke-speak"—a variant of English spoken widely in the Pentagon, nuclear strategy think tanks, political science departments, international relations programs, or wherever people gather to discuss in flat, dispassionate tones how to prevent the end of the world as we know it by threatening to produce the end of the world as we know it. We are far from neutral decoders. In our view, Kenneth Waltz, despite his fame and because of his influence, was also one of our era's most notorious nuclear bullshitters.

Okay. Deep breath. The format is identical for each of Waltz's propositions: first, Waltz, then Jim and janet (indented and with the identifier **J&j**). Here goes:

"First, international politics is a self-help system, and in such systems principal parties determine their own fate, the fate of other parties, and the fate of the system. This will continue to be so."[10]

> **[J&j:** Powerful countries have always, and will always, do what they damn well please, including equipping themselves with the most powerful weapons available, which are nukes. Sorry all you pipsqueaks, but the Big Guys always call the shots. Sure, the Non-Proliferation Treaty (NPT) of 1970 says the Big Guys will rid themselves of nukes, and others will avoid acquiring them. But really, treaty-schmeaty: the NPT and similar documents are just words on paper, a big bluff in the big poker game of international politics. The Big Guys, especially the U.S. and Russia, weren't serious. The nuclear "haves" were just bluffing, playing along, so as to try to claim some moral high ground, to keep the nuclear "have-nots" satisfied. (Feel free to suggest other interpretations.)]

"Second, given the massive numbers of American and Russian warheads, and given the impossibility of one side destroying the other side's missiles to make a retaliatory strike bearable, the balance of terror is indestructible."[11]

> **[J&j:** U.S. and Russian leaders, no matter who they are, no matter the situation, will always understand that they would be damned fools to use nukes against each other. But consider these implied corollaries: that the U.S. and Russia have never, and will never, be led by damned fools; or that leaders who are not damned fools will never inadvertently create situations in which the use of nuclear weapons seems like the least-worst option; and, that Kenneth Waltz had

never heard of the *Cuban* Cuban missile crisis. And oh, what is a "bearable" nuclear retaliatory strike anyway? (Feel free to suggest other interpretations.)]

"Third, nuclear weaponry makes miscalculation difficult because it is hard not to be aware of how much damage a small number of warheads can do. . . . War becomes less likely."[12]

[J&j: Nukes are the great simplifier. They take the guesswork out of trying to figure out whether to fight a war with a nuclear power. You just don't do it, you idiot! Note: this seems to imply that the Soviet loss in Afghanistan, the U.S. loss in Vietnam, the U.S. disasters in Afghanistan and Iraq, and numerous other asymmetrical wars either didn't happen, or else the small countries forgot that the Big Guys had nukes, and the Big guys either let the pipsqueaks off easy or themselves forgot about their nuclear arsenals. (Feel free to suggest other interpretations.)]

"Fourth, new nuclear states will feel the constraints that present nuclear states have experienced . . . Nuclear weapons make wars hard to start . . . These statements hold for small as for big nuclear powers. Because they do, the gradual spread of nuclear weapons is more to be welcomed than feared."[13]

[J&j: The Cold War was actually a kind of experiment to see if nuclear weapons keep the peace or encourage war. The Americans and the Russians haven't fought a big war since nuclear weapons were invented, and were subsequently proliferated massively in the military arsenals of the two countries. Before the nukes came online, huge wars between Big Powers were the norm. Not any more. So: no nukes = big wars; nukes = no big wars. Therefore: nukes should be spread as widely as possible (of course in an orderly fashion, according to whomever queues up for them at the global nuke supermarket). What seems to follow is this: volatile parts of the world—like the Middle East, Northeast Asia, parts of Southeast Asia—wherever war and conflict is rampant—should jump the nuke queue and acquire nukes ASAP, in order to bring peace and stability to their regions. Iran should definitely have nukes. North Korea should have a lot more nukes than their paltry dozen or so. Why not Iraq and Afghanistan? And maybe give them to the Kurds, who always seem to be in the midst of violence? Oh, why not blow the roll? Give them to the Taliban and Isis. That will pacify them, for sure. Note: in the late spring of 1999, India and Pakistan found themselves on the brink of war, just a year after each became a declared nuclear power. Only direct U.S. intervention prevented almost certain escalation that could have led to nuclear war. (Feel free to suggest other interpretations.)]

"[Fifth], the presence of nuclear weapons makes states exceedingly cautious. Think of Kennedy and Khrushchev in the Cuban missile crisis. Why fight if you can't win much and might lose everything?"[14]

[J&j: Okay, let's do that: let's think about Kennedy and Khrushchev in the Cuban missile crisis—an exercise with which, by this point, you are familiar. Are you on high ground? You'd better be, because the bullshit is going to get deep. Here goes. It follows from Waltz's statement that Khrushchev was cautious in placing nukes deceptively and secretly into Cuba and lying about them to the Americans, the world, and even to most of his own Soviet colleagues. Kennedy was cautious in responding to the discovery of the missiles in Cuba with an act of war, a blockade, which his administration renamed "quarantine" in order to claim that their action was not provocative. Kennedy was also cautious in his October 22, 1962, speech when he threatened to destroy the Soviet Union in a nuclear attack if any nukes stationed in Cuba attacked any country in the Western Hemisphere. Khrushchev was cautious when, in his response to Kennedy's speech, he defiantly told Kennedy that the Russians were going ahead with the deployment, no matter what. And both Kennedy and Khrushchev were cautious when they ordered their nuclear forces to high levels of alert, according to which each country could launch its nuclear forces more quickly. You see how "the presence of nuclear weapons makes states exceedingly cautious?" Hah! But wait a minute! Didn't Fidel Castro have something to do with the Cuban missile crisis? Didn't Fidel try to convince Khrushchev to nuke the U.S. as soon as the expected invasion of Cuban had begun? Weren't the Cubans willing to fight to the death against the world's most powerful nuclear force? You bet: the Cuban missile crisis veritably reeks of caution. (Feel free to suggest other interpretations.)]

The Cuban missile crisis that Waltz believes demonstrates the caution of leaders—that particular Cuban missile crisis never actually happened. It's the one that would have happened, if Kenneth Waltz could have written the script for it.[15]

But Kennedy, Castro, and Khrushchev didn't have a script. They had to invent one on the fly, with little accurate information about their adversaries, as they felt themselves being sucked into the vortex of the unthinkable. They and the world barely survived, by the combination of last-minute improvisation and a whole lot of luck. In the Cuban missile crisis, nuclear weapons did not prevent Armageddon. They nearly *caused* Armageddon. Khrushchev was seized by nuke envy. He thought magically that he could get away with the Cuban deployment and that Kennedy would adjust to the new reality of having Russian nukes in the U.S. neighborhood. Khrushchev returned to the real world only after Kennedy's October 22, 1962, speech threatening nuclear war against the Russians if even one Russian nuke was used anywhere in the Western hemisphere. Kennedy's speech was as reckless as Khrushchev's deployment, and most reckless of all was Castro's request to Khrushchev to nuke the

U.S. when the Yankees began their expected invasion of the island. The nukes created fear, which led not to caution, as in a script Waltz would have written, but to caution's opposite.

So: Do the nearly fifteen thousand nuclear weapons currently residing in the arsenals of nine nations pose a significant risk to human civilization? Not according to Waltz. Far from it! The possibility that the nukes might be used is why we are here today, instead of being ground into the dust by World War III.

And so we arrive once again at the nuclear variant of what the Princeton philosopher Harry G. Frankfurt characterizes as *bullshit.* Kenneth Waltz's views are bullshit, not lies, because his positions are meant to buttress his theory of the way international politics works. That is what he was about: constructing an airtight theory of the role of nukes in the world. He was a so-called realist: he believed that states are like tectonic plates that move and are moved according to the degree of force that is applied or threatened.[16] What Waltz describes is an alternative universe to the one in which the Cuban missile crisis actually happened, and in which leaders must actually make war and peace decisions now, often with insufficient time to think, with faulty information and misled by fallacious assumptions.

WALTZ'S BIZARRO WORLD

A Shopping Spree in the Nuclear Bazaar?

Kenneth Waltz is nothing if not consistent. Shortly before he died in 2013, Waltz began advocating a nuclear-armed Iran. As Waltz put it, "nuclear balancing would mean stability" in the Middle East, between Israel, long a nuclear power, and Iran, which has the technical capability to go nuclear, if it should choose to do so.[17] He cites as evidence for nuke-induced pacifism in the Middle East the absence of a nuclear war between India and Pakistan since they both publicly went nuclear in May 1998. Never mind that the two countries came very close to a nuclear war in 1999, during a crisis that was resolved only with the intervention of the U.S.[18] And North Korea? Waltz said in 2012 that since the behavior of all three of the Kims who have ruled North Korea since World War II has been bizarre, but has not involved nukes, then there is no reason for concern.[19]

So Harvard strategist Thomas Schelling was right, after all, about Waltz: he really did believe every shopping mall should have a nuke, including shopping malls in Iran, India, Pakistan, and North Korea. It's as if the nukes will somehow sedate or pacify the leaders of these countries so that that they will never resort to using their most destructive weapons. And of course, their arsenals are tiny compared to those of Russia and the U.S., so that if the unimaginable (to Waltz) were to occur and some nukes are detonated in these far-off places, U.S. interests will remain basically untouched, except perhaps for a little edginess right after the little nuclear war.

Waltz notwithstanding, as to whether North Americans should worry about the effects of a "small" nuclear war far from our shores, the answer is: absolutely, positively yes! But to understand why embracing a nuclear bazaar on the other side of the world is bizarre, we need to grasp what nuclear detonations will do to the earth's atmosphere, which is not broken up along the lines of national borders.

"THERE'S A SCENE MISSING"

Climatologists Write the Scene

Toward the end of the Academy Award-winning 1999 movie *Shakespeare in Love*, during a rehearsal, the famed actor Ned Alleyn (Ben Affleck) and the struggling young playwright Will Shakespeare (Joseph Fiennes) are discussing *Romeo and Juliet*. Alleyn is musing over the play, which he thinks is good but incomplete. In a moment of insight, he tells Will, "There's a scene missing, between marriage and death."

Here is the missing scene that Will then writes: After spending the night together, Romeo hears the song of the morning lark, signaling that he must leave or be found and killed. But Juliet resists, clinging to magical thinking: "Believe me, love, it was the nightingale"—which, if true means that they still have time together, hours before they must part. But Romeo sees the world as it is: "It was the lark, the herald of the morn. No nightingale"—there is no more time together. He must leave. They hold the hope that they will be reunited. But as we know, malign luck seals their fate. They reunite only in death.[20]

The missing scene vanquishes magical thinking and shows reality intertwined with luck—*bad luck*.

There is also a scene missing from our usual narrative of a nuclear war. We are afraid of being blown up, made to disappear instantly, when the bombs explode. If we think about the nuclear threat at all, we tend to think that is about all there is to it. Most of us believe implicitly that we will either be blown up or home free. A lot of us are vaporized or burned or otherwise mutilated and dead; the rest of us clean up the mess and build a new future, with the help of others, who are outside the blast zone, who have the means to assist us. The scene of nuclear terror bleeds seamlessly to the scene of sobriety and recovery. If we escape the big one, we'll be all right.

But we now know that this is magical thinking. The potential effects of nuclear war, whether an all-out war or a relatively "small" one, are complicated, global, and potentially longlasting. No matter where the explosions occur, we will all be affected. The basic reason for this is something you no doubt think about every day of your life: the *weather!* Any nuclear war will affect global weather in a particular way. The nuclear explosions cause cities to burn, throwing smoke and debris into the upper atmosphere, which absorbs light and heat from the sun. But this debris-filled atmosphere blocks the sun, and so turns the earth's surface and its lower atmosphere colder. If it turns cold enough, for long enough, crop failures occur, leading to food shortages and political and societal instability as people scrounge for food, and to mass starvation, famine-friendly diseases like cholera, and finally mass death on a scale unprecedented in human history.

If the deteriorating situation continues over a period of years, the damage to the human community may become irreversible as the world enters a "little ice age." Whether life that is recognizably human survives the ordeal is anybody's guess. But we shouldn't count on it. If worse comes to worse, the nuclear war in which some millions are killed by explosions would have led, via an alteration in the weather patterns, to the deaths of perhaps two billion people, or possibly more. Most of those who eventually suffer and die due to the war will have had no firsthand knowledge of it. Those who live longest after such a nuclear war may well envy the dead.

NUCLEAR WINTER

The Truth About a U.S.-Russian Nuclear War

What happens after the burning, vaporizing, and radiating are finished in the immediate vicinity of the explosions? What kind of a world do the survivors face? It will be cold and dark. Nuclear winter, the cooling of the earth's lower atmosphere and surface, will set in, leading to a scenario such as that depicted in McCarthy's *The Road.*

During the U.S.-Soviet Cold War, superpower adherence to the doctrine of Mutual Assured Destruction (better known by its wonderfully absurd acronym MAD), was supposed to prevent "a bolt from the blue," a preemptive first strike that would disable the opponent while (so the theory went) the attacker got off scot-free, having destroyed all the adversary's nuclear weapons before they could be used. Indeed, in the U.S. in the 1950s and early 1960s, this hypothetical scenario was sometimes called a "splendid first strike" (at least by hardliners who advocated it). During the Cuban missile crisis, General Curtis LeMay, the Air Force Chief of Staff, told President John F. Kennedy that the discovery of Russian missiles in Cuba was a perfect pretext for a preemptive strike on the Soviet Union—a suggestion that appalled Kennedy.[21]

But as climatologist Alan Robock now suggests, we no longer live in a MAD world, but a *SAD* world of *Self Assured Destruction*, where nuclear weapons are literally good for *nothing*, not even deterrence of an enemy nuclear attack.[22] Whether or not a nuclear response is given to a nuclear attack, the result is likely to be the same: enough debris caused by the nuclear explosions of the attacker's weapons will be sent aloft to the upper atmosphere to trigger nuclear winter, with its accompanying agricultural crisis, mass starvation, and the breakdown of societies all over the world. What little is left of the human race will be slogging along with Cormac McCarthy's Papa & The Boy, on *The Road* again, playing out Armageddon, in *slow motion*.

Skeptics say that nuclear winter is just a theory and that it can never be tested. As the recent work by Robock and his colleagues demonstrates—conclusively, in our view—nuclear winter deniers are bullshitting themselves, and the rest of us. Nuclear winter is an established scientific theory, and it *has* been tested, in the only way climatic theories can be tested, other than by the wholesale, purposeful disruption of the earth's atmosphere, which is of course unacceptable. It has been generated and tested against *analogues,* involving the careful examination of perturbations of the earth's upper atmosphere by volcanic eruptions, massive fires in cities hit by natural disasters such as earthquakes, and fires ignited by the large-scale violence typical of modern warfare.[23]

The beginning of wisdom regarding the potential of nuclear winter to produce Armageddon in Slow Motion is this: *cities burn!* We have known this for a long time: Union General W. T. Sherman burned Atlanta, Georgia, to the ground in the U.S. Civil War. San Francisco caught fire during the April 1906 earthquake and, driven by firestorms, burned to the ground. The Allied fire bombings of Hamburg and Dresden, as well as the fire bombing of dozens of Japanese cities, produced firestorms that reduced cities to ashes in a matter of hours. And the atomic bombings of Hiroshima and Nagasaki in 1945 proved that nuclear explosions over cities produce extraordinary firestorms—tornados of fire that incinerate almost everything in their path until there is nothing left to burn. The photos of Hiroshima and Nagasaki in the aftermath of being nuked are dramatic. They reveal charred, smoking ruins—formerly large and prosperous cities resemble huge lumps of burned-out charcoal, only hours after being nuked.[24]

In the early 1980s, climatological researchers using newly developed computers and innovative, multivariate climate modeling programs began to ask: What would happen to all the ash, dirt, smoke, and other materials emitted by burning cities in the event of a nuclear war? They calculated the level and type of pollution that would be created by a given number of nuclear explosions over or near cities. They then looked at the probable effects on the earth's climate when the upper atmosphere absorbs substantial levels of pollutants of the sort likely to be produced in huge, urban fires caused by nuclear explosions. The original research team, led by Carl Sagan of Cornell University, concluded that sooty smoke from firestorms ignited by nuclear weapons would be so dense as to block out the sun, turning the earth colder and darker, leading to the attrition of plant life and the radical shortening of growing seasons in agricultural areas. Nuclear winter would thus be characterized by mass starvation and the disintegration of human society.[25] This is the scenario inhabited by the ghostly figures of Papa & and The Boy on *The Road*.

The major recent addition to the climatologists' narrative of the aftermath of a Washington-Moscow nuclear war is this: the duration of the climate devastation would likely last at least *ten* years. The original computer simulations that led to the hypothesis of nuclear winter were limited to the year following an East-West nuclear war. The hardware and software available to the climatologists did not permit extrapolations beyond twelve months. Even so, the scenario for the year following a superpower nuclear war was grim. The new ten-year time horizon would follow something like a normal curve of devastation to the world's agriculture, with the surface of the earth being coldest and darkest at about the fifth year, before the earth began to brighten and warm up.

You might think: well, if we can just make it to year five, things will be looking up for the survivors. But you would be wrong. After five years of climate-induced famine and the rise of famine-friendly diseases like cholera, a substantial portion of the human race would already be wiped out. How many? It is hard to say, but most specialists put the figure in the billions of deaths from the direct and indirect effects of a U.S.-Russia nuclear war. Those who survived for five years or longer, like Papa & The Boy in *The Road*, would exist on canned goods from the prewar era or—what Papa & The Boy fear most of all—from cannibalism. But even for cannibals, edible, nourishing food would be a wasting asset, unrenewable and finite. By year five of the post-war period, recognizably human society, characterized by law, order, shared institutions—all the things that together constitute human civilization—would have disintegrated. If any members of *Homo sapiens* live to the tenth year, when the earth's own recovery from the nuclear war was well underway, if in fact there is a recovery, their habits would be those of hunter-gatherers, like those in a few surviving cultures in remote areas of the world today. With one important difference: they would have spent the preceding decade hunting and gathering prewar canned goods and/or human flesh to eat. It's anyone's guess whether human society could regenerate under these conditions, no matter what the pace of the planet's recovery from the war.[26]

NUCLEAR FAMINE

The Truth About a "Small" South Asian Nuclear War

Filling in the "missing scene" has become imperative now, in the 21st century. What if a regional nuclear war is fought between non-superpowers—a war that would not kill hundreds of millions of people in short order? Should nations and residents of the northern hemisphere be concerned about such a war, other than for humanitarian reasons?

A disaster of this magnitude would have no modern precedent; it might kill several million people outright. The war would put a severe strain on the global community's relief agencies, which would, at least in the initial going, likely be overwhelmed by the disaster, dealing with injuries, disease, massive refugee flows, and political chaos in the immediate wake of the war. But would the aftermath of the war *threaten* the global order? Would the post-war challenge to the international community be any different than it would for, say, a massive earthquake in a major urban metropolis?

The climate scientists' short answer is *yes!* They now suggest that the likely result of a regional nuclear war would be global Armageddon in Slow Motion. A "small" nuclear war would usher in some degree of nuclear winter: the deaths of tens of millions of people, throughout the world, due to the cooling of the earth's surface and lower atmosphere. The magnitude of the global severity would depend on the many factors that determine how much sooty smoke rises from burning cities to the upper atmosphere, how high it rises, and how it is distributed throughout the upper atmosphere.

Which brings us to South Asia where, according to many international security specialists, the standoff between India and Pakistan constitutes the world's greatest current threat of nuclear war.[27] Both countries have in excess of one hundred nukes apiece. Both believe they have excellent reasons for mistrusting, even loathing, the other side. Pakistan provides a haven for Muslim extremists. (Osama bin Laden, for example, was hiding in Abbottabad, Pakistan, when he was assassinated by U.S. Special Forces on May 2, 2011.) The Pakistani government underwrites armed terrorist groups in the disputed region of Kashmir; the Indian government typically responds to these frequent incursions by such groups with massive deadly force. There are daily clashes along what is called "the Line of Control" which, in light of the violence and chaos in its immediate environs, should probably be called "the Line Out of Control."

India and Pakistan have fought three major wars since independence was granted to both countries by Great Britain in 1948. The most recent war occurred between May and July 1999. It began as skirmishing along the Line of Control but soon escalated, with more than a half million fighters from both countries prepared to square off at their common border in the Rajasthan Desert. Pakistan is believed to have moved its nuclear warheads closer to their launchers in preparation for going nuclear in the event of a massive Indian invasion. Likewise, the Indians, it is also believed, began to prepare to launch a massive nuclear counterattack on Pakistan in the event the Pakistanis went nuclear. With the Americans mediating, the crisis was finally brought under control, but not before the world came closer to a nuclear war than at any time since the Cuban missile crisis.

South Asia today is a nuclear tinderbox. India's military is much larger than Pakistan's. In a head-to-head clash, therefore, Pakistan plans to go nuclear rapidly. India, on the other hand, has threatened massive nuclear retaliation against Pakistan if it goes nuclear first. Many Pakistani and Indian nukes are targeted at South Asian mega-cities, like Karachi and Lahore in Pakistan and Delhi, Calcutta, and Mumbai in India. These five cities have a combined population of approximately sixty million people. If war breaks out in these circumstances and goes nuclear, the loss of human life will be on a scale unprecedented in human history. Virtually all of the millions, possibly tens of millions, of casualties will be civilians. As India's and Pakistan's armies contest the Line of Control in Kashmir and their border in the Rajasthan Desert, huge cities behind these lines will have been destroyed.

The effects of a nuclear war between India and Pakistan, according to climate scientists, fall roughly into two broad categories: (1) the immediate consequences in South Asia; and (2) the delayed effects beginning in South Asia, then spreading across the globe.

The immediate result: roughly twenty million people would die from the direct effects of the explosions, a number equaling roughly half of the total fatalities worldwide in World War II. Moreover, the South Asian megacities targeted by the bombs, or exposed to the fallout from the bombs, would remain uninhabitable for an indefinite period of time, probably many years. The greatest humanitarian disaster in recorded history will have occurred.

This regional catastrophe would be only the beginning of a global nightmare. It will get colder and darker everywhere as the sooty smoke continues its deadly voyage around and through the earth's upper atmosphere. Growing seasons will shrink. Production of basic grains like rice, wheat, and corn will diminish. The approximately 870 million people who are already malnourished will starve to death if their caloric intake is reduced by as little as 10 percent, a state of affairs that is likely after the war. One billion people in primarily food-importing countries will be unable to obtain adequate caloric intake due to hoarding by exporting nations who will have difficulty meeting the basic needs of their own people. In China alone, one billion people will be at risk of starvation. It seems unlikely that the Chinese government will tolerate this situation for long before it will take aggressive measures, not excluding blackmail and violence on a massive scale, in an effort to coerce the formerly food-exporting nations of North America and Eurasia into providing foodstuffs for China. World markets will be in chaos. Extortion and blackmail will be rampant, from individuals to entire nations.

Approximately two billion people would die from these indirect effects of an India-Pakistan nuclear war. This means that nearly one-third of the globe's roughly 7.4 billion people will have died due to the war. By way of comparison, approximately 160 million people died due to violent conflict in the entire 20th century, which was the bloodiest century by far in human history. Were two billion to die in the aftermath of an India-Pakistan nuclear war, this single war would have killed more than twelve times the number of human beings who perished due to war in the 20th century. There is no meaningful precedent for such an eventuality.

Unanswerable questions arise that go beyond these population statistics and into the psychological reality of how life would be conducted under such circumstances. How would the survivors function? How far would human society devolve? Would other wars, perhaps other nuclear wars, be fought over the dwindling food supplies? How would the survivors tolerate the trauma in South Asia, and how would the survivors elsewhere deal with their own prospective starvation and the starvation of their children and other loved ones? We have no idea, but there is no reason for optimism. The way of life that we call "human" is unlikely to survive for long under such stress.

STATISTICS AND TRAGEDY VIA *ARMAGEDDON IN SLOW MOTION*

The Soviet dictator Josef Stalin is reported to have said, "A single death is a tragedy; a million deaths is a statistic."[28] In this chapter, we have thrown a lot of data at you: from nuclear strategy and arms control, South Asian politics, climatology, nutrition, agronomy, and even a bit of Shakespeare (the movie version). We have drawn on studies concluding that so and so many millions will die immediately in this kind of war; tens of millions later in that kind of war. And so on. These findings are, in our opinion, fundamental. They lead unambiguously to the conclusion that nuclear abolition must be our objective, ASAP. We must now think globally about the possibility of Armageddon in Slow Motion, deriving from nuclear wars that have heretofore been characterized by specialists as "small," not quite relevant to the lives of those of us who live in the northern hemisphere.

Still, Stalin's point is profound: *Statistics, no matter how great the horror they imply, are likely to remain implied, indirect, a matter for intellectual analysis. Even the statistics to which we refer in this chapter are unlikely to break your heart. And without a broken heart, you may remain unmoved by a mountain of statistics, no matter how many virtual bodies are piled up in the end. And if you remain unmoved, you are unlikely to support action to prevent similar catastrophes in the future.*

Maybe a rendezvous with Papa & The Boy in Cormac McCarthy's *The Road* can help bring us back to the emotional tragedy of a death. Imagine you are Papa. Then imagine you are The Boy. Imagine that you are on *The Road* because leaders did not have the wisdom and gumption to force nuclear nations and the entire international community to abolish nuclear weapons. Imagine spending years on The Road, in the manner that Papa & The Boy have spent it, as actors in the missing scene—the scene in which Armageddon occurs in slow motion.

Papa has known for some time that he is dying of some unnamed respiratory malady. Now he and The Boy have come to the end of The Road they have shared since The Boy's birth, just days after the nuclear bombs fell.

The man took his hand, wheezing. You need to go on, he said. I cant go with you. You need to keep going. You dont know what might be down the road. We were always lucky. You'll be lucky again. You'll see. Just go. It's all right.

I cant.

It's all right. This has been a long time coming. Now it's here. Keep going south, Do everything the way we did it.

You're going to be okay, Papa. You have to.

No I'm not. Keep the gun with you at all times. You need to find the good guys but you cant take any chances. No chances. Do you hear?

. . .

Just take me with you. Please.

I cant.

Please, Papa.

I cant. I cant hold my son dead in my arms. I thought I could but I cant.

You said you wouldnt ever leave me.

I know. I'm sorry. You have my whole heart. You always did. You're the best guy. You always were. If I'm not here you can still talk to me. You can talk to me and I'll talk to you. You'll see.

Will I hear you?

Yes. You will. You have to make it like talk that you imagine. And you'll hear me. You have to practice. Just dont give up. Okay?

Okay.

Okay.

. . .

He slept close to his father that night and held him but when he woke in the morning his father was cold and stiff. He sat there a long time weeping and then he got up and walked out through the woods to the road. When he came back he knelt beside his father and held his cold hand and said his name over and over again.

He stayed three days and then he walked out to the road and he looked down the road and looked back the way they had come.[29]

8

ARGAGEDDON OOPS?

Nuclear War via Mechanical and/or Human Screwup[1]

Dumb luck: The way in which something good happens completely by chance, without being planned or deserved.

—Macmillan Dictionary[2]

But in all my experience, I have never been in any accident . . . of any sort worth speaking about. I have never seen but one vessel in distress in all my years at sea. I never saw a wreck and have never been wrecked nor was I in any predicament that threatened to end in disaster of any sort.

—E. J. Smith, 1907, Captain, RMS *Titanic* (On April 15, 1912, the *Titantic* sank after a collision with an iceberg. More than 1,500 people perished including Captain E. J Smith)[3]

We have, thus far, focused on two paths to nuclear catastrophe, which we might refer to as: (1) *Armageddon Fast*, a war such as might have occurred if the Cuban missile crisis had exploded into a U.S.-Russian war, resulting in the destruction of at least three countries and the deaths of tens of millions of people, perhaps more, in a few hours time and, subsequently, the end of life on earth as we know it; and (2) *Armageddon Slow*, initiated by what is sometimes referred to by international security specialists as a "regional nuclear war," involving countries other than the U.S. and Russia, at least initially, in which climate cooling caused by the war has catastrophic effects on global agriculture, leading to mass starvation and social devolution of the human race to a level not seen since the dawn of human history. Both paths to Armageddon can produce the scenario in Cormac McCarthy's *The Road*: the last vestiges of human society, in which cannibalism becomes the dominant means of survival—for a while—for people who were once fully realized human beings. There is no guarantee of avoiding either Armageddon Fast or Armageddon Slow *other than* by reducing the world's nuclear arsenals to zero.[4]

We regret to inform you that there is yet another path to nuclear war we need to consider. We will call this third path to catastrophe *Armageddon Oops!* What if a nuclear missile is being moved and slides off the road and down a mountain, crashes and burns. (This actually happened to a Russian crew in eastern Cuba, near the U.S. naval base at Guantanamo Bay, during the Cuban missile crisis. Fortunately, the nuclear warhead had not yet been "mated" to its missile, so there was no nuclear detonation, although several Russian soldiers were killed. If the accident had resulted in a detonation, the Guantanamo base may have been destroyed, which would have elicited an immediate U.S. nuclear attack on Russian missile sites in Cuba.) What if a nuke is detonated due to rusty equipment? Or what if a sleepy launch officer in a silo out in Montana spills his or her coffee onto something and causes an electrical short, leading to an accidental launch? Or what if a pilot of a nuclear-capable aircraft misunderstands his instructions and believes he is supposed to drop his nuclear payload on an enemy target? And so on.

In cases like these is Armageddon Oops likely? No. Is it possible? Of course it is. We all know the truth of the adage "accidents *will* happen." We are familiar with the wisdom of intervening in a situation judged to be "an accident *waiting* to happen." There is no finite limit on the number of ways and occasions in which fallible human beings and their imperfect creations can screw up. The U.S. and Russia, who between them possess about 90 percent of the world's nuclear weapons, have gone to great lengths to build in safeguards against a screwup leading to the detonation of a nuclear weapon. Safeguards are necessary, but they are not guarantees. In addition, less is known about other nuclear arsenals, but it is presumed by specialists in the West that at least some cautionary steps—some, but not nearly enough—have been taken by the smaller nuclear powers to lower the risk of an accidental nuclear detonation.

The deep worry is that some sort of screwup will occur in a context permeated with mutual suspicion, stereotyped views between enemies, a high degree of military readiness, so as not to be caught off guard by an adversary —believed to be bent on your destruction—and, in general, a willingness to always believe the worst about the possible intentions of the enemy. Without this psychological context of intense enmity, a single accidental nuclear detonation, horrible as it would be to those exposed to it directly, would be the end of the unfortunate matter, not act one of Armageddon Oops. But in a context of mutual suspicion, an accident is unlikely to be regarded as an accident, a one-off screwup, but rather as a ruse to disguise the nefarious intentions by an enemy. The sequence to be feared looks like this:

Mutual Suspicion + Accident → Misperception → Crisis → Nuclear Catastrophe[5]

An accident actually happened during the early days of the Kennedy administration, in which a U.S. plane with nukes aboard crashed in North Carolina. The nuclear bombs almost, but did not detonate. In those days of deep mutual suspicion between the U.S. and Russia, what might have happened if a nuclear bomb had detonated in the crash?

THE GOLDSBORO INCIDENT, *LITERALLY*

The Literal History of a Cold War Footnote, January 23, 1961

On January 23, 1961, three days after the inauguration of President John F. Kennedy, a B-52 carrying two four-megaton hydrogen bombs (each with explosive power 250 times that of the Hiroshima bomb) split apart near the city of Goldsboro, North Carolina, and crashed in a tobacco field. Several members of the crew were killed. Others survived by parachuting to safety. Neither bomb detonated. For one of the bombs, every safety mechanism failed but one: the ready/safe switch in the cockpit. If it had been set to either GROUND or AIR instead of SAFE, the bomb would have detonated. That's what happened. Let's call that the *literal* history of what is commonly called "the Goldsboro incident."[6]

THE GOLDSBORO INCIDENT, *VIRTUALLY*

The Virtual History of How the End Began, January 23, 1961[7]

As is true of the Cuban missile crisis, our interest in the Goldsboro incident is not driven primarily by what happened, but by what might have happened, could have happened, (maybe even) would have happened, if that single switch had moved from the SAFE setting. We call this scenario, an exercise in virtual history, "*Hello White House, Goodbye World.*"[8]

It is January 23, 1961. President John F. Kennedy has been in office for three days. The president and his top advisers are trying to figure out their schedules, who they should appoint as deputies, how to deal with the thousands of requests and demands from constituents and members of Congress, and how to deal with the human traffic jam outside the oval office as ambassadors from around the world jockey to see the president and offer best wishes from their masters back home, and, generally, trying to figure out which end is up.

The disorientation that occurs when moving from off stage to center stage is most profound in the Defense Department, and its new secretary, Robert S. McNamara. He enters office with no relevant experience, other than his reputation for competence, organization, and an uncanny ability to get people to work efficiently, as he did as an executive at the Ford Motor Company before joining the Kennedy administration. McNamara has said publicly that he did not receive "one piece of paper" from his predecessor, President Eisenhower's Secretary of Defense, Thomas Gates—that is, McNamara knows nothing about the way the national security establishment runs, or what its more than two million employees around the world actually do. McNamara hates being ignorant of the beast that needs controlling—the Defense Department. In a national emergency, this could create huge problems, so McNamara hopes for smooth sailing, at least until he gets the lay of the land at the Pentagon.

Sometime after midnight, JFK is awakened by a call from McNamara on the secure line. McNamara says there has been an event somewhere in North Carolina—something has exploded, it seems, but he has no other hard information. As he is talking to McNamara, a Secret Service officer enters the president's bedroom and asks him to get dressed immediately, following which the officer will lead the president to an underground connecting pod from which Kennedy, McNamara, and other top-level officials will be taken to a secret location inside a mountain in West Virginia to, as the officer says, ride out what may have been a nuclear attack on the East Coast of the United States. JFK looks at the officer and realizes that this is not a joke, not some sort of initiation right inflicted on new presidents by their subordinates, but a real and present emergency of the first order. Apologetically, the officer informs JFK that the underground complex is not quite finished. It was set to open sometime next year.

Some hours later, Kennedy convenes his cabinet in their mountain retreat. The Secret Service officer was right. The place is only half finished. Communications are patchy and hard to understand. McNamara gives the briefing, having gathered what he can from calls he has placed to other Pentagon officials in the area. McNamara makes the following points:

- *A huge explosion has occurred in central North Carolina, around midnight on the 23rd.*
- *There is no confirmation on what has happened, but McNamara's assumption is that at least one thermonuclear bomb has detonated, an H-bomb being the only known device that can devastate so large a region.*
- *The bomb exploded near the Seymour Johnson SAC Air Force Base, which is near the city of Goldsboro, North Carolina, with a population of roughly fifty thousand. Wayne County, which contains Goldsboro, has a population of about eighty-four thousand. How many of those eighty-four thousand people may have already perished we don't know, but it may be more than half. We don't have hard data on any of this yet.*
- *Air Force surveillance planes have discovered a huge radiation cloud headed north, toward northern Virginia and Washington, DC. There is speculation that the radiation cloud may reach beyond Washington, DC, to Baltimore, Philadelphia, and perhaps New York City. McNamara tells the president: "I don't have to tell you the population counts of those cities."*
- *Low-level aerial reconnaissance reveals refugees—McNamara emphasizes that this is the word that his reporter used, "refugees"—are trudging away from the cities in the affected area. Having abandoned their cars due to unrelenting traffic or lack of gas, many are on foot. There appears to be no electrical power in Wayne County and possibly further out from there. We are investigating this.*
- *Hospitals in the area are becoming overwhelmed.*
- *McNamara tells the president that word of the explosion is spreading quickly and there is chaos across much of the East Coast.*
- *In a brief postscript to the briefing, McNamara says that his subordinates have made repeated attempts to contact the Kremlin, but without success. We have no idea, he says, what they think is going on or what they are going to do about what is going on. With that, the briefing ends.*

Kennedy, visibly shaken and with an unsteady voice, asks for reactions from his advisers. The first to speak is General Curtis LeMay, chief of staff of the air force (recently promoted from vice chief of staff). LeMay says that he is certain that the Russians have attacked the U.S. homeland. He believes that the U.S. has only a very limited amount of time to respond. LeMay says it is obvious that they are testing us—testing you, Mr. President—they would like us to capitulate, ask for mercy, whatever, shortly after nuking the East Coast. LeMay states that the Russians, whose missiles are notoriously inaccurate, were probably aiming for Washington, DC, which is roughly three hundred miles north of where the bomb detonated. Since they missed their main target, we need to be on the alert for another attempt. Therefore, LeMay has placed the U.S. Air Force on the highest level of alert short of war. LeMay concludes by requesting JFK to authorize a massive nuclear strike on the Soviet Union.

JFK's brother, Attorney General Robert Kennedy, shouts at LeMay, "Are you crazy?" To which LeMay responds, "No, I'm prudent and, unlike you, I know what I'm talking about."

JFK responds by saying that what happened is still unknown. Maybe the Russians are not responsible.

LeMay replies that it doesn't matter. If the Russians are responsible, then a full retaliatory nuclear attack is what U.S. strategy calls for, and it should be implemented at once. Whereas if the Russians are not responsible, Kennedy should take advantage of this event and order a massive preemptive nuclear attack on the Soviet Union and be done with the Soviet threat once and for all. LeMay, hot with anger because he sees the president hesitating, shouts: "If the Russians didn't do this to us last night, then they'll do it some other time when we'll least be expecting it. So we have to go now, Mr. President. Now!" Chairman of the Joint Chiefs of Staff General Lyman Lemnitzer says he agrees with everything LeMay has said. JFK looks at McNamara, who stares back at him blankly, as if to say, "You're on your own here."

At that moment, the lights go out. The emergency generators quickly restore the lights. The president asks, "What the hell is going on?" McNamara jumps to his feet to investigate.

McNamara returns, looking ashen. "Mr. President, there appears to be no electrical power in much of the East Coast." He can't speak about the rest of the country because so far he has been unable to reach anyone west of the Mississippi River. He's gotten word that panic is spreading. There are reports of clashes with the police as frightened people try to break into grocery stores in the middle of the night.

Kennedy signals to an aide to announce that the president will speak to the nation in one hour. Throughout the East Coast, the air force will drop millions of leaflets with text of the president's remarks.

As he is wondering what he will say, LeMay shouts, "What will you say? Will you announce that a counterattack is underway? We've got to retaliate. We've got to do SOMETHING!"

Kennedy asks if there is any word from Moscow.

There is none.

Meeting with his advisers in the Kremlin, Soviet Chairman Nikita Khrushchev is told that the Soviet military has no idea about what has happened in the U.S., but that his military advisers are 100 percent certain that the Kennedy administration, assuming they survived the blast, will blame the Soviets. That being the case, Khrushchev's advisers overwhelmingly recommend a preemptive nuclear strike on the U.S. We must use them or lose them, they say to Khrushchev.

What happens next is anyone's guess. The scenario just described was possible if the Goldsboro H-bomb detonated. Bear in mind that January 23rd falls three months before the crisis that would shape Kennedy's view of advisers who counsel confrontation and war: the Bay of Pigs disaster on April 17–20, 1961. His advisers swore the plan was foolproof: the CIA-backed Cuban exiles would land in southern Cuba, win a battle or two, whereupon the Cuban population would rise up in one voice, get rid of Fidel Castro, and agree to put someone in charge who was more amenable than Castro to "suggestions" from Washington. Although Kennedy tried to scale back the operation, in the end he let it go ahead, a passive capitulation to his hawks that nearly got him impeached and for which he was humiliated in the U.S. and throughout the world. Would the Goldsboro event be JFK's "Bay of Pigs"? If so, would he screw it up by trusting his hawkish advisers?

Khrushchev, for his part, is also in deep trouble if the Goldsboro H-bomb detonates. He and Kennedy have never met. Their correspondence, which would be so important in the resolution of the Cuban missile crisis, has not, by January 23, 1961, gotten beyond an exchange of pleasantries. Back channels do not yet exist. So decisions in Washington and Moscow would have to be made in almost total ignorance of what the other side is up to, what we call an "empathy-free zone," the zone in which the Cuban missile crisis began. Only this time, tens of thousands of people have been killed, many more than that are injured or ill, and the technical and social fabrics of the Eastern United States, including Washington and New York, have been shredded. Had one or both four-megaton H-bombs detonated over Goldsboro, North Carolina, in the crisis that ensued, neither Kennedy nor Khrushchev would have had the means to beat back worst-case scenarios with facts about the adversary's decision-making. The Cold War was raging; mutual suspicion between the U.S. and Russia was rampant. The relevant facts were unavailable. Where facts are few, paranoid fantasies are sure to tread.

THE WORLD'S NUCLEAR ARSENALS

"A Collective Death Wish; Potential Acts of Mass Murder"

In his 2013 best-selling book *Command and Control,* Eric Schlosser examines the known accidents that have occurred with the U.S. nuclear arsenals. The book is a cure for those afflicted with apathy about the nuclear threat. The scenarios, including the Goldsboro incident, are very scary, and in some cases, our escape seems almost as miraculous as our escape in October 1962 without a nuclear war. A few of them, had the damage not been contained, might have led to *The Road*, a panorama of a civilization destroyed in nuclear fire, as Papa & The Boy walk from the northeast United States to the Gulf of Mexico, where the father believes they have a better chance of surviving a little while longer because it is warmer—or so he hopes.

Schlosser ends his book this way:

> [We have] a false sense of comfort. Right now thousands of missiles are hidden away, literally out of sight, topped with warheads ready to go, awaiting the right electrical signal. They are a collective death wish, barely suppressed. Every one of them is an accident waiting to happen, a potential act of mass murder. They are out there, waiting, soulless and mechanical, sustained by our denial—and they work.[9]

And that is why we say, "You've got to get rid of the weapons."[10]

COLD WARS (PLURAL)

Welcome to Nuclear Danger in the 21st Century

Perhaps you think that the Goldsboro incident, but *with* the detonation of the bomb, might have led to Armageddon Oops. But that, you insist, was during the Cold War. Now things are not so risky. Maybe, you think, Armageddon Oops is off the list of things to worry about.

Sorry. It's still on the list. Why? Because while the global Cold War of yesteryear ended more than a quarter-century ago, it has been replaced by regional cold wars in volatile areas of the world. The perpetually tense and dangerous situation on the Korean peninsula is the very definition of a cold war. In the Middle East, a cold war with many players involves a nuclear-armed Israel ever vigilant against a bevvy of Muslim countries whose hostility toward Israel is intense. But many believe the most dangerous cold war at the moment may be the standoff in South Asia between India and Pakistan—a cold war that has turned into a hot war on three different occasions since the end of World War II.[11]

Consider the following scenario involving a close brush with a South Asian Armageddon Oops:

> *The U.S. has invited the prime ministers from both India and Pakistan to Washington, DC, to finalize and sign a peace treaty after decades of mutual violence, including three full-scale wars. But before the prime ministers can meet, a Pakistani aircraft*

crashes inside India's borders. The plane, as it happens, had a thermonuclear bomb on board. The U.S. secretary of state learns that without a team of high-level bomb squad experts to inspect it, the bomb could detonate at any time, devastating a huge area, potentially killing millions of people in India and also in Pakistan, and initiating a full-scale war between India and Pakistan who will blame each other for the devastation.

The Pakistani prime minister informs the secretary of state that a Pakistan team of experts is required to defuse the bomb, because only Pakistani munitions specialists are familiar with the bomb's design. But the Indian prime minister rejects this, claiming that only India has the right to inspect and defuse the bomb because it is located inside India's borders. U.S. decision-makers note that there is a great deal at stake: nuclear nations guard their merchandise zealously, fearing that enemies may blackmail them or attack them if they learn their secrets. The secretary of state, with authorization from the president, suggests that a U.S. team should lead the defusing process. In addition, the Pakistani team, according to the U.S. plan, will assist the Americans in defusing the bomb, while an Indian team will oversee the operation. The Americans strong-arm the Pakistanis and the Indians into accepting the plan, though each does so reluctantly. And so the bomb is defused successfully.

But another issue arises immediately that throws the diplomats into chaos once again. The issue is: Who gets to keep the defused bomb? Pakistan asserts its ownership and implies that it is willing to go to the brink of war to retrieve it, or even over the brink, thereby depriving India of its intelligence goldmine. But India refuses to hand it over to the Pakistanis, for the inverse of the Pakistani rationale for demanding custody of the bomb: Indian military and intelligence officials sense they are close to discovering their arch-enemy Pakistan's most significant nuclear secrets. The secretary of state finally convinces India to give the bomb to the U.S. Pakistan, however, refuses to accept U.S. custody.

The Pakistani prime minister is feeling intense political pressure to reclaim the bomb. Violent anti-Indian and anti-American protests have erupted all over Pakistan. It may be only a matter of days before the Pakistani government collapses. If it does collapse, it will probably be replaced by a military junta, which appears to be spoiling for a fight with India. Pakistan has already sent thousands of troops to the border with India in the Rajasthan Desert, in preparation for war. The Indian army has also mobilized and is at war readiness.

The American leaders decide that the situation in Pakistan is spinning out of control and that the political leadership will not survive unless it can claim victory in this crisis by recapturing the missing bomb. Only one solution is possible. The Indians must be forced to swallow hard and agree to let the U.S. return the bomb to Pakistan. Consequently, the U.S. secretary of state and the U.S. president meet with the Indian prime minister. They tell her the bomb must be given back to Pakistan. It is an ultimatum. The U.S. will deliver the bomb to the Pakistanis. The Indian prime minister is furious. She and her government are also under intense pressure from the Indian military to keep the bomb. She implies that whatever may be her personal view of the matter she may not be able to prevent her military from shooting down the U.S. plane carrying the bomb.

The U.S. president turns on her and strongly implies in what he says, and by his icy stare, that shooting down the U.S. plane would be a very, very stupid thing for India to do, an act that the U.S. will make them regret for a long time to come. The president may be bluffing. But the Indian prime minister and her government do not call the president's bluff, if that is what it is. Pakistan gets its wayward bomb back in custody after having come within a hair's breadth of war with India, a war that would have raised the odds sky-high that South Asia would have been the site of the world's first two-sided nuclear war, a war with the possibility of escalating to the level of a world-threatening climate disaster within months of the war's initiation.

This scenario was compellingly dramatized in an episode of the CBS primetime series, *Madam Secretary* on March 27, 2016. The episode, called "On the Clock," was scripted with input from specialists on the nuclear threat associated with the highly respected *Bulletin of the Atomic Scientists*.[12] Many discussions we have had over the years with Pakistani and Indian decision-makers and scholars lead us to this conclusion: the only implausible feature of the scenario on *Madam Secretary* is the ending: the capitulation of the Indians in the face of blackmail, or worse, from the Americans, and the subsequent happy end of the crisis via the return of the bomb to Pakistan.

Can the world really be brought to the brink of a nuclear war over ownership of a defused, now unusable, thermonuclear bomb? Is custody of a pile of nuclear junk really worth the cost of millions of people's lives in South Asia? As crazy as this scenario sounds, we should recall that, at its core, the Cuban missile crisis of October 1962 was about the location of a few dozen Russian nuclear weapons in Cuba. About that crisis, leaders eventually asked: Is this really worth Armageddon? They concluded that it was not, but by the time they grasped the danger and reached this conclusion they were unsure whether they could extricate themselves from the crisis in time to avoid it.

The beginning of wisdom in assessing the likelihood of any given scenario leading to nuclear war is the suspension of belief that, in a crisis, leaders will make decisions according to some classical definition of "rationality." In other words, they will decide in the same deliberate, calm, objective manner that characterizes (say) your decision about where to take your vacation a couple of years hence. They might be cool, calm, and collected in the midst of a deep nuclear crisis; they might act as if they are inhabiting Waltz's fantasy world. But the Cuban missile crisis proves decisively that they also might not. The psychology of crises is what the Waltz's of the world leave out. It's why we put **crisis** in the very center of our understanding of what nearly happened in October 1962.

In the onrush of confusing events, under crushing pressure not to be caught off guard, in which every minute counts, leaders may make decisions that would have been unthinkable prior to the crisis. This being the case, you need to ask yourself whether, in light of what happened in October 1962, you are comfortable looking forward to a South Asian nuclear crisis knowing that leaders might, *or might not*, act according to some classical notion of rationality when the nuclear chips are on the line.

With regard to the *Madam Secretary* scenario, ask yourself: What if the Indians did indeed shoot down the U.S. plane carrying the Pakistani bomb back to Pakistan? What happens next? Does Pakistan launch a preemptive strike against India? If it does, will India respond in kind? And what will the U.S. do, now that it is deeply implicated in the events? And how will the Russians or Chinese respond to whatever the Americans do? Whatever happens, it will constitute big trouble for India, for Pakistan, for the U.S., and for the world. It may or may not lead to nuclear war in South Asia.

But let's imagine that it does. Armageddon in Slow Motion begins.

Wouldn't it be wise to abolish nuclear weapons soon, before something like this actually happens?

9

ON *THE ROAD* AGAIN VIA CLIMATE CATASTROPHE

From a 19th Century Volcanic Eruption to a 21st Century Nuclear Winter

The boy stood up and got his broom and put it over his shoulder. He looked at his father. What are our long term goals? he said.
What?
Our long term goals.
Where did you hear that?
I dont know.
No, where did you?
You said it.
When?
A long time ago.
What was the answer?
I dont know.
Well. I dont either. Come on. It's getting dark.

—Cormac McCarthy, *The Road* (2006)[1]

. . . Stupid mists—fogs—rains—and perpetual density . . . a celebrated dark day, on which the fowls went to roost at noon, and the candles lighted as at midnight.

—George Gordon, Lord Byron, Letter from Geneva (July 22, 1816)[2]

Cormac McCarthy did his homework. The world of *The Road*—the gun-metal light, the ubiquitous ash, the end of agriculture, the shuffling through a dead planetary junkyard, the panic, the violence, the desperation, the futility of action when one is freezing and starving—all of this is well documented in histories of what happens to human society in the wake of huge volcanic eruptions. It is no accident that many climate scientists who uncovered the dimensions of nuclear winter also happen to be experts in volcanism: the study of volcanic eruptions. Big eruptions have global effects. *Global* is the key word. If the debris from an erupting volcano rises to the upper atmosphere, the eruption will have global consequences due to the disruption of global weather patterns.

Given a sufficiently large and explosive volcanic eruption, a scenario such as that described in *The Road* could occur. There would be no precedent for this, of course. The significance of past momentous volcanic eruptions for our understanding of nuclear winter is this: the erupting volcanoes, together with the degree to which they result in a cooling of part or all of the earth's surface, provide a laboratory in which to test ideas about the probable effects of a nuclear war, leading to nuclear winter. The key factor is how much soot is thrown by the eruption into the upper atmosphere, where it can persist for months, or even years, if it is propelled high enough. In addition, the higher the debris is thrown the more likely the consequences will be global due to the prevailing tendency for atmospheric material of all kinds to rotate in a reliable west-to-east direction. The beauty of linking volcanism to estimates of nuclear winter under various kinds of nuclear wars is that the *source* of the exploded, propelled debris does not matter. What matters are: (1) the amount of soot that is produced by the explosion (or explosions); and (2) how high into the atmosphere it is thrown. Contrary to the arguments of many nuclear winter deniers, it is not necessary to actually experience a nuclear war in order to make rational, empirically based estimates of the degree of global cooling that would follow it. An exploding volcano, in other words, acts as a proxy for a nuclear detonation.

We know about the atmospheric effects of huge explosions, not from theory or from computer simulations or science fiction, but from historical facts regarding the year 1816—known as "the year without a summer." What happened that remarkable year, and the two years following, has been vividly described by the Australian scholar Gillen D'Arcy Wood, in his recent book *Tambora: The Eruption That Changed the World*:

> The so-called "Year Without a Summer"—1816—belongs to a three-year period of severe climate deterioration of global scope caused by the eruption of Mt. Tambora in Indonesia in April 1815. With plummeting temperatures, and disruption to major weather systems, human communities across the globe faced crop failures, epidemic disease, and civil unrest on a catastrophic scale . . .

> To be alive in the years 1816–18, almost anywhere in the world, meant to be hungry. Across the globe during the so-called "Year Without a Summer"—which was, in fact, a three-year climate crisis—harvests perished in frost and drought or were washed away by flooding rains. Villagers in Vermont survived on hedgehogs and boiled nettles, while the peasants of Yunnan in China sucked on white clay. Summer tourists traveling in France mistook beggars crowding the roads for armies on the march.
>
> . . . When the crops failed that year, and again the next, starving rural legions from China to Ireland swarmed out of the countryside to market towns to beg for alms or sell their children in exchange for food. Famine-friendly diseases cholera and typhus stalked the globe from India to Italy, while the price of bread and rice, the world's staple foods, skyrocketed with no relief in sight. Across a European continent devastated by the Napoleonic wars, tens of thousands of unemployed veterans found themselves unable to feed their families. They gave vent to their desperation in town square riots and military-style campaigns of arson, while governments everywhere feared revolution. In New England, 1816 was nicknamed "Eighteen-Hundred-and-Froze-to-Death," while Germans called 1817 "The Year of the Beggar.". . .[3]

In the midst of what Gillen D'Arcy Wood calls "a tsunami of famine, disease, dislocation and unrest," human empathy quickly eroded.[4] With parents selling their children in exchange for food, with the massive breakdown in the human infrastructure—especially the family—we can begin to see the year without a summer as a kind of prequel to *The Road*. It followed roughly this sequence:

> *Mt. Tambora Eruption → Climate Disruption → Crop Failure → Starvation → Societal Collapse → Erosion of Empathy → Armageddon in Slow Motion (aka* The Road*)*

The sequence of climatic events that would have led to *The Road* differs from what happened in 1816 in two respects: their root cause is different (nuclear war versus a volcanic eruption); and the duration of the devolution of human society (Papa & The Boy have been on the road for approximately ten years; only one year has elapsed between Tambora's eruption and the beginning of the 1816 climate catastrophe in Western Europe). But if following 1816, the cold, dark year of starvation and dislocation had repeated itself for ten consecutive years there is no telling how miserable and inhumane human life on earth would have become or, indeed, whether the apocalyptic trend could have been reversed if the weather had turned around. In the climatic catastrophe of 1816–1818, hundreds of thousands still died of disease and starvation, millions were dislocated, and violence driven by desperation erupted all over Europe.[5]

The eruption of Mt. Tambora was the largest in recorded history; that is, in the last 2,500 years. It was an atmospheric proxy for a small nuclear war, of perhaps a couple of dozen Hiroshima-sized nuclear bombs (roughly fifteen kilotons each). Cities didn't burn, but Tambora burned mightily, its explosions propelling massive quantities of debris into the upper atmosphere, overspreading the earth, causing chaos in global weather patterns and immense suffering for years to come.

SEQUEL TO THE ROAD

Byron's 1816 Letter to Our Nuclear-Armed World of the 21st Century

The cause of the misery in this climatic catastrophe in Europe and elsewhere was a volcano eruption in Indonesia roughly seven thousand miles away. The epicenter of European devastation turned out to be in Switzerland. Conditions in many Swiss cantons became horrific, with substantial areas becoming uninhabitable. The weather remained unseasonably cold and wet into, and through, the spring, stretching into the summer and beyond. Between mid-spring and summer's end 130 days of rain fell in and around Geneva, submerging the city to a degree reminiscent of what happened to New Orleans in the Hurricane Katrina disaster of August 2005. It was so cold in the mountains that the usual spring melt never occurred, swelling the bulk of the glaciers until some broke off and crashed, sending cascades of lethal ice chunks through entire valleys full of villages and farms, destroying everything in their paths.

The disastrous weather was only the beginning of the human catastrophe in Switzerland and throughout Western Europe. Crops were planted but were drowned by the relentless cold rain. Grain surpluses were quickly exhausted. People had literally nothing to eat—at least nothing they were used to eating. The "diet" of the Swiss, according to one report, consisted of "the most loathsome and unnatural foods—carcasses of dead animals, cattle fodder, leaves of nettles, swine food . . . ."[6] Starving families hit the road. Children became beggars. The number of homeless may have reached more than one million people. Mortality in 1816–1817 was over 50 percent higher than it was in 1815 (which was already higher than usual due to the violent conclusion to the Napoleonic Wars).[7]

The weather was more than disastrous. Its weirdness almost defied belief. Sometimes the entire sky turned blood red; other times it was so dark, even in the middle of a summer day, that candles were necessary during lunch. The Scottish-English poet, George Gordon, Lord Byron, spent all summer near

Lake Geneva, which was then a popular summer tourism destination for the English upper classes. Byron had rented a luxurious property called the Villa Diodati, on the balcony of which he wrote his poetry and correspondence. In a letter written in the last days of July 1816, he reported enduring "stupid mists—fogs—rains—and perpetual density" and "a celebrated dark day, on which the fowls went to roost at noon, and the candles lighted as at midnight."[8] Nocturnal thunderstorms were reported to have gone on for hours, with lightning illuminating the sky the entire time, with the brilliance of midday.

Byron is equally well known for his short, scandalous life and his brilliant long poems. The scandals are irrelevant to our purpose. But one of his medium-length poems, written in Geneva during late July 1816, should be required reading for everyone concerned about the threat to human survival posed by climate change, including a nuclear winter, via "Armageddon in Slow Motion." The poem is called simply "Darkness." The poem, all eighty-two lines of blank verse, is given below, along with some context supplied by us.

In reading this extraordinary poem, it is necessary to keep in mind both what Byron knew and what he didn't know about the catastrophe unfolding around him in mid-1816. First, here is what he knew: (1) the *weather* was strange beyond strange; (2) people across Europe were *starving*; (3) the social fabric of European society was disintegrating—for example, many of the usually staid and stable Swiss, driven by hunger and fear, had begun to behave erratically, in ways that seemed to Byron to reveal a kind of incipient *madness*; and (4) although he was not religious in the formal sense, Byron knew well the biblical Book of Revelation, in which the end of the world is foretold, and he had begun to wonder if the *end of days* described in Revelation was upon them.

Sitting comfortably, at least for the moment, within the protective shell of privilege provided by his residence in the Villa Diodati, there was also a lot that Byron did not know: (1) the *cause* of the disruptive weather (the connection to the eruption of Mt. Tambora would not be discovered for another 150 years); (2) the *trajectory* of the catastrophic weather—it might get worse, or better, or get worse before it got better; (3) the *duration* of the disruption—would it last for a year, or ten years, or longer? Finally, (4) Byron had no way of identifying *the point of no return*, when the deterioration of society would be irreversible.[9]

Frightened and agitated by the cold, dark, and inexplicable world that suddenly confronted him, Byron sat down at his table on the balcony of the Villa Diodati and feverishly wrote "Darkness" sometime during the last two weeks of July 1816. Climatologist Alan Robock of Rutgers now routinely recites long passages from Byron's poem in public lectures on nuclear winter.

He reports first learning about the poem from Russian scientists in the 1980s, who had read it in an 1847 Russian translation by the great Russian writer Ivan Turgenev.[10] After Robock read it (in the original English), the Russians asked him what he thought of it. Robock remembers telling them "it sounds just like nuclear winter," a proposition with which the Russian climatologists enthusiastically agreed.[11]

Here is "Darkness."[12] Think of it as a letter from a great 19th century poet to those of us in the 21st century seeking to avoid a catastrophe such as Byron witnessed in Geneva in 1816—or worse. Written with the vision of a great artist, "Darkness" describes the extremity to which a climatic catastrophe might lead. "Darkness" is the sequel to *The Road*. It is the road beyond *The Road*.

Periodically, we give our take (indented, italicized, and with the identifier ***J&j***) on what we think the poet is driving at. Like Cormac McCarthy's *The Road*, "Darkness" presents us with an attempt to imagine the unimaginable: a world without human beings, as conceived by a human being, in human language, written for other human beings. Its variegated portrait of the horror that would accompany a nuclear winter can, we believe, show us what is at stake if efforts to abolish nuclear weapons fail.

Darkness[13]

By George Gordon, Lord Byron
(written in Geneva, Switzerland, July 1816)

I had a dream, which was not all a dream.
The bright sun was extinguish'd, and the stars
Did wander darkling in the eternal space,
Rayless, and pathless, and the icy earth
Swung blind and blackening in the moonless air;
Morn came and went—and came, and brought no day,
And men forgot their passions in the dread
Of this their desolation; and all hearts
Were chill'd into a selfish prayer for light:

> *[**J&j:** Byron describes what he sees and what he feels. Some of what follows he has observed with his own eyes. Some he has read in newspapers and in letters from friends all over Europe. Some is speculation, informed by his experience and imagination, but still speculation. He seems to say that we human beings were not meant for the cold and*

the dark that was gathering all around him. If the climatic catastrophe continues unabated, the cold and the dark may be, for all we know, our new environment for all time. Try to imagine that everyone you know is praying for light—something we take for granted every day of our lives. In the cold and the dark, you feel alone and helpless. Hearing the voices of others does not reassure you. It frightens you. Psychologically, there are thus only two conditions in these catastrophic circumstances: formless anxiety about what may lie waiting for you out there in the cold darkness; and outright fear of whomever might speak to you, for you know that the individual is also cold, also starving.]

And they did live by watchfires—and the thrones,
The palaces of crowned kings—the huts,
The habitations of all things which dwell,
Were burnt for beacons; cities were consum'd,
And men were gather'd round their blazing homes
To look once more into each other's face;
Happy were those who dwelt within the eye
Of the volcanos, and their mountain-torch:
A fearful hope was all the world contain'd;

***[J&j:** The poet scarcely recognizes Geneva and its surrounding area. Like the rest of Europe, packs of starving humans roam across the countryside with but one objective: to locate food. Starvation is the common enemy, and it is ever present. Yet having a common foe does not bring the people together. Communities have not formed in the cold and dark to work out equitable arrangements for sharing whatever resources they may have, as a group, to generate heat and light, and to share what little they may have found to eat. Instead, unable to get warm, to eat, to see, they set themselves against one another. There are isolated cases of beneficent behavior. But they are few, as the violence of the hungry becomes greater, with each passing day. And even those who find food have no fuel for their fires. What a choice: to huddle shivering inside one's abode, with little or nothing to eat, or to burn one's home in order to keep warm, oh so briefly. Hopelessness sits heavy on everyone's shoulders. Imagine a world in which those living near active volcanoes are, as Byron's suggests, the luckiest people on earth, because they have a source of light and of heat.]*

Forests were set on fire—but hour by hour
They fell and faded—and the crackling trunks
Extinguish'd with a crash—and all was black.
The brows of men by the despairing light
Wore an unearthly aspect, as by fits

The flashes fell upon them; some lay down
And hid their eyes and wept; and some did rest
Their chins upon their clenched hands, and smil'd;
And others hurried to and fro, and fed
Their funeral piles with fuel, and look'd up
With mad disquietude on the dull sky,
The pall of a past world; and then again
With curses cast them down upon the dust,
And gnash'd their teeth and howl'd: the wild birds shriek'd
And, terrified, did flutter on the ground,
And flap their useless wings; the wildest brutes
Came tame and tremulous; and vipers crawl'd
And twin'd themselves among the multitude,
Hissing, but stingless—they were slain for food.

> *[**J&j:** As the cold and the dark close in on everyone, an epidemic of madness has also set in. Fires are kept burning by the addition of human and other corpses—those portions of corpses deemed impossible to eat. The eyes of many have begun to bulge out, as if they are seeing visions of horror that others can't see. Some have taken to howling like wolves, or screeching insanely at objects visible only to themselves. Bryon implies that madness may be a prerequisite for those preparing to eat snakes. Even the animals seem to have gone mad: perhaps they sense catastrophe, in their ways, just as human beings do. Perhaps, in a world gone horribly wrong, the only proper response is to give way to madness. In the madhouse of climatic catastrophe, the mad are oddly normal, while those few who remain temporarily normal in the usual sense are oddly abnormal. Such has human society been perverted by the ongoing climate catastrophe.]*

And War, which for a moment was no more,
Did glut himself again: a meal was bought
With blood, and each sate sullenly apart
Gorging himself in gloom: no love was left;
All earth was but one thought—and that was death
Immediate and inglorious; and the pang
Of famine fed upon all entrails—men
Died, and their bones were tombless as their flesh;

The meagre by the meagre were devour'd,
Even dogs assail'd their masters, all save one,
And he was faithful to a corse, and kept
The birds and beasts and famish'd men at bay,
Till hunger clung them, or the dropping dead
Lur'd their lank jaws; himself sought out no food,
But with a piteous and perpetual moan,
And a quick desolate cry, licking the hand
Which answer'd not with a caress—he died.

*[**J&j:** Human empathy has evaporated into the dank, dark air. Our feeling for one another diminishes to nearly nothing. We no longer look at one another or listen to one another. Many ask What is the point? Why follow the old ways, the old moral codes, when everything is leading to a common outcome, which is oblivion? Wars break out daily—small wars, primitive wars, compared with the recent wars in Europe involving Napoleon Bonaparte, with his gigantic armies and modern weapons. The new wars are fought with sticks and stones by groups of bandits vying for access to food. The consumption of human flesh is no longer taboo. For those involved in the violence, there are only the good cannibals, who kill their victims before consuming their flesh; and there are the bad cannibals, who dismember their victims, as their flesh is needed. And dogs are no longer man's best friend, but are instead a much-coveted meal. The singularly heroic dog in "Darkness" is modeled on Byron's own beloved Newfoundland dog, Boatswain, to whom he composed an epitaph in 1808, which concludes this way:*

> To mark a friend's remains these stones arise;
> I never knew but one—and here he lies.*]*

The crowd was famish'd by degrees; but two
Of an enormous city did survive,
And they were enemies: they met beside
The dying embers of an altar-place
Where had been heap'd a mass of holy things
For an unholy usage; they rak'd up,
And shivering scrap'd with their cold skeleton hands
The feeble ashes, and their feeble breath
Blew for a little life, and made a flame
Which was a mockery; then they lifted up

Their eyes as it grew lighter, and beheld
Each other's aspects—saw, and shriek'd, and died—
Even of their mutual hideousness they died,
Unknowing who he was upon whose brow
Famine had written Fiend.

> *[**J&j:** Human beings have, in their extremity of cold, dark and hunger, become dehumanized. Empathy between human beings is no longer possible. Everyone is your enemy, and vice versa. For a time, you try to sustain yourself by constructing a narrative along these lines: although it is difficult, you have succeeded in remaining human in these terrible circumstances. You remember your former self, before the cold and the dark set in, a world of friends, neighbors, relatives, and the ordinary tasks of getting on with life in that long gone time. You imagine that you still adhere to a moral code, perhaps do unto others as you would have them do unto you. At least, you convince yourself that you are doing the best that can be done in the situation in which you find yourself. You imagine, further, that if the weather would only turn around—and it will, you think, or at least you desperately hope it will—then you and the others who have survived the nightmare can begin to rebuild the world and your lives in ways that approximate the life you used to know. This is your hope. But you soon discover that you have unwittingly mistaken a hope for statement of fact. Your narrative—your fantasy life—comes crashing down when, for the first time in a long time, you stare in the face of someone and are paralyzed by two reactions: that the individual whom you are staring at, and who is staring at you, is but a wild animal; and that you too have become a wild animal. There will be no rebuilding, regardless of what happens to the weather. It is too late. You and the human race are doomed. Death is the only escape.]*

The world was void,
The populous and the powerful was a lump,
Seasonless, herbless, treeless, manless, lifeless—
A lump of death—a chaos of hard clay.
The rivers, lakes and ocean all stood still,
And nothing stirr'd within their silent depths;
Ships sailorless lay rotting on the sea,
And their masts fell down piecemeal: as they dropp'd
They slept on the abyss without a surge—
The waves were dead; the tides were in their grave,
The moon, their mistress, had expir'd before;

The winds were wither'd in the stagnant air,
And the clouds perish'd; Darkness had no need
Of aid from them—She was the Universe.

*[**J&j:** Life has been extinguished. Byron tells us that all is cold and darkness, although in saying so he encounters the limits of language in describing a situation of which we have no experience, and can have no experience. It's a world without us, without others, without anything that lives or breathes or grows; it's the end. Byron tries to envision the ultimate cold and dark, which is the direction he seems to think, from his standpoint in Geneva in July 1816, we are headed. This is the sequel to* The Road, *but without even Papa & The Boy.]*

WHY "DARKNESS," WHY NOW?

You may wonder what is left for us to say in this chapter after we have subjected you to *The Road* and Byron's "Darkness." Something *is* left. We need to be as explicit as possible about what it at stake. We find ourselves recalling the contemporary American poet Mary Oliver, whose short poem, "The Uses of Sorrow," says in a personal context what we would like to say to you about the discussions of nuclear history and nuclear policy:

(In my sleep I dreamed this poem)

Someone I loved once gave me
a box full of darkness.
It took me years to understand
that this, too, was a gift.[14]

In this dark beyond darkness, it makes no difference whether you have your eyes open or closed. You can't see any way out. It's that dark. But you mustn't give up.

Having grappled with the Cuban missile crisis as history and warning—Armageddon almost happened; it can happen at any time—we urge you to keep your eyes open as you turn the page to part IV. In this final section, we light a candle that reveals, we believe, the possibility of defying the pitch-black possibility of nuclear Armageddon: by using the Cuban missile crisis as a catalyst for a new way of thinking about how to abolish nuclear weapons.

PART IV

THE DARKNESS DEFINED AND DEFIED

(Nuclear Abolition Via The Black Saturday Manifesto)

Look at how a single candle can both defy and define the darkness.

—Attributed to Anne Frank[1]

Where do you go from here? You need a way to stay focused on the necessity of moving to zero nukes, by ignoring distractions thrown at you by those unable or unwilling to grasp what actually happened on the island of Cuba during the Cuban missile crisis. You will require some tools to weed out the many fairy tales written about the crisis, all of which state or imply that moving to zero nukes is unnecessary, unwise, or downright impossible. In this book, we call their views (provocatively, but we believe accurately) "bullshit." The chapters in part IV provide the tools for avoiding the bullshit going forward, a guide to the fundamental lessons of the Cuban missile crisis sufficiently concise that you can tape them to the door of your fridge or put them on a thumbnail and stick it in the corner of your computer screen, and a way to defy the darkness. They are:

- *A bullshit detector for identifying the darkness-deniers—the pseudo-historical falsehoods, half-truths, and agenda-driven nonsense that continues to accumulate more than a half-century after the crisis (chapter 10)*
- *A figurative flashlight with which to illuminate how the takeaways and lessons of the Cuban missile crisis can be applied to nuclear danger now, in the 21st century (chapter 11)*
- *Finally, a way out: The Black Saturday Manifesto: toward the annual, global commemoration of October 27, 1962, the most dangerous moment in human history (chapter 12)*

10

BE ANYBODY WABAC

Empathy, Not Sympathy, Is the Key

Ty Webb: Just be the ball, be the ball, be the ball.

—Caddyshack, a film by Harold Ramis (1980)[1]

Ethical integrity originates in empathy. . . . Our thoughts, words and deeds are based on a sense of what we have in common rather than what divides us.

—Stephen Batchelor, *Buddhism without Beliefs* (1997)[2]

The trick [of empathy] is to figure out what the devil they think they are up to.

—Clifford Geertz, *Local Knowledge* (1983)[3]

PLEASE: "SECOND THAT EMOTION"

Do You Feel It? Is It Real? Might It have been Real? Is It important?

Habitable history permits us to enter a deeply foreign event, to empathize with those who experienced it long ago and far away as their history of their present moment moved forward, with the outcome unknown; with highly imperfect information, loaded with misperceptions and misjudgments as the protagonists stumble forward, trying to avoid the worst and hoping for the best. *Never forget that people in the past were living their own version of the present.* This is easy to recommend but difficult to implement. You can never, for example, study the Cuban missile crisis without knowing the outcome. Actually, already knowing the outcome has a lot to do with why you are interested in it in the first place. It's important, to say the very least, that the world was not blown to smithereens on the last weekend of October 1962. So you want to know why the world was almost toast, and why ultimately it was not.[4]

What difference does it make whether the work of history, from whatever genre, sucks you into the stream of forward-moving events? Here are two one-word answers; both apply in spades to the Cuban missile crisis: *emotion* and *crisis*.

Emotion! Lived history is *felt* history—it is funny, ridiculous, uplifting, embarrassing, frustrating, aggravating, satisfying, and, in the case of the Cuban missile crisis, scary as hell. Repeat: scary as hell. Scared people sweat, and, in general, live life out at the edge of what they can tolerate. This kind of life does not take place in a library cubicle, or in front of a computer screen, or on a movie set. In this kind of life, people can get hurt, or killed, or—as leaders found themselves in the Cuban missile crisis—be on the brink of making decisions and committing acts that would have been inconceivable just days or hours or even minutes before. Every significant moment in your life is tinged with emotion, driven by emotion—it's what makes life worth living and is what makes losing one's life a tragic affair. The rock era's great countertenor, Smokey Robinson, sang, apropos of love, "I second that emotion."[5] You should too, apropos of the history you encounter.

Crisis! What happens in a crisis?[6] The stakes are high, you suspect that you don't quite understand what is going on, time suddenly seems short, and your heart begins to palpitate. Your preparations, your plans and schemes, are called into question by some unexpected confluence of events. You thought she would say yes to your proposal of marriage, but she didn't. You thought that the college of your choice would accept you, but it didn't. You thought your best friend would never betray you, but he did. You are at a fork in the road, and you don't know what to do. On the last weekend of October 1962, the leaders of the U.S., Cuba, and Russia reached such a fork, and either direction, so it seemed to them, might lead to Armageddon and the end of the world, as we know it. No one ever prepared for such a decisive moment. How in the world would you prepare for *that?*

If the history feels like real life, populated by real people facing real dilemmas, and if the people and events correspond to actual people and events that are consistent with the historical record, then go with it. *Inhabit it.* Commune with your fellow human beings via the author's or filmmaker's WABAC machine. Whereas, if the history leaves you cold, if the characters seem more like stick figures than living human beings (largely devoid of human emotion), and/or the history seems warped, artificial, and just plain wrong (invented characters and events), then you face the following choice: give it up as bullshit history or, if the artist has talent, enjoy it as fiction that happens to have some characters whose names and circumstances correspond to those of people known to have been real.

BULLSHIT VERSUS HABITABLE HISTORY

A Tale of a Historian's Fiction, and a Novelist's Habitable History

Alas, in practice, it is often difficult to assess the veracity of a WABAC machine. You might be swept along by something totally implausible. (We are no exception. We are fans of the X-Men movies, which overflow with ridiculous plot lines, time and space travel, cameo appearances by U.S. presidents John F. Kennedy, who may or may not have been murdered by a mutant, and Richard M. Nixon, who famously and inaccurately exclaimed, "I'm *not* a crook!") Or the history may be accurate but you can hardly stay awake during your encounter with it. (Many docudramas strike us this way.) Dare we say it? We are about to throw you once again onto what Hilary Mantel calls "the great marshy ground of interpretation," along with this sage advice: hang in there, grasshoppers; don't panic; be the history, both as to its accuracy and its capacity to compel empathy.

What we can do is provide you with two prototypes: one of bullshit history, and one of habitable history. The irony is that the fictional bullshit is due to one of the English-speaking world's most famous historians, Niall Ferguson; while the habitable history comes from Hilary Mantel, a novelist whom virtually everyone regards as a writer of fiction.

Niall Ferguson: Historian-Bullshitter

Fasten your seat belts, hold on tight, and be assured that the following two paragraphs appear unaltered, exactly as they appear in Ferguson's book, *Virtual History*, a book of "counterfactuals"—of history that might have been but wasn't, written by eminent historians. Ferguson himself weighs in on JFK and Cuba. Alas, we are not kidding. According to Niall Ferguson:

> *No American Prime Minister did more to deepen American-Japanese confrontation than John F. Kennedy, the son of Roosevelt's Anglophobe consul in London, Joseph Kennedy.*

> *By a huge margin—mainly owing to the Catholic vote in the North's crowded cities—Kennedy won the 1960 election. The following year, he scored a minor triumph when a successful invasion reclaimed Cuba from the last remaining Nazi forces in Latin America. Emboldened, he began to examine the possibility of another military intervention, this time in support of Ho Chi Minh's Vietnamese revolt against the Japanese-backed regime of Ngo Dinh Diem.*
>
> *In many ways, JFK was a lucky Prime Minister. He was spared the difficulties of the black suffrage movement which plagued the political career of his Southern counterpart, Lyndon Johnson. He survived an assassination attempt while visiting Johnson in Dallas in November 1963. His Centralist party smashed the states' righters led by Barry Goldwater in the elections of 1964. But Kennedy's good luck deserted him in Vietnam. True, the war was popular; but Kennedy could not win it. When he was forced to resign in 1967, following revelations that his brother, the Attorney-General Robert Kennedy, had authorised phone-tapping of political opponents, no fewer than half a million troops were fighting alongside the North Vietnamese forces. But the Japanese-backed regime was better equipped than had been expected, not least because of the rapid development of Japanese electrical engineering. When Richard Nixon swept to victory in the 1968 election, it was with a mandate to end the war. In a television debate with Nixon before his impeachment, a haggard Kennedy made his bitterness clear. "If I had been shot dead back in 1963," he exclaimed, "I would be a saint today." Although . . . Kennedy had a point, his remark was universally derided at the time.*[7]

And you thought Alice was confused in Wonderland? There are at least seven significant inventions by Ferguson in the first paragraph, and at least twelve in the second. Of course, whether or not you agree with this estimate of nineteen "significant" "what-ifs?" depends on what one understands as "significant." There are at least two to three times this number of events embedded in Ferguson's two paragraphs that never occurred, or are misattributed, misnamed, or in some other way at variance from the facts as we understand them. But who's counting? Well, we are. Ferguson's literary performance art lacks all plausibility, any believable characters, and is totally without the power to make us care about JFK or anyone else. This is, for us, useless bullshit, written by a famous historian, presented apparently without irony, as something from which we can learn something important. We present it here as a kind of prototype of perfectly *un*-inhabitable history.

Hilary Mantel: Historian-Novelist

You have already encountered in chapter 4 an example of exceptionally habitable history from the conclusion to Hilary Mantel's 2012 masterpiece,

Bring Up the Bodies: Thomas Cromwell, alone in his study, picking up the pieces after having dispatched King Henry VIII's wife, Anne Boleyn, to the scaffold for her beheading. Mantel invites you to please be quiet, step into Cromwell's room, and inhabit this extraordinary man as he plots his next moves. Cromwell has carried out his orders from King Henry VIII. It's all in a day's work. But still, many sorts of influential Englishmen hate him for a variety of reasons (much of it class related, Cromwell being a blue-collar upstart who, the gentry believe, has no business in such a high position). Many want Cromwell dead ASAP.

Hilary Mantel allows us, in very economical language, to inhabit Cromwell's response to his new situation: a new queen, Henry VIII's third, Jane Seymour, and new dangers and opportunities. Cromwell lives out a crisis every day. At the Tudor court of Henry VIII, one false move can mean death and, if Henry is sufficiently angry at the victim, it will be a slow death accompanied by some of the most horrifying forms of torture ever invented. We can feel Cromwell's determination, his competitiveness, and his ambition. Cromwell, writes Mantel, intends to be "stuck like a limpet to the future"—the limpet being the primitive creature with the most powerful grip in all of nature. "Go ahead and try to get me, you fools," we can imagine Cromwell thinking. Mantel's ability to convey Cromwell's personality so vividly—while honoring the known historical evidence—is one reason so many eagerly anticipate the third and final volume in the Cromwell trilogy, when history's "limpet" loses his grip, along with his head, on the scaffold of the Tower of London.[8]

EMPATHY NOT SYMPATHY

What Would You *do in a Deadly Situation?*

One feature of Mantel's Cromwell that bears on our own portrait of Fidel Castro on the last weekend of October 1962 is that both men behave in ways that can be difficult to comprehend, as we look back at them. In fact, their behavior may seem not just unusual but reprehensible. We think: Omigod, I would never have done what those guys did. They were just awful! This is an understandable reaction, but we urge you not to confuse *sympathy*—which is the feeling that you approve, you favor, you admire what someone has done—with *empathy*—the capacity to put yourself in the skin of another human being, in another time, place, and context. Sympathy is an act of agreement that accompanies your feeling of approval; empathy is harder work, an act of understanding, whether you approve or not. It is your effort to determine, as Geertz puts it, "what the devil *they* think *they* are up to."[9] Empathy requires us to step outside the bubbles of our own viewpoints and consider the viewpoints of people who hail from very different circumstances than we do.

Habitable history, in essence, is history that is accurate, that exhibits *empathy* toward its characters, and that facilitates empathy for us, on the receiving end.

Some enterprising scholar of the court of Henry VIII has determined that for the eight or so years Thomas Cromwell served as chief minister to the king, he personally arranged, or approved, or in any event did not object to, the killing of thousands of people.[10] Even if we grant that it was a tough neighborhood, ruled by a sometimes barbaric and cruel monarch who happened to be his boss, any modern officer of state who kills this many of his fellow citizens stands a good chance of being added to the black list of Human Rights Watch. Circumstances like these make Mantel's believable portrayal of Cromwell a remarkable achievement. A blue-collar author writes about a blue-collar guy who scratches his way to the top, and remains there for quite a while, before his time runs out and he too loses his head on the chopping block. The implied question on every one of Mantel's 942 pages so far published about Cromwell is: "Okay, you brilliant 21st century skeptics who claim that Cromwell was *just* a nasty, cruel opportunist; what would *you* have done in Cromwell's circumstances—not in some imaginary world, but in the true grit of the court of Henry VIII?"

The problem with Fidel Castro is that, having decided wrongly but plausibly that Cuba is on the brink of total destruction, he prefers annihilation and martyrdom to survival and capitulation. By what right, we may want to know, does a leader presume to take his country into nuclear oblivion on the assumption that all Cubans want what Fidel wants: martyrdom, to be provided by a presumed Russian nuclear attack that totally destroys the United States of America? Do the Cuban people really value their martyrdom over the futures of their children? Could Cuban patriotism, communist ideology, and the chance to stick it to Uncle Sam, really be worth more than life itself? On what basis does the fiery Fidel presume to speak for all 7.5 million Cubans? And what about the roughly 180 million citizens who in 1962 make up the population of the U.S. who, in Fidel's view, are to be turned into nuclear toast by a Russian nuclear attack? Don't they matter? Is the incineration of the U.S. justified? These are all good and necessary questions.

Our response to these and related moral queries about Fidel's judgment is a variant of the question that drives Hilary Mantel's treatment of Thomas

Cromwell: What would you have done in his position? Fidel Castro didn't just appear on the Cuban scene during the Cuban missile crisis. He had led a civil war against a U.S. puppet, Fulgencio Batista, in the 1950s. He had been jailed, tortured, and exiled. After coming to power, he was the target of dozens of assassination attempts by Cuban exiles on the CIA's payroll. In late October 1962, his island nation is surrounded by the world's most powerful military machine, gearing up for what looks remarkably like a large-scale attack and invasion of Cuba.

If you are Fidel on that weekend, that is who you are. You believe that the American terms are unconditional surrender or nothing. If you are Fidel, you are not the surrendering type. In fact, everything in your background suggests that, not unlike Thomas Cromwell, you relish your role as an outsider and underdog. You are David. The U.S. is Goliath. And in your sling are Russian nuclear weapons. That's the situation you are in. So we say: "Okay, you 21st century geniuses, you say Fidel Castro must have been some suicidal maniac, but what would *you* have done if you had been Fidel in that situation? Not: you, now, with your comfortable upbringing and nice manners, but Fidel Castro, the survivor of a brutal history in a very tough neighborhood that is ruled by the United States of America, to him, the world's biggest bully."

We urge you to reread the previous three paragraphs. Now consider this: the Cuban missile crisis would never have occurred if John F. Kennedy and Nikita Khrushchev had taken to heart the message in those paragraphs. But they didn't. In fact, it never occurred to them that such an effort at empathy with the Cubans was relevant to their interests and concerns. They thought that Cuba was just a little pipsqueak country that mattered little. Kennedy and Khrushchev were wrong about that.[11] As a result, their nations, and the world, came within a hair's breadth of total destruction.

11

DARKNESS VISIBLE

Findings, Takeaways, and Imperatives of the Cuban Missile Crisis

No light, but rather darkness visible
Served only to discover sights of woe

—John Milton, *Paradise Lost* (1667)[1]

Darkness honestly lived through is a place of wonder and life.

—Robert Lowell (October 1957)[2]

HOW THE END OF EVERYTHING MIGHT HAVE BEGUN

There But for Fortune Went Our Ancestors (and the World)

There are many scenarios from October 1962 in which a nuclear war might actually have happened. Here is one. (The comments in parentheses refer to events that actually occurred!)

> *The Cubans and/or Russians shoot down several U.S. reconnaissance planes on October 27, 1962.* (The Cubans were firing at all U.S. low-flying reconnaissance planes, but failed to bring any down; the Russians shot down one high-flying U-2 spy plane on the morning of October 27th.) *JFK can no longer restrain his hawks; he*

orders a retaliatory air attack on targets in Cuba. (He had been under constant pressure to authorize military actions against Cuba ever since the missiles were discovered.) *The joint Russian-Cuban forces in eastern Cuba, led by Raul Castro, attack the U.S. naval base at Guantanamo Bay with short-range nuclear weapons, killing several thousand Americans.* (On October 27th, unknown to JFK, the Russian nukes were moved into position near Guantanamo and made ready to fire.) *The U.S. then begins its invasion of Cuba, and is met with Russian nuclear fire against U.S. forces at sea and on the beaches of Cuba.* (Unknown to JFK, Russian short-range nukes were ready to fire and Russian commanders were determined to use them.) *The U.S. responds with a nuclear attack against Soviet sites in Cuba, killing thousands of Russians and Cubans near the missile sites, which would have been the initial targets of a U.S. air strike.* (U.S. nuclear-armed aircraft were an eighteen-minute flight to targets in Cuba; the plan was for 1,200 bombing missions with non-nuclear bombs on day one of the attack. If the Russians had used their nukes, the U.S. would have retaliated in kind.)

The crisis quickly escalates beyond the Caribbean, whether or not any Russian rockets are fired from Cuba, and whether or not they hit targets in the U.S. The war spreads first to Europe, where the Russians have seized West Berlin, to which the U.S. responds with short-range nukes targeting Russian troop formations. (The Russians have several million men within 100 miles of Berlin; the U.S. and its allies have a mere 12,000 stationed in West Berlin; this is why they conclude that the only way to counter the Russians in Europe is with nuclear weapons.) *Finally, the Russians and the Americans attack each other's homelands, killing tens, or perhaps hundreds of millions of people, effectively bringing the era of human civilization to an abrupt end.* (Both U.S. and Russian nuclear forces are mobilized at the highest degree of readiness short of war, so that an attack by one upon the other will trigger a convulsion of unprecedented violence, from nuclear armed missiles, planes, and submarines.)

Think Cormac McCarthy's *The Road*; think Papa & The Boy. The survivors envy the dead. (When we read the novel, we like to listen to the score from the movie, by Nick Cave and Warren Ellis, which is simple, heartbreaking, and bleakly beautiful.) We believe this is more or less what would have happened in October 1962 if war had commenced in Cuba over the missiles the Russians had deployed on the island.

REPEAT THIS— "BUT STILL, NOTHING MUCH HAPPENED"

The Problem of Anxiety Management in the Nuclear Age

Did nuclear war happen? Obviously not. Could it have happened? Yes. Were these events, or scenarios of comparable deadliness, *possible*? Yes. The nuclear attack on Guantanamo may have occurred, in the frenzied circumstances of the moment, whether or not the U.S. attack had begun. In the Old West metaphor: the nuclear guns were loaded with live ammunition. The gun barrels were aimed. The hammers were cocked. The trigger fingers in Washington, Moscow, Havana, among the NATO and Warsaw Pact forces in Europe—in fact, wherever U.S. and Russian forces happened to be across the globe—were twitchy, poised to respond to almost any provocation, or even a rumor of a prospective provocation.

You may hasten to add, "but still, nothing much happened." Repeat this a few times: "but still, nothing much happened." Notice that with each repetition, ever more anxiety about what might have happened is drained out by the statement of what did happen—"nothing much." *Armageddon*, the catastrophic event that didn't quite happen, seems progressively less plausible each time you repeat "but still, nothing much happened" due simply to the repetition of its particulars. This is natural. Psychologist Sigmund Freud noted a century ago that the "compulsion to repeat" is one way we human beings try to manage our anxiety.[3]

So here we are now, more than a half-century after the Cuban missile crisis, awash in the accumulated repetitions of each passing day, week, year, and decade: "but still, nothing much happened." With each repetition, those who inquire into the crisis focus increasingly on explaining the actual "nothing" and ignore the raw human experience of trying to prevent from happening what could have been Armageddon. In this way, nearly every statement ever made about the crisis after the fact—anytime, anywhere, with whatever view of its level of danger—only adds to the lulling effect of the compulsion to repeat, because for more than fifty years we have begun with the null outcome and worked our way backward in time to its supposed causes. The subtext of all such statements, both explicit and implicit, is a riff on British poet Elizabeth Barrett Browning's famous "How do I love thee? Let me count the ways."[4] Or: Why did the Cuban missile crisis, which seemed so dangerous at the time, have a happy ending? Let me count the ways.[5]

The tendency is irresistibly to try to explain why, in spite of some non-quantifiable level of danger of Armageddon, it did *not* happen, rather than try to inhabit the forward-moving chaos and anxiety of the crisis from the inside—from the viewpoints of those who did not know the outcome, who in fact had the primary responsibility to manufacture an acceptable outcome. Former Secretary of Defense Robert McNamara was unusual in his insistence on remembering and reliving the danger at the time. But for the most part the crisis has, over more than a half-century of scholarly commentary, been transformed from a terrifying moment that could have resulted in the end of everything to an event that is regarded as interesting, even fascinating, but no longer anxiety provoking.

It has not always been like this. In the 1960s, many ordinary people intuitively understood that our journey to, through, and beyond the heart of darkness in October 1962 was mostly due to *luck*, and that Armageddon is almost inevitable. In 1963, the iconic and much-covered singer-songwriter Phil Ochs wrote "There But for Fortune."[6] The song title tells it all. Phil Ochs and hundreds of other young artists of that far-off time *got it!* In the age of nuclear weapons, no political gizmo or technical gadget can ensure that another Armageddon-threatening event will not occur and, if it does, none can guarantee that we will be as lucky next time as we were in October 1962.

This was, and remains, a horrifying thought: that we are here today largely due to the good fortune of those who in October 1962 came within a hair's breadth of producing a radiating ash heap of a dead planet. Why is it so scary? Because no one knows what to do with such a conclusion. Do we hope that we are also lucky next time? This has been the implicit conclusion of the nine nations currently with nuclear weapons, and the two dozen or so others who rely on one or more of the nuclear nations to guarantee their security, up to and including the necessity of using the nukes on their behalf.[7] In other words, we'll just hang on to the nukes perpetually and hope we remain lucky and don't have another Cuban missile-type crisis.

How do we learn from a fluke, from happenstance, from a fortunate roll of the nuclear dice? The short answer is: we don't, and we don't even try. Instead, we by and large deny that the peaceful resolution of the Cuban missile crisis was a fluke—we assume we weren't just lucky, leaders did not pull a rabbit out of a hat at the last minute and thereby save the world from a nuclear holocaust. We manage our anxiety about "another Cuban missile–type crisis" claiming that, after the fact, we now *understand it*—we can tell a story that yields identifiable causes and effects and lessons as to how to proceed in the future. Fluke? What fluke? There are no flukes in international affairs. Instead, in the view of Kenneth Waltz, the anti-hero of our chapter 7, nukes make us safe, and a lot of nukes make us very safe. We weren't lucky in October 1962, according to Waltz. Instead, "the presence of nuclear weapons makes states exceedingly cautious. Think of Kennedy and Khrushchev in the Cuban missile crisis. Why fight if you can't win much and might lose everything?"[8] Waltz's answer: you don't, which is why the outcome of the Cuban missile crisis was predictably peaceful, just like all other Cold War crises, none of which ended in nuclear war. End of story. As Waltz never tired of telling his readers: sleep well; don't worry.

THE "LUCKY FOOL SYNDROME"

The Fundamental Attribution Error Really **Is** *Fundamental*

A quick dip into a little social and behavioral science strongly suggests that our minds seem wired in such a way as to reject or deny the degree to which our personal lives, and the fate of nations, is governed by chance—by *plain dumb luck*. Luck doesn't lend itself to a good story, with heroes and villains, a coherent plot, and an outcome that pulls it all together, the way a novelist constructs a narrative or a filmmaker frames a movie.

The leading thinker these days emphasizing the significance of luck—both good and bad—is Nassim Nicholas Taleb. He writes that most of us, most of the time, are what he calls "lucky fools," who are pleased to take credit for what we perceive to be our successes but to blame our "bad luck" (on scheming, dishonest adversaries, or stupid advice from underlings, or perhaps the weather, etc.) when we fail.[9] The attitude is: I deserve all of the credit, but none of the blame.

The evidence is overwhelming that we were just such "lucky fools" in October 1962. Carl Richards, whose weekly column on the *New York Times* financial page is called "The Sketch Guy," has applied Taleb's insight to Richards' professional world of financial planning. In a 2014 piece called "Avoiding 'Lucky Fool Syndrome,'" Richards wrote:

> Knowing that these issues exist, we have a choice. We can continue to float along on a cloud of serotonin, playing the fool and suffering the consequences, or we can challenge our biases. It's not easy to make the right choice, but it's doable. It starts with getting a better handle on the difference between skill and luck. [10]

Distinguishing between skill and luck is harder than it probably sounds to you. This is because of the courage it takes to face the reality that your perceived success may not be due to your superior intellect, practical acumen, or energetic pursuit of your objective. Instead, it may be due to luck—luck that you were born, luck in having the parents who raised you, luck in meeting the right people in the right place at the right time, and so on and on. We prefer not to face the fact that whatever iota of brilliance or competence we may have is predicated upon an oceanic quantity of plain dumb luck.

You may recognize aspects of your own behavior in "The Sketch Guy's" drawing of the syndrome he has named.[11]

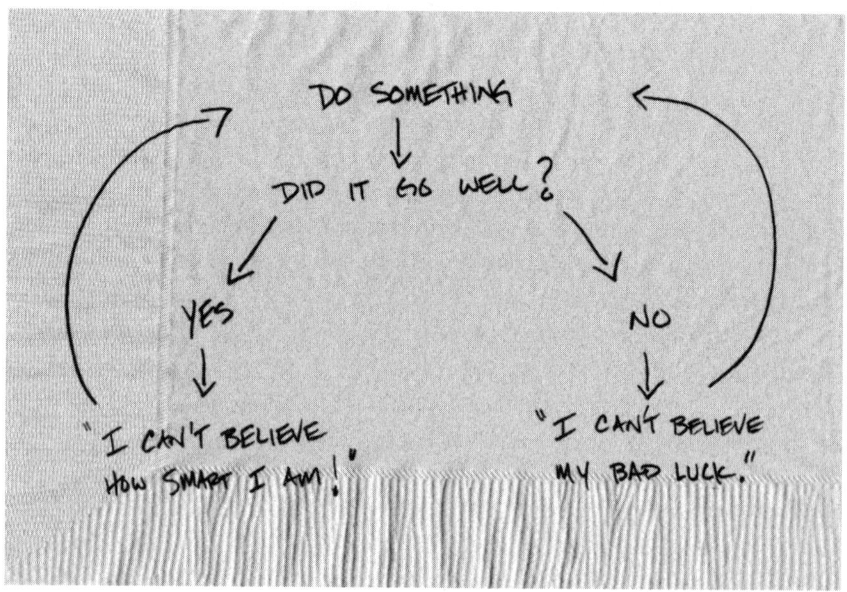

Whether or not you recognize your own behavior in "The Sketch Guy's" napkin drawing, we recognize in it the retrospective view of the Cuban missile crisis as it *misinforms* the discussion of nuclear weapons globally: in this view we weren't lucky, we were smart, skilled, and we understood, at least intuitively, that the Cuban missile crisis was going to work out okay. Reasonable people—that is, Kennedy and Khrushchev—reached a reasonable solution, toward which events were pointing all through the crisis. Unreasonable people—that is, Castro and the Cubans—were ignored because they really had nothing to do with the nuclear weapons in Cuba, or with nuclear risk generally. In the terms of "The Sketch Guy's" drawing, yes, it ended very well, luck had little or nothing to do with it, and we have to conclude, as Kenneth Waltz and his followers conclude, that there is something about nukes that makes those in charge of them very smart, very cautious, very responsible. It was skill, and full awareness of the situation in Washington and Moscow, not luck, that was responsible for the peaceful outcome. The explanation makes us feel less anxious and more confident about avoiding nuclear war with thousands of nukes in the world. But it does so at the expense of the lived truth as experienced by those who lived through it with the fate of the earth on their shoulders. In other words, it is *bullshit!*

Psychologists believe the "Lucky Fool Syndrome" is driven by what they call the Fundamental Attribution Error, following Stanford psychologist Lee Ross, who first named it in an influential 1977 paper.[12] The Fundamental Attribution Error is ubiquitous, insidious, and when it holds leaders in its grip when war and peace is on the line, it can be disastrous. Where empathy is absent, the Fundamental Attribution Error is virtually unavoidable. Basically, when we make the error, our thinking goes something like this: *Your hostility toward us is unprovoked. Our hostility toward you is only a necessary reaction to your hostility.*[13] The tendency to commit the Fundamental Attribution Error is an important component of our human fallibility, elements of which were threaded all through decision-making in Havana, Moscow, and Washington in October 1962.

Fallible human beings nearly sent human civilization to kingdom come in October 1962, and they might do it again because, ultimately, no one knows how to fix the "problem" of human fallibility. In addition, thousands of nuclear weapons are still scattered around the globe, many on a hair-trigger alert, just as they were in October 1962. Only now, in the 21st century, twice as many countries have nukes as had them during the Cuban missile crisis, and the newer nuclear powers (China, Israel, North Korea, India, and Pakistan) are located in volatile regions of planet earth.

Accordingly, with this book, we seek to recover some of the chaos and confusion of the anxiety that the *actual* Cuban missile crisis *actually* produced in leaders in the U.S., Russia, and Cuba, and to harness some of the anxiety and use it as a pivot toward the abolition of nuclear weapons. In short,

Feel the Chaos of Oct '62 + Thousands of Nukes Now
= Fear of Armageddon = Nuclear Abolition

WHAT WE NOW KNOW

Our Findings about the Moment Armageddon Almost Began

We now hold the following inconvenient truths about the Cuban missile crisis to be self-evident:

- *Millions Dead.* If the Cuban missile crisis of October 1962 had erupted into all-out war between the U.S. and Russia, tens or hundreds of millions of people would have died.
- *Destruction of Nations.* The war that followed the Cuban missile crisis would have destroyed many nations, including the U.S., Cuba, and Russia; the dust in the atmosphere from the nuclear detonations would have produced a nuclear winter, possibly leading to the death of plant and animal life necessary for the survival of human life.
- *Superpower Anxiety.* It was known in Washington and Moscow at the time of the crisis that war was possible, and that if war broke out, escalation to a catastrophic global nuclear war was likely, and that such a war might destroy human civilization. Anxiety over the possibility of such a war led Washington and Moscow to retreat just barely in time to end the crisis short of war.
- *Cuban Defiance.* The Cuban leadership and Cuban people did not share the anxiety over nuclear annihilation that was widespread in the U.S. and Russia. Instead, believing (not without reason) that the U.S. was determined to destroy the Cuban Revolution, invade the island, and install a U.S.-friendly government, the Cubans were convinced they were doomed. Resolving to fight honorably to the death, they prepared for Armageddon, as did the tens of thousands of Russian troops on the island. Indeed, they moved to provoke the war they saw as inevitable by shooting at U.S. planes overflying Cuba.

- *Cuban Martyrdom; U.S. Annihilation.* The Cuban leadership believed (not without reason) that the Russians would redeem Cuba's total destruction by destroying the U.S. in retaliation for the U.S. attack and invasion of the island.
- *Both Superpowers: Clueless in the Caribbean.* Neither Washington nor Moscow had a clue as to the strength of the impulse toward martyrdom that swept across the island of Cuba between the Bay of Pigs invasion of April 1961 and the outbreak of the Cuban missile crisis, eighteen months later. The superpowers believed the Cubans' mindset and motives were irrelevant. We now know they were wrong to ignore the Cubans. If the U.S. airstrike and invasion had commenced, the Americans would unexpectedly have been met by nuclear fire from Russian forces, inspired by the Cubans to use every war-fighting weapon they possessed against the U.S. onslaught. Mutual and comprehensive annihilation would have soon followed.

We were extraordinarily lucky in October 1962. The key question now, in light of these findings, is this: Do we believe that we will be this lucky the next time a deep crisis occurs involving nations in possession of nuclear weapons? If we believe this, we will be anywhere from apathetic to downright hostile to calls like ours to abolish nukes. But if we really believe this, we will be irresponsibly foolish. Once foolish (in October 1962), we say, twice abolish (and de-nuke the 21st century).

THE MEANING OF OUR FINDINGS

Three Takeaways from the Cuban Missile Crisis

- *Armageddon is Possible.* A catastrophic nuclear war nearly happened in October 1962. We know this not from science fiction, nor any other kind of fiction, nor from hypothetical scenarios, prophecies, or trend projections. We know it because it is now a matter of historical record. On the final weekend of October 1962, the world came within a hair's breadth of being blown to smithereens. This actually happened.
- *Armageddon is Possible, Even If Big Nuclear Powers Don't Want It.* A nuclear catastrophe will likely be inadvertent. It will involve a series of conscious decisions that were unthinkable prior to a crisis, like the Cuban missile crisis. As the crisis deepens, time will seem short, and

the stakes skyhigh, and the pressure to attack first may become impossible to resist. Smaller involved nations, believing their best option is martyrdom, and unaware (or not caring) that any nuclear war will likely destroy nations, may seek to drag nuclear powers into the conflict, with catastrophic results.

- *Armageddon is Virtually Inevitable.* The indefinite combination of nuclear weapons and human fallibility will eventually result in the destruction of nations, possibly all nations. Arguments to the contrary defy credibility.

The U.S. created nuclear weapons to expedite the end of World War II. After the war, many believed the nuclear arsenals of the U.S. and Soviet Union prevented World War III because both sides understood that an attack by one against the other with nuclear weapons would bring retaliation in kind and the ruination of both countries. (This was "mutual assured destruction," or MAD.) But in the Cuban missile crisis, leaders of the two superpowers unexpectedly saw the massive arsenals turn on them, threatening to set off the global doomsday machine, like a Frankenstein's monster for the nuclear age.

"NOT MISSION DIFFICULT"

Two Imperatives from the Cuban Missile Crisis

- *Armageddon Must Be Made Impossible.* Armageddon must be made not merely improbable—based on subjective judgments of highly fallible human beings—but impossible, based on the abolition of such weapons as swiftly and safely as possible. This must be made a top global priority.
- *The Risk of Armageddon Must Be Nipped in the Bud.* Big powers must learn to take seriously the security needs of adversaries or allies who are smaller, weaker, and poorer, especially when weapons of mass destruction are involved. Otherwise they risk igniting a crisis in slow motion, such as the Cuban missile crisis, which began with the April 1961 Bay of Pigs invasion and culminated with the U.S., Russia, and Cuba on the brink of catastrophe in October 1962.

We are reminded of an exchange from the second of the Mission Impossible movies:

HUNT (Tom Cruise): I don't think I can do it.
SWANBECK (Anthony Hopkins): You mean, it will be difficult?
HUNT: Very.
SWANBECK: This is not mission difficult, Mr. Hunt, it's mission impossible. Difficult should be a walk in the park for you. [Hunt undertakes the mission, *and succeeds.*][14]

Is the abolition of nuclear weapons mission really *impossible*? Many believe it is. They believe this because of the undoubted difficulty of the task, and/or because they don't believe that moving to zero nuclear weapons is a particularly urgent matter. But what we now know about the missile crisis proves that it *is* an urgent matter. Armageddon is possible, at any moment, no matter how implausible it may seem as you read these words. After all, the nuclear war-threatening horror show known as the Cuban missile crisis seemed equally implausible right up to the moment it nearly exploded in the faces of leaders and nations whose imaginations proved unequal to the macabre possibilities of the nuclear age.

"Possible" and "impossible" are elastic concepts. The abolition of slavery in the U.S. was once considered impossible by all but a radical few who believed abolition was an urgent imperative. Besides, the message in this book, unlike the messages given to the Impossible Missions Force (IMF), will not self-destruct in five seconds, or five years. The message will become irrelevant only under one of two conditions: either the world is destroyed in a nuclear catastrophe, or the human race collectively succeeds in abolishing nuclear weapons.

12

THE BLACK SATURDAY MANIFESTO

Abolishing Nuclear Weapons One Anniversary Per Year, for as Long as It Takes

October 27 was the day that would come to be known around the White House as "Black Saturday." Five days had gone by since Kennedy's televised address to the nation revealing the presence of Soviet nuclear missiles in Cuba, and events were spinning out of control. Earlier that day the Soviet premier, Nikita Khrushchev, had upped the ante in the diplomatic negotiations by demanding the withdrawal of American missiles from Turkey. An American U-2 spy plane had been shot down over eastern Cuba. The island had been sealed off by an American blockade, and U.S. warships were challenging nuclear-armed submarines in the Caribbean.

—Michael Dobbs (2008)[1]

Anniversaries encourage us to reflect on the past, relive an important moment in the present and look ahead to the future. Our personal lives are filled with a wide range of anniversaries—both happy and sometimes sad. In business we also mark key milestones. Yet the external PR potential of these celebrations is often left unrealized.

—Website of CooperKatz, a New York City public relations firm, posted on June 4, 2013, the firm's 17th anniversary.[2]

Catalyst: An agent that provokes or speeds significant change or action.

—Merriam Webster Dictionary

THE GREAT REPRIEVE OF OCTOBER 27, 1962

In October 1962, we nearly blew up the world. All the conditions were in place for us to destroy ourselves, our nations, and our human civilization. No one saw it coming. All were shocked by what seemed to be the unexpected and threatening actions of others. Leaders in Havana, Washington, DC, and Moscow became convinced that the risk of Armageddon was sky-high by *Black Saturday,* October 27, 1962.[3] They wondered if they would still be alive, and whether their nations and the world would survive for another hour, day, or week. People all over the world were horrified by the very real prospect of all-out nuclear war.

But it didn't happen. Instead, we got a stay of execution due to a combination of plain dumb luck and a virtuosic, last-minute escape improvised on the fly by the leaders of Russia, the U.S., and Cuba.

Since that Great Reprieve of October 1962, two antithetical processes—one a cause for deep pessimism, the other offering a glimmer of hope—have evolved in parallel. First, the number of nations possessing nukes has grown from four to nine. Together these nations control nearly fifteen thousand nuclear weapons, many located in the most volatile regions of the world.[4] If even a tiny fraction—less than 2 percent—of these weapons were detonated in a conflict, human civilization could be destroyed either directly by the nuclear blast and radiation effects or indirectly via disease and starvation during the nuclear winter following the detonations. The persistence of the nuclear threat demonstrates that we have learned nothing useful about the extreme volatility and danger of the continued coexistence of human fallibility and nuclear weapons.

Yet a second development has occurred over the past thirty years. We have learned a lot about nuclear danger in what has become the great nuclear laboratory of the Cuban missile crisis. The crisis has been figuratively peeled, layer by layer like an onion, by hundreds of investigators all over the world, until its hard core of undeniable reality is visible to anyone who cares to look. The documentation—including declassified written material, authoritative oral testimony, and scholarly commentary—is immense. We have been involved in this research process continuously since its origins in the mid-1980s. This is what it all adds up to:

- if history were a game of roulette;
- and if exactly those conditions present by Black Saturday, October 27, 1962, could be reinstituted by some process of black magic;

- and if we were to spin the roulette wheel of history one hundred times;
- in our estimation, we will get Armageddon on at least ninety-five of those spins.[5]

We now know for certain how supremely lucky we were that the Cuban missile crisis did not explode into Armageddon. However you define "lucky," most of us would agree that we would be fools to expect to be that lucky the next time the possible use of nuclear weapons comes into play.

The world we live in today has a surfeit of thousands of horribly destructive nukes and billions of highly fallible human beings, a few of whom are charged with deciding, in some unforeseen deep crisis, whether or not to order the use of these weapons. So we face a choice: to continue to sleepwalk toward the nuclear abyss into which we nearly fell in October 1962; *or* to bring the insights derivable from the Cuban missile crisis—the Armageddon that almost-but-didn't-quite-happen, that probabilistically *should* have happened—to bear on a process that stands a chance of leading to the abolition of nuclear weapons.

In the Old Testament Book of Deuteronomy we are told: "I set before you life or death, a blessing or a curse. Choose life then." In the context of the effort to abolish nuclear weapons and the threat of Armageddon, we believe that going forward, to "choose life," must be to derive, learn, and apply the lessons of the near-death experience of the human race more than a half-century ago. We must henceforth exhibit a new kind of virtuosity, commensurate with the virtuosity of John F. Kennedy, Fidel Castro, and Nikita Khrushchev by Black Saturday. We must show one another the means for vicariously experiencing the look and feel of nuclear danger, for getting inside that experience in all its horror and multidimensionality, until the clarity of Black Saturday leads to a commitment to create a new reality in which Black Saturday will remain history's scariest one-off. The new reality will exclude nukes, in principle and in fact.

Millennials—those born in the years just before or just after the turn of the 21st century—must do the heavy lifting in making nukes of strictly historical interest. But paradoxically, millennials are on the whole serenely uninterested in the threat of Armageddon. That needs to change quickly and profoundly. For even if everyone on planet earth were to decide by this evening that nukes must be abolished, it would still take years, likely decades, before all the nukes are destroyed and, as important, until everyone comes to *believe* that they have been, in fact, destroyed. So millennials: you are the ones who must see the Black Saturday Manifesto through to its implementation to abolish nuclear weapons. This one is for you!

THE FUMBLING, FUTILE, FRUITLESS BACKSTORY

Knowing That *We Must Abolish Nukes, But Not Knowing* How

Now what? Now that we have told you the truth about the October 1962 Cuban missile crisis; now that we have documented how the world hung precariously and frighteningly like a spider and her gossamer web over a red-hot fire, primed to plunge momentarily into fiery nothingness; now that we have explained to you that the risk of Armageddon today is no different than what it was during the East-West Cold War that spawned the Cuban missile crisis; now that we have alerted you to the one mistake that fallible, mistake-prone, often uninformed leaders with access to nukes must never make, even once; now, with all that on your mind, what in the world are you supposed to *do* about it? What are we—any of us, all of us, and especially millennials—supposed to *do* about it?

Good question. Necessary question. Tough question. It is a question that we believe has an unambiguous answer. But first, here is the backstory of why we have been spinning our wheels during the seventy-plus futile years of the nuclear age.

A little philosophy will help reframe what needs to be done to abolish nukes. The British philosopher Gilbert Ryle made a distinction we find useful in trying to understand what needs to be done to begin to chart a path toward the abolition of nuclear weapons. In a famous example, Ryle pointed out that knowing *how* to ride a bicycle is very different from reading a description of the various things *that* have to happen to keep a cyclist moving forward and not falling off the bike. You cannot learn to ride a bike solely, or even mainly, by reading about it in a book of instructions, containing words of wisdom like: turn handlebars to angle X, reduce speed by amount Y, and resume progress toward trajectory Z. Try it sometime. Even if you already know how to ride a bike, just thinking about getting all your angles and trajectories in sync will cause you to lose control.[6]

Virtually from the moment the U.S. dropped two nuclear bombs on Japan (on Hiroshima, August 6, 1945; and on Nagasaki, August 9, 1945), the conversation about how to abolish these terribly destructive weapons has focused on knowing *that* they can inflict such horrendous damage, or *that* exploding relatively few of them could end civilized life on earth. Most people advocating nuclear abolition have assumed implicitly that once we grasp *that* these weapons can destroy all of us, we will find a way to learn *how* to abolish them. Like Michael Jordan in his famous Nike Air Jordan sneakers, we'll "just do it!"[7]

Well, we haven't done it, even though we've had more than seventy years to try. Why not? Because knowing *that* nukes are terribly destructive tells us nothing about *how* to get rid of them in a world of perpetual conflict, diminishing resources, monstrous inequalities, mistrust, misperception, and mistaken assumptions about one another. Instead, magical thinking has prevailed, along the following lines: nuclear Armageddon is possible; therefore, we will simply all do what is necessary to abolish nuclear weapons; where there is a will to do so, a way will be found. But the evidence is overwhelming clear: we are not magicians. *We just don't know how.* Repeat: we just don't know *how,* though most of the nuclear abolitionists seem to think knowing *that* it is necessary should be enough.

Confronting a problem this big, this global, this complicated can be overwhelming. Many of our own students, confronting for the first time the reality of the Cuban missile crisis and its connections to the 21st century nuclear threat, have told us they have had trouble sleeping. A few have even said they wish they had never learned the truth, because doing something constructive to eventually reduce the threat seems impossible.

Although the problems are immense, the first task—let's call it "telling *that*"—is a familiar one for writers, filmmakers, scientists, artists, scholars, politicians, and in fact anyone interested in publicizing humanity-threatening dilemmas. You describe the apocalyptic dimensions of a huge global problem. This is the easy part. In *Dark Beyond Darkness*, from the beginning of the Prologue through the closing lines of chapter 11, we have been "telling *that.*" The standard way of telling "that" the Cuban missile crisis happened emphasizes dates and times on which this happened, or that happened, or the other thing happened. It might or might not be interesting. But it probably will never be more than interesting.

We've been striving to tell you what "that" Cuban missile crisis was like, in a new way, via habitable history: via vicariously being there, feeling the terror, the shock, the psychological disorientation of feeling the burden of responsibility on your shoulders when nuclear war seems all too plausible an outcome of the situation in which you find yourself. If you are able to inhabit the history as we are telling it—focused on the experience of Robert McNamara and Fidel Castro—then to an obviously limited but we hope nontrivial extent, you should have immersed yourself in some portion of the uncertainty, anxiety, and confusion of that extended moment leading toward, and through, Black Saturday, October 27, 1962.

We have given the psychological component what we believe is its due, when conveying what "that" thing was that happened by Black Saturday, 1962, a "that" that would necessarily have included such exclamatory reactions as: what the f★★★ is going on; what the f★★★ is about to happen; and what the f★★★ should I or can I do about it? It incorporates emotion. It's a deeper, darker shade of telling "that"—what THAT would have been LIKE in real time and in that place. Habitable history tries to raise the odds of replacing a reader's typical "huh," when finishing the reading, with OMG, what is to be done about that?

But for all that, habitable history is still about telling "that." In proposing the Black Saturday paradigm, we shift from telling you *that* to telling you *how* to take meaningful steps toward the abolition of nuclear weapons. You know what the endpoint must be, which is zero nukes, but you haven't a clue as to how to get there.

You are not alone. Countless plans and schemes have been advanced over the past 70-plus years whose authors have believed they know *how* to rid the world of nukes. There is an immense literature that might be summarized this way: if you (nuclear nations) would only focus for a moment on the unspeakable horror of nuclear war, and follow our instructions, the nukes would be abolished in X or Y or Z years, or possibly a couple of decades.[8] But seventy years on, here we are: fallible human beings, still with the capacity to destroy ourselves in minutes, hours, days, or years, depending on the size, number, and location of the nuclear detonations in some conflict that cannot, as we sit here today, be foreseen. The instructions of the nuclear abolitionists have been ignored by those with their fingers on the nuclear buttons all over the world. Knowing *that* the fate of the world is on the line doesn't necessarily tell us anything useful about *how* to fix the problem in a world fraught with crises, mistrust, conflict, and killing on a vast scale, even without the use of nuclear weapons.

We are stuck in neutral. It's time to put down the clutch and shift the paradigm.

BLACK SATURDAY REMEMBRANCE DAY

The New Paradigm in Forty-Two Words

Here is how to begin the process of abolishing nuclear weapons:

> **Establish *Black Saturday* as a global day of reflection, each year, on October 27th, emphasizing: (1) the near Armageddon**

> **of the Cuban missile crisis; (2) the threat of Armageddon today; and (3) the necessity of abolishing the nukes before they abolish us.**

That's the idea. That is, we believe, how nuclear weapons might someday be abolished. We are not joking. We urge you to read on.

We believe that the success or failure of such an initiative will depend on our ability to exploit one of our least rational, but occasionally very useful, human characteristics. The ancient Romans called it *anniversaria in Virtute* ("the power of an anniversary"). Everyone everywhere seems to be a sucker for anniversaries, especially (in our experience) anniversaries divisible by at least ten, without remainder. Why this is so is a psychological mystery. But that it is so is not in doubt.

You can experience *anniversaria in Virtute* for yourself in the following example. On November 22, 2013, people all over the world remembered, many in meaningful ways, the assassination in Dallas fifty years earlier of U.S. president John F. Kennedy. The city of Dallas was inundated with tourists who wanted to make a solemn pilgrimage along the route Kennedy's limo took on the day he was murdered. Newspapers, magazines, TV shows, movies, books, plays, and much else overflowed with stories about Kennedy. Incredibly, more than 140 new books on Kennedy appeared in 2013 in English alone.[9]

One year later, in 2014, on the 51st anniversary of the assassination of JFK, virtually none of the above took place. Few went to Dallas. There was almost no media coverage of the anniversary. In November 2013, it seemed as if all news was Kennedy news. In November 2014, there was no Kennedy news. Think about it: You don't find the contrast surprising, do you? Both make sense: the all-Kennedy channel in November 2013; the absence of any Kennedy channel in November 2014.

Keep in mind the power of an anniversary, particularly if it is divisible by at least ten, without remainder.

A BLACK SATURDAY ROADMAP

Follow the Arrows to a Paradigm Shift, from the Numbers Game, to Remembrance of the Moment Armageddon Nearly Began

The Old Paradigm Is Broken

Millennial Ignorance, Disinterest, and Denial

Most anti-nuclear activists are all about numbers: of warheads, launchers, distance between warheads and launchers, size of nuclear arsenals, and so on. The idea is: these are not weapons in the traditional sense; they are instruments of mass destruction that, taken together as a global problem, constitute a global doomsday machine. We don't disagree with any of this. The problem is that very few people care about it. Anti-nuclear organizations are small, underfunded, and their very existence is unknown to the vast majority of citizens in developed countries, including many who count themselves among the reasonably well informed.

The net effect of this apathy toward the nuclear threat is particularly discernable in young American college students. A poignant and devastating short film by Jonathan Deaton demonstrates this in spades. Deaton's prize-winning 2016 film, which he made while he was an undergraduate at Elon College in North Carolina, is called "Joining the Conversation on Nuclear Weapons."[10] It runs for only four minutes, but it is a compelling four minutes. College students arrive at a studio, chat with each other, and get ready to answer the filmmaker's questions or address the filmmaker's comments. "What do millennials have to say about nuclear weapons?" is projected onto the screen. As Deaton's Errol Morris–like interrogation of the students proceeds, it is obvious that these millennials have virtually *nothing* true or useful to say about them. Deaton talks to the students in pairs; they represent many ethnicities, they are gender balanced, and all seem articulate when chatting informally on camera, until it comes time to comment about nuclear weapons and the nuclear threat.

Here are examples of Jonathan Deaton's questions and comments, followed by representative student responses:

- *When I say "nuclear weapons," what's the first thing that comes to mind?*
  Big bombs.
  Mass destruction.
  Mushroom clouds.
- *How many nuclear weapons do you think the whole world has right now?*
  I hear it's a lot.
  Maybe a few hundred.
  I have no idea.
  Seven.
- *We actually have over fifteen thousand nuclear weapons [as of 2016].*
  Oh, shit.
  Fifteen thousand? Why?
  That's scary.
- *We accidentally dropped two nuclear bombs on ourselves in North Carolina [where the filming is taking place], and each of those bombs were 250 times the power of the Hiroshima bomb, and would have spread lethal doses of radiation as far as New York City.*
  How does this happen?
  Shit.
  That's unbelievable.
- *Right now with every hour that passes, we spend 2.2 million dollars of taxpayers' money every hour to pay for nuclear weapons.*
  Shit! (Gulp).
  That's crazy!
  There are so many things that that money can go to.
  What the f***! I didn't know about that until just now!
  We better start thinking in another way.

These responses are consistent with our own experience teaching about the nuclear threat to undergraduates in the U.S. (at Brown University) and in Canada (at the University of Waterloo). In a recent film announcing the launch of a new anti-nuclear project called "NSquare," Eric Schlosser, author of the prize-winning 2013 book on nuclear accidents, *Command and Control*, rightly says that we are afflicted with "historical amnesia" about nukes that is especially powerful among young people.[11]

Nowhere on websites of leading anti-nuclear organizations do we find any meaningful, informed reference to the Cuban missile crisis, or any other political or military crisis in the nuclear age. It's just numbers, numbers, and more numbers, followed by exhortations to get rid of the nukes.

Problem? What Problem?

Why Millennials Have No Fear, No Narrative, No Memory, and No Interest

The reason why young people have close to zero awareness of the nuclear threat is straightforward. Unlike their parents and grandparents, who grew up in the scary days of the Cold War, millennials are simply not afraid of nuclear weapons, either because they believe the nuclear threat evaporated when the Cold War ended or because they have other overriding interests, or both. Even when informed, as they were in Jonathan Deaton's revealing film, it is pretty obvious that while they are surprised by what the filmmaker tells them about the numbers, they are not really afraid. Mainly, they giggle at how wrong their answers are. From their point of view, what is there to be afraid of? So what if we spend ourselves nearly bankrupt maintaining nuclear arsenals? So what if we develop ever more sophisticated ways of delivering them to hypothetical enemies presumed to deserve being vaporized? So what?

Discussions about numbers are abstract and inconclusive, for a good reason. There is no scary story to hold onto, no realistic path that was actually experienced by decision-makers who found themselves unexpectedly on the brink of having to do what they (like our students) believed was the most irrational and horrendous thing imaginable, which is to initiate a catastrophic nuclear war. They have only the numbers of weapons in mind. They have been told that more is worse and fewer is better, but they fail to see why this is necessarily the case. They have no narrative of trial and redemption, no collective memory of actual personalities behaving heroically or stupidly, or clumsily, or in any other way.

There is no fear because there is no narrative. Because there is no narrative, there is no memory. Because there is no memory, there is little awareness of a problem, and even less interest in it.

Chapin Boyer (born in 1991) illuminated these issues in a remarkable 2016 essay. He graduated from one of America's elite eastern colleges and majored in history. He then moved to the West Coast and began work as a graphic designer, specializing in designing games that involved virtual reality experiences. Project NSquare, the anti-nuclear effort mentioned in the previous section, hired Boyer to create some virtual reality experiences that, to some obviously limited degree, might provide young people with some idea of what it would be like to be present at or near a nuclear detonation. The work with NSquare provided Chapin Boyer with his first exposure to the problem of nuclear danger. After his contract work with NSquare was finished, he pulled together his thoughts in an essay in the *Bulletin of the Atomic Scientists*—the group that promotes and maintains the "Doomsday Clock." The closer the clock is set to midnight by the board members at the *Bulletin*, the closer the world is said to be to nuclear war.

Here is part of what Chapin Boyer had to say:

> My generation grew up believing that the problem of nuclear weapons had been solved. The United States' main nuclear opponent, the Soviet Union, is no more. Our president has agreed to reduce the nuclear arsenal, and we no longer practice hiding under our desks in case the bombs drop. We have no context for the kinds of danger that these weapons present.
>
> . . .
>
> My generation has no context for nuclear weapons. We do not have the fear that our parents confronted; we do not have the stakes that our parents grew up with; and for most Americans, nuclear weapons seem like a non-issue. Things have yet to go terribly wrong, so why should we worry.
>
> . . .
>
> I do not know how to garner the attention of young people. I would love to claim that my generation can be easily plied by this or that tactic, but I cannot. Without a context, how can young people hope to understand the issue of nuclear weapons? We see racism, sexism, classism, environmental destruction, immigration issues, refugee issues, economic issues, and so many more all around us. These are the issues that occupy my generation, because these are the things that we are most afraid of.
>
> Maybe it comes down to fear. Perhaps that is what context provides for us, along with a spark to move toward a better future. I do not think there is any easy fix to make us fear nuclear weapons in the way we should. I have studied this issue, have worked with activists on this issue, and yet I still find myself more preoccupied with other problems. Even after all my work, I do not have the context.[12]

We believe Chapin Boyer speaks for many of his generation. Our generation—baby boomers—had a compelling narrative: the Russians are out to get us, and they will nuke us the first chance they get if we don't credibly threaten to nuke them in return. (Keep in mind that a compelling narrative can be completely or mostly false.) Chapin Boyer and his fellow millennials find our Cold War narrative curious and unreal, but they have nothing comparable with which to replace it.

The Black Saturday 'Solution" in 651 Words

Remember Black Saturday on Every October 27th Until We Are De-nuked

"Solution" is inside quotation marks for this reason: remembering Black Saturday, October 27, 1962, is, we believe, a potential solution to the problem of apathy, disinterest, and denial with which so many respond to news of the nuclear threat. Without an overwhelming and sustained demand for nuclear abolition all across the global community, we believe there is virtually no chance of achieving it. Leaders whose governments control nuclear weapons, or whose nations have their security guaranteed by the potential use of nukes from an ally, have powerful reasons for refusing to consider relinquishing their nukes: they know their adversaries can destroy them, and they don't trust them. For the leaders of the nuclear nations to agree to abolish their nukes, all of them would need to simultaneously cease to fear their adversaries and learn to trust them. And they would have to continue trusting them for years, or perhaps decades, until abolition is achieved. The probability of such a sustained period of international benevolence under current circumstances is, we believe, nil.

Focusing on Black Saturday, not as allies or adversaries but simply as members of the human race, can act as a catalyst to force leaders to listen to what we are saying: we must abolish nukes and raise the odds that we will survive as a species, or we can sit on our hands and be destroyed together by the Frankenstein's monster that the nuclear arsenals of the world have become. That is at the heart of the psychological paradigm shift: from the numbers in a spreadsheet to the narrative of the most dangerous moment in the Cuban missile crisis—Black Saturday—a collision of real, fallible human beings with the power to destroy human civilization if they made the wrong moves.

How do we get the paradigm to shift not just in our minds, but also out there in the real world where the missile silos, bomb factories, and nuclear war plans actually exist? How do we arrive at an endpoint for which the word *solution* need not appear in quotation marks? *We should move toward the abolition of nuclear weapons by beginning with the facts, especially the psychological facts, of the October 1962 Cuban missile crisis, particularly as it was experienced in Cuba.* We should stop pushing the bullshit and stick with the truth, which can be the catalyst for the movement toward abolition of nuclear weapons. To rev up the engine of global public opinion for the abolition of the nukes, the United Nations, along with its constituent and associated agencies devoted to the abolition of nuclear weapons, should establish October 27th, the anniversary of Black Saturday, as a global day of reflection each year on "the most dangerous moment in human history."[13]

This will require on or about every October 27th a literal and virtual assemblage of a critical mass of creative talent and the resources to support that talent. If the UN drops the ball, the private sector will need to supply the ideas and the energy. In any case, the invitation list should be long and distinguished: artists, filmmakers, poets, sculptors, composers, musicians, playwrights, and other artists should submit art they believe captures what happened, and what did not happen (but nearly did), on the last weekend of October 1962. The creative artists should also dig deep and connect that long ago and faraway crisis to the nuclear threats now, some of which we have discussed in *Dark Beyond Darkness*. Winners in all categories would be announced every October 27th. Analogous sculpted outdoor pieces should be placed conspicuously in Washington, Moscow, and Havana, and elsewhere. Above all, artists must continue to search for ways to portray the downward spiral of the Cuban missile crisis, and the miraculous escape, in ways that move people to understand that the experience of October 1962 proves that the right number of nuclear weapons in the world is zero.

The Anniversary Heuristic

Why the Black Saturday Manifesto Can Succeed by Focusing on the Anniversary

Every so often an example of social science research comes along that is clarifying, and which can also claim to be based on sound empirical research. We are referring to research on decision-making pioneered by Daniel Kahneman, a Nobel laureate, and the late Amos Tversky. What they and their colleagues have shown is that biases, what they call *heuristics*, often short-circuit whatever proclivities toward rationality we may have.[14] As Kahneman recently wrote, at the heart of every heuristic is the inexhaustible human desire for narratives, for stories that make sense of events in our lives.[15]

The difference between successful and failed decision-makers is not between those who tell themselves stories and those who don't. All are awash in their stories. But good decision-makers tend to be those who can adopt a critical attitude toward the degree to which their stories do or do not map onto external reality, and thus adjust their stories in line with the real-world requirements. As Kahneman said recently, "Most of us, most of the time, are in the business of predicting the past."[16] We make our predictions in ways that stick pretty close to what we know has already happened, rather than something that may be off the wall but is actually more likely than we think. The reason the more likely outcome escapes us is that we cannot tell ourselves a story within which it makes sense.

Stories need not be entirely, or even mainly, factual, but they must be compelling; they must organize experience in line with what we believe is our place in the order of things. Narratives of "the same" event can conflict radically, even totally, as they almost always do in international conflicts. Think, for example, of the names given to the conflict that raged in North America between 1861 and 1865. To northerners, it was the *Civil War*, a war started by rebellious, slave-holding firebrands who tried to break away and destroy the Union. The rebels were what we today would call *terrorists*. To the southerners, or Confederates, the conflict was *The War for Southern Independence*, a conflict brought on by arrogant, prejudiced northerners bent on extending their hegemony over patriotic southerners, many of whom ultimately gave their lives for the honorable cause of southern independence. And so on.

Narratives like these are incompatible when they develop in an empathy-free zone. Whatever else they may do, the stories add to the sense of worth of those who subscribe to them, and offer membership in a group with distinguished roots, heroes, and deeds courageously done. And of course, the most compelling *national* narratives also identify enemies: misguided, possibly evil, altogether malevolent entities whose principal purpose is the destruction of all who share your narrative.

What Kahneman and Tversky discovered is that in the construction of our stories, we use heuristics, or mental shortcuts, that make it possible for us to develop and retain a coherent sense of who we are and what we are about. They also discovered the lengths to which we are often willing to go—how "irrational" we are willing to be—to preserve and protect the integrity of our narratives. If we can tell a compelling story about our experience, or the experience of others, we are more likely to remember that story. In fact, it may be our only reliable strategy for remembering anything. We are more likely to "recall" events that never happened, if they are embedded in a compelling narrative line, than we are events that actually happened but are not so embedded. If an experience is not embedded in a story, it will be forgotten, as if it never happened. We remember stories, not isolated facts or fictions. We have a preference for smooth, coherent, self-protective narratives over our raw, confusing, often threatening experience, as it happens. Our stories help make us the human beings we are.

In this context, we want to introduce *The Anniversary Heuristic*. (With a tip of the hat to Daniel Kahneman and Amos Tversky, we dare to suggest, with some trepidation, that we have discovered, and named, a new heuristic.) Look at your yearly calendar. Look for dates in the calendar that you want to remember because they are personally meaningful to you: wedding anniversaries; dates of births and deaths; your own secret anniversaries (such as the first time you pledged your love to your mate, and vice versa, for example); lots of firsts. Notice that when you contemplate the anniversaries that are personally meaningful, you find that you want to stop and review the memories that flood your mind—some good, some bad—the stories that collectively define you and your relationship to the world.

Bottom line: *anniversaries are irresistible*; to the degree that we are in touch with our past, we are connecting the dots of a virtually infinite number of meaningful anniversaries as we untangle the web of who we are, and weave the strands into a skein of stories that help us make sense of our lives and the lives of others who are important to us. People in public relations and commercial sales have always known about the power of anniversaries. You publicize your announcements and make your sales by hooking them onto anniversaries.

The Anniversary Heuristic in Action

How Remembrance of Four Black Saturdays Since 1987 Produced a Revolution

Disgruntled students, forced by some requirement or other to take a history course, have been known to complain as follows: "History is just a bunch of stupid dates you are forced to memorize and regurgitate on exams." Many of us have had history courses that felt like that. But while dates are undeniably important in history, we discovered while carrying out our research on the Cuban missile crisis that not all dates are created equal. Anniversaries of recent world historical events have extraordinary power to move people emotionally, and to attract their interest to a degree unimaginable under other circumstances. Anniversaries of the Cuban missile crisis—four of them—were absolutely critical to our success. These anniversaries were the 25th (1987); 30th (1992); 40th (2002); and 50th (2012).

In our research on the Cuban missile crisis, we used an innovative method called *critical oral history (COH)*. With COH we can build a bridge between the confusion of lived experience—where we don't know how things will turn out—and the relatively cut-and-dried after-the-fact rendering of that experience. It works by combining, in highly structured conferences, (1) decision-makers with the lived experience, (2) declassified documents (which provide added accuracy and authenticity to the conversation), and (3) scholars who studied the event, knowing full well the outcome.[17] We discovered during the

Cuban missile crisis project that critical oral history often yields rich and surprising insights into what it looked like and felt like for decision-makers, then and there, thus yielding more accurate analyses and applicable lessons for decision-making now and in the future. COH can allow us to enter the WABAC machine and inhabit the lives of the key players.

The linchpin in the method of critical oral history is the group of former and/or present high-level decision-makers we can bring to the table. When asked how to describe our role, our answer (borrowed from the late New York Yankees owner George Steinbrenner's description of his job) is: "We put the appropriate butts in the appropriate seats."

This is hardly the place to go into detail about the operational logistics of pulling off a critical oral history conference on a contentious event like the Cuban missile crisis. One example must suffice of how the anticipation of one of these mystically magical anniversaries (25th, 30th, 40th, or 50th) can facilitate dialogue between former enemies. Once we convinced Robert McNamara to go to Cuba and listen to what Fidel Castro had to say about the Cuban perspective on the crisis, we knew (only then) that Fidel would find a way to participate, even though he was, in January 1992, the sitting head of state with much more to do than attend a historical conference. Once we knew we had Fidel, much else was possible: declassified documents came flooding in our direction; people called us at all hours asking for invitations; and it suddenly became possible to do what in normal circumstances would have been virtually unthinkable: we were able, with considerable effort, to raise the funding to pay for what was, by our standards, an enormous and complicated undertaking, full of political uncertainty (because the U.S. and Cuba did not have diplomatic relations at the time).

And that, we can say now with respect for the former U.S. Defense Secretary and the former Maximum Leader of the Socialist Republic of Cuba, is how Bob's butt and Fidel's butt wound up in the appropriate seats at a conference table in Havana, Cuba, from January 9–12, 1992. Once in those seats, the two men astonished us, and our colleagues, and everyone everywhere with their interest in the peace of the world. (We omit discussion of what it took to get those butts in the seats, but it required a lot of shuttle diplomacy between Washington and Havana, thirteen trips by us to Cuba between January 1989, when we first met the Cubans at our Moscow conference, and the Havana conference in January 1992.)

Let's remind ourselves, in the form of headlines, what we now know of the *dark beyond darkness* of the Cuban missile crisis. Let's borrow from T. E.

Lawrence ("Lawrence of Arabia") and call them "The Seven Pillars of the Black Saturday Revolution" that we now derive from the events that culminated in the Armageddon-threatening crisis of October 1962.[18]

1. *Danger.* The Cuban missile crisis was much more dangerous than previously imagined.
2. *Complexity.* The crisis was far more complex, and involved events in Cuba far more centrally, than previously imagined.
3. *Crisis in Slow-Mo.* The crisis did not last just thirteen days, as most people believe, but grew slowly over several years of mutual incomprehension by Washington, Havana, and Moscow, coming to a slow boil with the failed U.S.-sponsored Bay of Pigs invasion eighteen months before the crisis.
4. *Empathy-Free Zone.* The pivotal variables were psychological: empathy between the three parties to the crisis was almost nonexistent. Actions taken by each side for defensive reasons were misunderstood by others to be offensive and threatening.
5. *Inadvertence.* The onset of the crisis and its ultimately very close proximity to nuclear war were due to inadvertent acts by all sides. In part because of the absence of mutual empathy, leaders were unable to foresee the consequences of their actions.
6. *Pipsqueak Power.* The unwillingness of Moscow and Washington to take Cuba's security needs seriously, and to credit what the Cubans claimed were their rights, nearly pushed the crisis over the brink and into nuclear war.
7. *Now.* The risk of nuclear Armageddon exists today, in a world of thousands of nukes. It could happen fast, slow, or as a consequence of some screw up that is misinterpreted as a hostile act, requiring a nuclear response.

This array of "pillars," taken together, constituted a *substantive* revolution, an *intellectual* paradigm shift, in our understanding of the most dangerous moment in human history. The Cuban missile crisis did not last just thirteen days, as many still believe; it festered and grew over many years of mutual, three-way incomprehension. Everything else we learned is consistent with this simple revision of a myth that dominated the first thirty or so years of commentary on the crisis, including just how close we came to doomsday by Black Saturday, October 27, 1962. This is not your parents' and grandparents' Cuban missile crisis. Millennials, this is *your* Cuban missile crisis, the true Cuban missile crisis. It is useful in three critical respects: it is true, it is scary, and it points the way unambiguously to the necessity of abolishing nuclear weapons.

It's the Black Saturday Anniversary, Stupid

A Shout-Out, in Case You Doubt the Seriousness of Our Main Point

Excuse us, if you will, for "shouting," but—

> **Very nearly 100 percent of what we (and now you) know about the Cuban missile crisis—beginning with the Seven Pillars of the Black Saturday Revolution—was made possible by hooking critical oral history conferences to anniversaries regarded by many, for whatever reasons, as significant. In particular, the 25th, 30th, 40th, and 50th anniversaries facilitated a huge critical mass of personalities, press coverage, publications, events and appearances, movies and TV shows—a series of multifaceted, multitudinous "happenings" that few believed possible before they actually happened.**

No anniversaries, no critical oral history. It is that simple. Anniversaries, properly massaged and exploited, made possible a revolution in our understanding of history's most dangerous moment. It is definitely *not* that easy, but we believe it *is* that simple.

Our question is this: If this much could be accomplished by exploiting four anniversaries over fifty years, how much more might have been accomplished if it had been possible to exploit all the anniversaries of Black Saturday after the Havana conference in 1992, when the bullshit Cuban missile crisis dissolved under the weight of evidence given by participants from all three countries involved in the crisis? Anniversaries are powerful force multipliers. What if—using the catalytic power of anniversaries—we could have organized meaningful activities on October 27th and received comprehending appreciation from millions all over the globe? Might annual, globally reiterated remembrances of Black Saturday have built the groundwork for eventually abolishing nuclear weapons? How far along would we be, with decades of momentum-building global activities? The path is far from easy (and far from quick), of course. But with a simple shift of our paradigm, we think it may be possible to build a global constituency for nuclear abolition.

We agree with those who emphasize the tremendous difficulties involved in any eventual effort to concretely and confidently ensure that nukes have been abolished. It will be complicated. It will require the expertise of technical experts from a wide variety of disciplines. And it will take time to work through all the details, including many that we are not, in advance of the process, able to foresee. Yet our point is that the experts won't be needed in advance of a global commitment to abolition. Repeat: the experts won't be needed in advance of a global commitment to abolition. The annual Black Saturday remembrances have one and only one purpose: *to render the abolition of nukes an uncontroversial no-brainer to the world's leaders*. When that happens, the phones of the relevant nuclear specialists will begin ringing night and day, and they will go to work on making the no-brainer a reality.

We have given anniversaries a good deal of thought over the years. At first, we did not get their potential to act as intellectual force multipliers that might allow us to do things we never dreamed possible. (We still don't understand the weird but undoubted power of anniversaries to rivet people's attention.) Some might argue that the periodic eruptions of fascination with the Cuban missile crisis were produced not by the strange magic of anniversaries divisible by at least ten without remainder. Instead, they would emphasize the crucial participation in our conferences, books, and movies of figures of historic significance like Robert McNamara and Fidel Castro. Obviously, their participation, and that of many others, was necessary both for substantive reasons and for the undoubted public relations bonanza they helped to provide, which allowed us to disseminate word of our revolutionary findings to a wide global audience.

Bob and Fidel were necessary, but so were the anniversaries. Bob and Fidel needed the anniversaries as occasions to come forward, tell their stories, and ask their questions. The anniversaries provided the "magic moments" and yielded the following benefits:

Participants focused on determining the proximity to nuclear war, especially on Black Saturday. From the first conference, the agenda was driven relentlessly by the participants' recollections, stimulated by the declassified documents, toward the question of how dangerous the crisis actually was. Of course, lots of details were discussed at the meetings—how many Russian ships carried warheads to Cuba; or how high and how fast did the low-flying U.S. reconnaissance fly over Cuba as Black Saturday approached? That sort of thing. But the big-ticket discussion items all had to do with the level and causes of nuclear danger: How close did we actually come, they asked each other across the conference table on these occasions, to committing the policy-makers' ultimate unpardonable sin of destroying the world? We always came back to this question, over and over again: How dangerous was it on Black Saturday? What might have happened if . . . . Eventually, we began to call this category of issues "the look and feel of nuclear danger."

The former officials inadvertently acted as surrogates for ordinary citizens. The participants asked each other more or less the questions ordinary citizens might have asked if they had participated, whether or not they were old enough to actually remember the Cuban missile crisis. In other words, the engine that connected these men on the anniversaries was the honesty, pathos, sadness, and theater of the absurd humor that regularly arose and proved irresistible to the participants and, via journalists' accounts, television coverage, books, articles, movies, and other means, to the world outside the conference room as well.

If you were watching television news, or reading a newspaper or magazine during these Black Saturday remembrances, you could with relative ease vicariously pull up a chair to the conference table in Marathon, Florida; or Cambridge, Massachusetts; or Havana, Cuba; or Moscow, USSR; and listen, fascinated by the real-life horror stories the participants told one another. It was terrific theater, but it was theater of a special kind: it was the theater of the *real.*[19]

WELCOME TO PLANET BLACK SATURDAY

It's Time for Millennials to Carry the Fire in the 21st Century

If you have ever tried to organize anything—a birthday party, a study group, a vacation, anything at all—image, then, inventing millions of your events, actually or virtually. Then you can get a feel for the monumental task it will be to organize, over a period of years, perhaps even decades, an internationally recognized, compelling remembrance day for October 27, 1962, the day when not very much happened but during which the key participants believed they may have been on the verge of destroying entire human societies, perhaps all human societies. We get that: the road to nuclear abolition will be a slog.

But we want *you* to get this: we see no alternative. It will be difficult. But if it were easy, someone else would already have done it. We want you to understand both horns of your dilemma. Establishing a meaningful yearly global commemoration of Black Saturday will doubtless be harder than you can possibly imagine. The dimensions of such a project are staggering. But even if you are able to achieve yearly global attention for Black Saturday—by who knows when, by who knows how many dedicated people, and who knows how—you will at that point merely have achieved an amazing global theatrical event, like the World Cup of soccer or the Olympic Games. You still would not yet have reduced the nuclear arsenals of the world by a single weapon. The "solution" to the nuclear threat would still be in quotation marks. You would then need to find a way to carry your abolitionist momentum to the governments of nuclear nations. Only governments can reduce and eventually eliminate the nukes they currently possess and control. But they won't do it on their own. They will need to be pushed by a global consensus, at the core of which is an accurate understanding that the indefinite combination of human fallibility and nuclear weapons will destroy all of us. That is the lesson of the Cuban missile crisis.

Implementing this lesson is not for the faint of heart. It is a task for what we call "raging incrementalists"—those with passion, persistence, and patience.

But we offer you a model, President John F. Kennedy. On the evening July 26, 1963, Kennedy announced to the nation the signing of the Limited Test Ban Treaty and its potential for reducing the risk of nuclear war with the Russians.

> . . . No one can say whether the time has come for an easing of the struggle. But history and our own conscience will judge us harsher if we do not now make every effort to test our hopes by action, and this is the place to begin. According to the ancient Chinese proverb, "A journey of a thousand miles must begin with a single step."
>
> My fellow Americans, let us take that first step. Let us, if we can, step back from the shadows of war and seek out the way of peace. And if that journey is a thousand miles, or even more, let history record that we, in this land, at this time, took the first step.[20]

If you embrace The Black Saturday Revolution, we believe you will have taken the first step toward creating the conditions within which the horrific danger posed by nuclear weapons begins to realistically frighten people. After that, the abolition of nuclear weapons will become a no-brainer for millenials, as it was for Kennedy, Khrushchev, and Castro by the end of their respective lives.[21]

We do not expect to live long enough to see the first time Black Saturday is commemorated globally in a way commensurate with its significance. We hope we are wrong, but we believe we are right. It will take time to shift the paradigm, under the best of circumstances. In the 1962 book that introduced the idea of "paradigm shift" to the world, Thomas S. Kuhn tells us why shifting the paradigm is difficult, time-consuming, and not always successful:

> Led by a new paradigm . . . it is rather as if the professional community had been suddenly transported to another planet where familiar objects are seen in a different light and are joined by unfamiliar ones as well. In so far as their only recourse to that world is through what they say and do, we may want to say that after a revolution scientists are responding to a different world.[22]

Kuhn goes on to say that the purveyors of a new paradigm should not expect to convert many of the Old Guard to the new way of approaching the relevant problems. They have too many sunk costs; their reputations have been established entirely within the traditions of the old paradigm; and—let's face it—the most eminent tend to be the oldest, the most set in their ways, and the least mentally flexible. Kuhn's "solution"? Go after the young people. Get them on board. Offer them "citizenship" on the new planet. Old paradigms, according to Kuhn, disappear in a manner rather like old soldiers, in the famous phrase of U.S. general Douglas MacArthur: "Old soldiers never die, they just fade away." As members of the Old Guard retire and ultimately die, their paradigm fades with them, according to Kuhn. It's like, he says, suddenly seeing both a rabbit and a duck in the famous optical illusion, where before you saw only one or the other:[23]

According to Kuhn, we need to see "revolutions as changes of world view."[24] First, there is the new idea—say, that the earth orbits the sun rather than the other way around—an idea that the old paradigm can make no sense of but which a new and emerging paradigm easily explains. This is followed by resistance, attack, and counterattack (science, according to Kuhn, is not so different from politics), which is followed by either the victory or defeat of the new paradigm. Important revolutions are only completed when the old guard fades from the picture and the Young Turks take over.

Imagine, for the moment, a campaign to establish a global Black Saturday Remembrance Day every October 27th. Keeping in mind the rabbit-duck illusion and Kuhn's application of it to cognitive revolutions. Ask yourself: What might be the dimensions and the nature of the revolution we seek? Try this on for size. Before the revolution (i.e., *now*), the majority of the world's people either know nothing of the nuclear threat or don't care about it, or both, while leaders of the nuclear nations operate within a context that requires a nuclear weapons capability for the basic security of their nations. At least, that is their pre-revolutionary belief.

Pack your bags: it's time to head for another planet. Over time, millions begin to reflect on the nuclear threat, at least once a year. The cumulative effect eventually becomes obvious as people all over the world begin to speak out publicly about their belief that nuclear weapons are terribly dangerous and that their possession does not increase their security. A cognitive crisis begins to occur. First one, then another, leader of a nuclear nation, sensing which way the wind is blowing, says that, well, they have also been wondering why nuclear weapons are needed. There is resistance. But there is also counter resistance: people return again and again to the Cuban missile crisis, the moment when leaders nearly blew up the world, and in fact drew the conclusion that they were only a hair's breadth from Armageddon and that they may have lost the means to prevent it. Artists of all kinds dramatize this relentlessly and effectively, leading up to, through, and beyond every Black Saturday anniversary. Suddenly—it will seem sudden, even if it takes twenty years—it's a no-brainer. Nuclear abolition is something everyone wants to take credit for originating. The leaders call in the specialists on disposal and verification, who set to work with their essential, labor-intensive, and years-long tasks.

And on the first Black Saturday anniversary following the announcement of the global intention to destroy the nukes, the ghosts of Kennedy, Castro, and Khrushchev appear simultaneously at celebrations in Washington, Havana, and Moscow, much to the surprise of even the most ardent citizens of "Planet Black Saturday." These ghosts of the Black Saturday Past express their joint satisfaction that their descendants have used the events of October 27, 1962, to raise the odds, for the moment, that the human experiment shall not perish from the earth.

If you build it, they will come. Guaranteed. We'll come too. We'll hitch a ride with them.

10/27/62
Because Luck Is Insufficient (Go For It!)

We can't personally lead any group, or convene meetings, or beat down doors in the corridors of power until the decision-makers listen to the message of Black Saturday. We are baby boomers, born just after the dawn of the nuclear age, roughly seventy years ago. The hand-to-hand combat with the forces of nuclear inertia is, we think, better left to the young and energetic: the paradigm-shifters of the 21st century. Leaders of revolutionary movements should not have to take naps and medications as often as we do.

But wait! We're not quite finished yet. We have more to say about The Anniversary Heuristic and its use as a catalyst for nuclear abolition. We intend to follow up *Dark Beyond Darkness* with another small book focused on ideas in this manifesto. That, and what we hope will be a surprise constituent of the Black Saturday Catalyst in a couple of years.[25]

But for right now, here are five ideas for you to consider:

• *Message*. In her marvelous 2014 post-apocalyptic novel *Station Eleven*, Canadian novelist Emily St. John Mandel introduces us to one of her lead characters, a feisty young woman named Kirsten Raymonde. Kirsten has a tattoo on the inside of her left forearm. It reads: "Because Survival Is Insufficient." The text is from *Star Trek*, but it refers in *Station Eleven* to the philosophy of the group to which Kirsten belongs: a traveling company of actors and musicians who, now twenty years after a pandemic has wiped out 99 percent of the human race, travel around northern lower Michigan and southwest Ontario performing Shakespeare and giving concerts to the handful of survivors who are eking out their existence in small settlements. The slogan, "Because Survival Is Insufficient," becomes ever more poignant as the novel progresses toward something quite rare in contemporary post-apocalyptic fiction—an uplifting, optimistic conclusion. The people in the traveling company, like many they meet along their route, have made a commitment to remain as fully human as possible, even in very dangerous and primitive conditions.[26]

Having recently read and reread *Station Eleven*, we asked ourselves: If we were tattooing types—which we are not—what might we have inked onto our forearms? What are we committed to, as embodied in our Black Saturday Manifesto? How would we try to capture, in a phrase, our basic message? We came up with this:

10/27/62

Because Luck Is Insufficient

This is as close as we can come to stating what we are about in a phrase and a half—what everything we have discovered over thirty years of work on the Cuban missile crisis boils down to. We're not going to ask you to get tattooed or even to stencil a T-shirt. But we are asking you, having gotten this far in the book, to keep this super shorthand reference to Black Saturday in mind in such a way that you still remember it long after you've finished with the book. This is the essence of the fire we hope you carry throughout as much of the 21st century as it takes to abolish the nukes.

• *Starting Up*. Reread this book. Write down what most interested you or surprised you about it. If the circumstances allow, write a paper on it for a class, or discuss it at your book group, or both. Go to Armageddonletters.com. to extend your knowledge of the Cuban missile crisis. Pay special attention to the film, *Who Cares About the Cuban Missile Crisis?* Start a conversation. Pick the audience. Share your thoughts about *Dark Beyond Darkness* and anything you think connects with it. Find partners and stick with it.

• *Getting Going*. Why not ask your friends what they know of the nuclear threat, just as Jonathan Deaton did in the film we discussed earlier in this chapter? If you can muster some enthusiasm among your friends, why not organize a study group devoted to the objectives of the Black Saturday paradigm shift, beginning with establishing the anniversary of 10/27/62 as a global day of remembrance of the most dangerous moment in recorded history?

• *Contacting Anti-Nuclear Groups*. Go to the Wikipedia entry for "anti-nuclear groups": https://en.wikipedia.org/wiki/Anti-nuclear_organizations. The entry lists 125 organizations, most of them headquartered in the U.S., although some are located in Europe. We will not tell you which to contact. Use your own intuition and judgment. Send them an email asking whether they would be interested in incorporating a Black Saturday component into the mission and their activities. If they answer "no," ask them: "Why not?" Without being rude, you might suggest that they go to *Who Cares About the Cuban Missile Crisis?* available at Armageddonletters.com, and on our YouTube page. You can tell them about *Dark Beyond Darkness.* Talk with them about their ideas about what we are calling a paradigm shift in the effort to rid the world of nuclear weapons.

Here is the issue: the anti-nuclear groups are an important source of support because they have already dedicated themselves to abolishing nuclear weapons. But they are mostly about numbers, as we have discussed in *Dark Beyond Darkness*. If we can encourage them to supplement their abolitionist proclivities so as to provide room for the historical component required by the Black Saturday Manifesto, we would be off to a running start.

• *Going Global.* Get to know others who share your interest in working toward a global, annual 10/27/62 Remembrance Day. Familiarize yourself with the United Nations Office for Disarmament Affairs (UNODA). You can begin your immersion at its website: https://www.un.org/disarmament/. You should instantly see what is something like the Mother of All Problems facing those of us committed to **10/27/62: Because Luck Is Insufficient**. This organization is obviously important. To go global on the issue of preventing nuclear war, the UN should be involved. In fact, they should be leading the way. But nowhere in their portfolio, as represented by their complicated website, does there seem to be any interest in *any* historical issue, let alone Black Saturday. The reasons for this are complex and connected to the UN's modus operandi generally, which requires a degree of consensus that usually rules out the adoption of paradigm-shifting ideas. We have the impression that in this area, as in others, the UN is a follower, not a leader. Still, you will need to familiarize yourself with the general outlines of the activities in which they are engaged.

But we must go global in ways that the UN has never dreamed of. Get involved, to the degree your interests and talents and time allow, in a grassroots campaign to connect with people all over the globe about producing significant works of art and significant gatherings of people (face to face and online) each 10/27/62. It will no doubt begin with what might seem to be a rag-tag band of oddballs. Don't worry about being odd. What you will be standing for has an unimpeachable track record: the idea works in spades. Observing the anniversary of the Cuban missile crisis has been our tried-and-true method of getting noticed, discovering the truth about the crisis, and getting the word out to a global audience. The annual observance, when sanctioned by the nations of the world, is the best means available to build a critical mass of momentum toward the abolition of nukes as no-brainer.

And remember: you are not alone; you are involved in something whose stakes are infinite, and you will be embarking on an adventure of a lifetime.

In telling what we know about October 1962 and its connections to the risk of nuclear war in the present and future, our principal purpose is to carry the fire to you millennials: to those of you who were born just before, or just after, the turn of the 21st century. *This is your century.* For a variety of reasons, you should not expect to be as lucky as we baby boomers have been for the entire length of our lives so far, particularly in October 1962, but also throughout the Cold War and the entire nuclear age. Remember: your generation has the capacity to blow up the world, as ours nearly did during the Cuban missile crisis. Now that you know how lucky we were in October 1962, we hope you will not trust your luck.

Following a tradition begun by Karl Marx and Friedrich Engels in their 1848 *Communist Manifesto*, it is customary for a document calling itself a "manifesto" to conclude with a stirring exhortation. Very well: *Millennials of the world unite around Black Saturday! You have nothing to lose but the weapons that could destroy all of us today, next year, any time!*

EPILOGUE

SHOW US YOUR DARKNESS

Warning Given! Warning Received?

Light is easy to love;
Show me your darkness.

—R. Queen, *Darkchylde* (2016)[1]

Cormac McCarthy's *The Road* is that rare book (and film) that deals compellingly with both the cosmic and the personal—the end of the world, as we know it, and the end of a relationship between a father and his son. From the moment we encounter Papa & The Boy, we are immersed in a compelling and believable post-apocalyptic tale that is heartbreaking and poignant. This is how the book begins:

> When he woke in the woods in the dark and the cold of the night he'd reach out to touch the child sleeping beside him. Nights dark beyond darkness the days more gray each one than what had gone before. Like the onset of some cold glaucoma dimming away the world. His hand rose and fell softly with each precious breath. He pushed away the plastic tarpaulin and raised himself in the stinking robes and blankets and looked toward the east for any light but there was none.[2]

Form follows substance: it doesn't take long for McCarthy's infrequent, unpredictable punctuation and odd syntax to feel natural, as if a world this devoid of the props of civilized life *should* be presented in a language in which some of the usual grammatical props are degraded or missing.

When Papa & The Boy awaken in the morning—"morning," in *The Road*, refers to a period of near darkness that follows a period of total darkness—they resume their journey south, toward the Gulf of Mexico, in search of warmth. (Papa believes they will freeze to death during the coming winter if they stay where they are.) "Then," we are told, "they set out along the blacktop in the gunmetal light, shuffling through the ash, each the other's world entire."[3]

Human empathy is virtually nonexistent in *The Road*, except for the feelings Papa & The Boy have for each other. They inhabit a world in which all human contact, other than between them, is to be avoided because it is assumed that all other momentary survivors in their post-apocalyptic world are what Papa has taught The Boy to call "bad guys," a euphemism for cannibals. Papa & The Boy are starving, and they live in fear of being eaten by creatures resembling what before Armageddon they might have called their fellow human beings. In *The Road*, others are instead just hungry carnivores. As they push their rickety grocery cart containing all their earthly belongings through the cold and the dark, Papa & The Boy are simply trying to buy a bit of time. Eventually they, like the other survivors, will starve or freeze to death, or die of nuclear-winter-friendly diseases such as emphysema or pneumonia, or be killed and eaten by "bad guys."

We are told nothing about the events that preceded the dog-eat-dog existence that Papa & The Boy experience on The Road. We are led to believe there was a nuclear war, but only obliquely, and we are told nothing about whatever political crisis, if there was one, led to the war. But we don't need to know the geopolitics of the war, because *The Road* is the story of what happens to human empathy following a climatic catastrophe. Until the very end of the novel, when another family materializes to care for The Boy following Papa's death, all the empathy left on earth, as far as we know, exists between Papa & The Boy. We discover what it might be like to live in a world in which human beings no long treat one another as human beings.

In the Prologue to this book, we imagined that you had been sucked by some dark magic into John Hillcoat's movie adaptation of McCarthy's *The Road*.[4] Fortunately, you don't live in that world. You are not on the run from cannibals. You are not starving. The world as you remember it, from before you read this passage, or this book, is pretty much unchanged. Every evening, it will get dark, or as dark as cities and their suburbs get, nothing like the "dark beyond darkness" in which the events in *The Road* take place. Every morning, the sun will rise in the East, and the darkness will recede.

Having read our book, you now know that if nuclear weapons are not abolished, *The Road* may be transformed into reality at any time. You know this can happen, whether or not anyone, at this moment, seeks to initiate a nuclear war. You know it because, in October 1962, Armageddon came within a hair's breadth of occurring in just these circumstances. You also know we escaped mostly by luck.

Now you know what it took us thirty years to uncover. And what we have uncovered is unremitting darkness: a darkness so profound and overwhelming that it seems at first that it must reside only in science fiction. No more. Anyone who claims the contrary is bullshitting you. Try very hard to keep the darkness visible. This is the difficult part. Addressing this difficulty is what this book is about. As the contemporary graphic novelist R. Queen puts it,

> Light is easy to love.
> Show me your darkness.[5]

Stay focused, from time to time, on the moment-to-moment danger we are all in. Whatever mode of action you may choose to help move the world toward zero nuclear weapons—political, literary, artistic, scientific, or simply using your conversations and your vote constructively—remember what is at stake, which is everything.

Keep shifting the paradigm. Keep looking for ways to make the Cuban missile crisis come alive for us inhabitants of the 21st century. Keep returning, at least annually, to Planet Black Saturday—

10/27/62

Because Luck Is Insufficient

ACKNOWLEDGMENTS

We have been trying for thirty years to understand the Cuban missile crisis. The debts we have accumulated during that time are as various as they are multitudinous. None of our conferences, books, articles and films on the crisis is conceivable without the support of so many, over so long a time. We are grateful beyond words to one and all.

Publisher. We have been extraordinarily fortunate in our long-term relationship with Rowman & Littlefield. *Dark Beyond Darkness* is our tenth book with them. Our editor Jonathan Sisk and publisher Jed Lyons have been with us every step of the way, since the late 1980s when we signed our first contract with R&L. They are helpful in all the relevant ways, and then some. Thanks to Jon and Jed for making this unusual book a high priority for R&L. We also thank Christopher Utter and Kate Powers, who have assisted Jon at various stages of this journey, as well as Desiree Reid who has done a fine job of copy-editing. Finally, we thank senior production editor Elaine McGarraugh for her patience and guidance through the final phases of producing this book.

Readers. We were fortunate in recruiting several friends and colleagues to read our manuscript—many times—as it evolved, and to give us comments of whatever sort they deemed useful. The group included the following: Mark Garrison, a retired U.S. foreign service officer and a well-informed student of nuclear danger; Matthew Heys, a high school social studies teacher, whose knowledge of both our subject matter and the idiosyncrasies of communicating with the millennial generation are staggering; Edward T. Linenthal, the former editor in chief of the Journal of American History, and a paragon of teaching dedication and brilliance; James Mercer, a high school English teacher, who provided us with a detailed critique and much good advice on how to get millennials to sit up and pay attention to something that they need to know about, even when the necessity of knowing about it is not initially obvious;

and Sonya Stejskal, Queen of Social Studies, who in April 2016 arranged for us to come to Omaha, Nebraska to lecture to, and receive some thought-provoking feedback from, more than 200 advanced placement students in history, social studies, Latin American studies and political science. Thanks to our readers and Sonya's recruits, we feel as if we have passed through the ring of fire, and that our book is much better because of their efforts.

Millennials. Dark Beyond Darkness is targeted at the millennial generation, a cohort that, for the most part, is uninformed and uninterested in the history of the Cuban missile crisis and whatever it might imply for nuclear danger in their century, the 21st century. For years, we have wanted to reach out to young people with a book on the crisis that is not dumbed down, but which enables them to rise up and meet the challenge of the history to which they are the heirs, and the danger they must live with, until such time as nuclear weapons are eliminated. This book is their book. One of our mantras has been: *"this book will not present your parents' and grandparents' Cuban missile crisis."* Consequently, we asked a dozen students to give an early version of this book a test drive, and to report back from October 1962 on what they liked, didn't like, or didn't understand. We also asked them what scared them. They focused us on how to communicate to their generation without lecturing, but without sacrificing substance. We thank the members of our seminar, "Managing Nuclear Risk: From the Cuban Missile Crisis to the Breakthrough With Iran," winter term, 2016 at the Balsillie School of Internatonal Affairs: Nazmul Arifeen, Olivia Auston, Joshua Darby-MacLelland, Ousmane Diallo, Kathleen Fryer, Nicole Georges, Kayla Grant, Lema Ijtemaye, Caleb Lauer, Patrick Segsworth, Alexander Smith and Ruxanna Vlad.

Colleagues. Our home institutions, the Department of History, and the Balsillie School of International Affairs, at the University of Waterloo, have provided us with unwavering support for all our endeavors, including the writing of this book. Particularly instrumental in helping us secure a half-sabbatical leave on short notice, we thank Gary Bruce, Andrea Charette, Heather MacDougall and Douglas Peers. We also thank Bonnie Bishop and Donna Hayes of the History Department for their multifaceted assistance. Thanks are also due to our Balsillie School Director, John Ravenhill, and his two ace deputies, Tiffany Bradley and Joanne Weston. They make the running of a complex institution look much easier than it no doubt is. The unorthodox authors' photographs are the work of Trevor Hunsberger, multimedia producer at our sister institution, the Centre for International Governance Innovation (CIGI). His uncommon mix of technical skill and human empathy were much appreciated by his subjects.

Filmmakers. In the midst of writing the first draft of this book, The Showtime Network bought the rights to develop a multi-part TV miniseries based on our previous book, *The Armageddon Letters: Kennedy/Khrushchev/Castro in the Cuban Missile Crisis* (Rowman & Littlefield, 2012). Showtime then asked Phil Alden Robinson ("Field of Dreams"; "The Sum of All Fears"; etc.) to both write the script and direct the miniseries. Phil Robinson has been a revelation. He has had his pedal to the metal ever since signing with Showtime, sending us questions and drafts and, generally engaging us in a non-stop conversation about the Cuban missile crisis. Phil is, as we have told him, learning in a little more than a year, what it took us thirty years to figure out for ourselves. Our "dangling conversation" has been immensely useful to us—at least as useful as anything we have provided to Phil, or so we believe. The miniseries is being produced by Ruddy Productions and Phoenix Pictures. We are grateful to Albert Ruddy and Todd Martens of Ruddy Productions, and to Mike Medavoy and Ben Anderson of Phoenix Pictures, for their interest in our work, and for steering Phil Robinson to it.

Life. All the while a book is being written, life goes on beyond the screens of the laptops of the authors. For indispensible support, both voluminous and varied, we owe a debt of gratitude to those who enabled us, amid some storms and stress, to carve out enough quality writing time to compose this book. We are grateful to: Stephanie Bradley-Swift, Cristian Danescu, Gregory Fichter, Eileen Kirkbride, Jesse Kirkbride, the late John Limber, Julie Maidment, Alexandra McGraw, Kristin McGraw, James Romoser, Bruce Sanford, Dan Swift, Anita Venugopal, and the Well-Fit Community at the University of Waterloo. Thanks to one and all.

Subtitle. Two-thirds of our subtitle is borrowed from the subtitle of a remarkable book, *Black Earth: The Holocaust as History and Warning.* It is by our friend Tim Snyder of the Yale University History Department. Like Tim, we are in the business of looking, in sometimes frightening and horrifying detail, at recent history for clues as to how to conduct ourselves in the present.

Cover. Amy Dale's program design for the Kitchener, Ontario's Grand Philharmonic Choir's performance of Beethoven's *Missa solemnis* provided inspiration for our cover design. Katherine Hurley, friend and choir member, invited us to the performance, which was scary and moving.

Cinque angeli di Bellagio, Italia. The run-up to submitting a book to a publisher can get a little crazy; typically, the tasks are many and varied, many having little to do with the substance of the book, and a great deal to do with the look, marketing, endorsements, permissions, and of course the cover. It may or may not be true that you shouldn't judge a book by its cover, but try telling that to obsessive authors. For this crazy phase, we shifted the venue from Waterloo, Ontario, where we live, to the beautiful, laid-back calm of Bellagio, Italy. On this, our ninth visit to the jewel of the Italian lake country, all went well until each of us developed serious health issues. Bellagio is isolated and thinly populated, and both factors contribute to its charm. But for visitors in need of urgent medical care, its isolation seems less charming than alarming. For extraordinary assistance to us as we navigated these crises, we are deeply indebted to our "five angels of Bellagio": Nadia Gilardoni, conference coordinator at the Rockefeller Foundation's Bellagio Center; Daniela Martinelli, whose logistical knowledge and skill we shall long remember; Elena Ongania, who retired recently as the Residents' Coordinator at the Rockefeller Foundation's Bellagio Center, and one of the strongest women we've ever met; Pilar Palacia, the Managing Director of the Rockefeller Foundation's Bellagio Center; and Helen Shields, professor of medicine at Harvard Medical School, and our candidate for the title of "world's greatest clinician." Helen sent us diagnoses and instructions, via email, from 5,000 miles and six time zones away. All were declared "assolutamente giusto" by the doctors at the San Raffaele Medical Center in Milan, Italy. Underneath your jackets, ladies, we see wings.

Dedication. This book is dedicated to the memory of Robert S. McNamara, JFK's secretary of defense during the Cuban missile crisis. During a more than twenty-year collaboration with Bob, we revolutionized our understanding of the proximity to Armageddon on Black Saturday, October 27, 1962, the most dangerous moment in recorded history, along with the significance for our 21st century world, of that long ago and far away crisis. Who knew that "Maximum Bob," as we often called him, a pillar of the national security establishment, would turn out to be an anti-nuclear revolutionary? Bob's belief in the necessity of nuclear abolition was galvanized by the research we did together on what was happening in Cuba during the crisis in which he was centrally involved. The McNamara we knew, *McNamara in winter*, was the little research engine that could, and did, turn our understanding of the crisis inside out and upside down.The revolution in understanding that this book represents is unthinkable without Bob—Bossy. Brilliant. Gruff. Demanding. Kind. Vulnerable. Generous. Curious and Courageous—all of the above. We miss him.

J&j
Waterloo, Ontario
September 5, 2017

NOTES

NOTES TO PROLOGUE

1. Cormac McCarthy, *The Road* (New York: Vintage, 2006), 10.

2. *The Road*, a film by John Hillcoat, distributed by Dimension Films, November 2009. The film stars Viggo Mortensen, Kodi Smit-McPhee, and Charlize Theron. The musical score, by Nick Cave and Warren Ellis, is haunting and evocative.

3. We call this mode of thinking "possibility logic." If a hypothetical event is catastrophic—as, for example, a nuclear war is catastrophic—then we believe it makes sense to abandon traditional probability logic, believed to be the basis of human rationality, and focus instead on what is possible, without regard for how probable it may seem at any specific moment. The idea developed in conversations with former Secretary of Defense Robert McNamara, at the very beginning of our project on the Cuban missile crisis in the late 1980s. McNamara reconstructed his own thinking in the missile crisis this way: "I didn't think that . . . [nuclear war] . . . was probable, but . . . I'm not interested only in probable risks if they may lead to disastrous consequences. That's what motivated me." In James G. Blight and David A. Welch, foreword by McGeorge Bundy, *On the Brink: Americans and Soviets Reexamine the Cuban Missile Crisis* (New York: Hill and Wang, 1989), 192. Most of McNamara's colleagues in the Kennedy administration did not think this way; they felt the risk of nuclear war was small. Many of them urged an attack and an invasion of Cuba. But McNamara, like Kennedy himself, believed that because a catastrophic conclusion to the crisis was entirely possible, whatever could be done to exit the crisis without a war of any kind should be done. Today, those embracing zero nukes do so because Armageddon is *possible*, while those who oppose nuclear abolition do so because, among other reasons, they believe Armageddon is *improbable*.

4. See "Who Cares About the Cuban Missile Crisis," directed by Koji Masutani. This is a four-minute, partially animated introduction to the Cuban missile crisis. It may be found among the short films at http://www.armageddonletters.com or at: https://www.youtube.com/watch?v=zObCklM5LPw.

5. Bobby Pickett and the Crypt-Kickers, "Monster Mash," released on August 25, 1962, by Garpax Records. The Wikipedia entry for the record contains the following sentence: "The 'Monster Mash' single was #1 on the *Billboard* Hot 100 chart on October 20–27 of that year, just before Halloween. It has been a perennial holiday favorite ever since." In light of what was happening in the Cuban missile crisis at exactly that moment, this statement must be regarded as (dare we say) cryptic, even gothic.

6. Kennedy may have forgotten about the game, but those who saw it will not. With runners at second and third, and two outs, trailing by one run, the San Francisco Giants first baseman Willie McCovey hit a vicious line drive that was snagged by Yankees' second

baseman Bobby Richardson. The "damn Yankees" had won another World Series. The last pitch of the game is at: http://m.mlb.com/video/topic/6479266/v13062809/62-ws-gm-7-nyysf-richardsons-snag-yanks-win.

7. These propositions are copiously documented in the chapters that follow. The endnotes to those chapters provide ample resources with which to evaluate our claims, and to follow up various points for clarification and verification. For many subjects, increasing familiarity can lead to ho-hum interest, even outright boredom. But immersion in the details of the Cuban missile crisis, for most people, renders the event scarier than they ever imagined it before.

NOTE TO PART I

1. Theodore Roethke, "In a Dark Time," in *The Collected Poems of Theodore Roethke* (New York: Doubleday, 1961). The poem is also widely available online. See, for example: poetryfoundation.org for the text of the poem, as well as a short but informative biographical sketch of Roethke.

NOTES TO CHAPTER 1

1. Several ideas in this chapter had their origins in a piece we wrote for *Truthdig*. See our piece "The Scream and the Cuban Missile Crisis Still Echo" at http://www.truthdig.com/arts_culture/item/scream_and_the_cuban_missile_crisis_still_echo_20150501 (posted May 1, 2015).

2. Edvard Munch's *The Scream* may well be the most famous painting in the world. There are at least four versions of it painted by Munch, one of which is accompanied by a woodcut containing a poem he wrote commemorating in words his terrifying experience by the Oslo fjord. *The Scream* was the centerpiece of a 2016 exhibition at New York's Neue Galerie. It was displayed elegantly, along with the entire poem Munch wrote to accompany it. See: https://www.facebook.com/Neue.Galerie.New.York/photos/a.10150257220130822.34521.15715400821/10154045108610822/?type=3&theater. There are two versions of Munch's poem he wrote to accompany *The Scream*—one from his diary, and one that he revised slightly and carved into the wooden frame of one of the versions of the painting. Both versions are quoted in their entirety and given context in: Presca Ahn, "'The Great Scream in Nature': Edvard Munch at MoMa." It is available at: http://theamericanreader.com/the-great-scream-in-nature-edvard-munch-at-moma/. A recent, concise introduction to Munch, *The Scream* and other of his paintings, is in Peter Schjeldahl, "We All Scream," *The New Yorker*, February 29, 2016, 73–75.

3. Stephen King, *Pet Sematary: A Novel* (New York: Simon & Schuster, 1983), 293.

4. Carol Vogel, "'The Scream' Is Auctioned for a Record $119.9 Million," *New York Times*, May 3, 2012.

5. There is a mind-boggling collection of *Scream* images at this address: https://www.google.ca/search?q=%22The+Scream%22+merchandise&biw=1138&bih=755&tbm=isch&tbo=u&source=univ&sa=X&ved=0ahUKEwi_w5XrkMDSAhWlx4MKHagoBEUQ7AkIOg#imgrc=j1q6NBm_AF0tjM.

It seems altogether possible to wear a different image of *The Scream* every day for a year without repeating any of the images. And that is just the images on apparel. Alexandre

Nodopaka, in his satirical poem, "The Scream of Edward Munch," imagines going for a walk on the bridge by the Oslo fjord with his friend "Ed" Munch, and the two of them marveling at how a child's crayon drawing of a screwy face has fetched so much money. See: https://www.poemhunter.com/poem/the-scream-by-edvard-munch/.

6. At some point in every course we teach, we append to the end of a class a photo session in which the students (as a group) each give their best shot at mimicking Munch's *The Scream*.

7. The evidence points to the conclusion that Munch's primal scream experience actually happened in more or less the way it is depicted in his famous painting. The surprise is that it happened in the autumn of 1883, more than a decade before he painted *The Scream*. During November of that year, the Norwegian sky did indeed turn blood red, just as it did all over the northern hemisphere, due to the eruption of Mt. Krakatoa, in Indonesia, beginning on August 27, 1883. In 2004 three intrepid scholars—two physicists and one teacher of English—went to Oslo and, using geographical indicators from the various versions of Munch's painting, found the precise location where Munch was standing, and the direction he was looking, when the blood-red sky lit up over Oslo. See Donald W. Olson, Russell Doescher, and Marilynn S. Olson, "The Blood-Red Sky of the Scream," *American Physical Society News* 13, no. 5 (May 2004). See also the links in note 1, above.

8. Milan Kundera, *The Book of Laughter and Forgetting*, trans. from the Czech by Michael Henry Heim (New York: Knopf, 1980), 3.

9. Milan Kundera, *The Unbearable Lightness of Being*, trans from the Czech by Michael Henry Heim (New York: Knopf, 1984), part 6, "The Grand March." Elsewhere in the book he says, "Kitsch causes two tears to flow in quick succession. The first tear says: How nice to see children running on the grass! The second tear says: How nice to be moved, together with all mankind, by children running on the grass!" (Ibid., part 6) Applied to Munch's *The Scream*: It's not about terror, or existential anxiety run amok, or a vision of the end of the world as we know it; instead, it's "cute" (say) on compression pants or in a fuzzy doll, and people who give such things as gifts are "nice."

10. Jonathan Schell, *The Fate of the Earth* (New York: Knopf, 1982), part 1, "A Republic of Insects and Grass." It is available in a more recent publication that combines the book with Schell's *The Abolition* (New York: Knopf, 1984). Both books originally appeared as pieces in *The New Yorker. The Fate of the Earth* was shocking in its time, and it still has considerable shock value now, in an era in which our collective awareness of the nuclear threat is minimal and we are, in general, much less worried about Armageddon than in the tumultuous 1980s, when fear of nuclear war gripped many Western societies. We often assign this in classes, and a not uncommon response after the book is read and digested by the students is one of unease, of feeling that there was this potentially huge, disruptive horror show waiting to happen about which, to that point in their lives, they knew nothing about. Most think that the nuclear threat ended with the end of the U.S.-Soviet Cold War. Schell's detailed account is horrific. He explains dispassionately what would happen to New York City, where he resided, in a nuclear attack consisting of one thermonuclear bomb. It is horrific but fact-based. It has also been given a renewed sense of cogency by the 9/11 terrorist attacks in New York and Washington, DC. It now no longer seems an exaggeration, in light of the damage caused by two jetliners to the World Trade Towers, to say that New York City and the surrounding area would be utterly, completely destroyed by a nuclear bomb.

11. The Cuban missile crisis provides the backdrop for season 2, episode 13, of *Mad Men*. The crisis itself, however, only exists on black-and-white TVs spread around the office, and it is distinctly secondary in importance to the revelation Peggy makes to Pete that she had his baby a while back and gave the baby away. *X-Men: First Class* (2011) is

great fun, but when the Mutants start bending the trajectories of Russian missiles fired at sea, well, let's just say it didn't really happen like that in October 1962. A highly capitalized and very successful video game supposedly based on the crisis is *The Cuban Missile Crisis: The Aftermath*. The premise is that when an American U-2 is shot down over Cuba by a Russian anti-aircraft missile on October 27, 1962, nuclear war breaks out, and the world becomes an incinerated, radiating ruin. (A U-2 was, in the crisis, shot down on October 27th, but the pilot, Major Rudolf Anderson, became the only known U.S. casualty in the crisis.) A lot of the action takes place in Cuba—or rather on the island that used to be Cuba before it was totally destroyed in the nuclear war—a dubious premise, to say the least. The Russians and the Americans go at it with tanks, jets, missiles—the works. But this is nothing but pure, unadulterated *kitsch*. The problem is that following a nuclear war of the magnitude implied, civilization would be wiped out. There would be no commandos, no tanks, no planes, no war after the war, because the air would be poisonous, food would be nonexistent after a few weeks or months, there would be no fuel for the machines that support combat operations. Instead, in such an aftermath, Cuba, like the rest of the world, would be silent, cold, dark, and almost entirely uninhabited. Sorry, gamers, but that's the truth. A non-bullshit variant of something that might accurately be called "The Cuban Missile Crisis: The Aftermath" would consist of the few surviving human beings slogging fearfully across the landscape, like Papa & The Boy in *The Road*, only with perhaps the occasional husk of an incinerated palm tree.

12. Diane Sawyer, interview with Fidel Castro, Havana, Cuba, March 13, 1993. Castro's use of the thumb-forefinger embodiment of nuclear risk came a little over a year after Castro and Robert McNamara met at a conference in Cuba to discuss the crisis. Neither, we believe, used the image before the Havana conference; both used it repeatedly for many years after the conference—after they understood the comprehensive readiness of Moscow, Washington, and Havana to begin a war that almost surely would have escalated to apocalyptic proportions. See also, on Castro's estimation of the proximity to Armageddon in the crisis, Robert S. McNamara and James G. Blight, "The Miracle of October: Lessons from the Cuban Missile Crisis." The paper, written in 2001, is available at: http://the-puzzle-palace.com/files/OctMiracle.pdf.

McNamara used the image in Errol Morris's 2004 Academy Award–winning film *The Fog of War*, on which we served as principal substantive consultants to both McNamara and Morris. The high-voltage intensity of McNamara is focused eerily on his left thumb and forefinger, as they almost touch, and as he says, "We came that close to nuclear war at the end." A video of McNamara making his statement is at: https://www.youtube.com/watch?v=CtUfBc4qQMg.

The entire transcript of *The Fog of War* is available on Errol Morris's website: http://www.errolmorris.com/film/fow_transcript.html.

13. William James, "On a Certain Blindness in Human Beings," in *The Writings of William James*, ed. John J. McDermott (Chicago: University of Chicago Press, 1977), 629–45, 629.

14. The Cuban missile crisis is far from a one-off of superpower cluelessness and self-destructive arrogance. The American war in Vietnam, which began in earnest in the spring and summer of 1965 and lasted until April 1975, claimed three million lives, including nearly sixty thousand Americans, and tore the U.S. apart politically and embarrassed it in most parts of the world. Later, the 2003 U.S. invasion of Iraq, allegedly in search of (non-existent) Iraqi weapons of mass destruction, would leave millions homeless, destroy the balance of power existing in the Middle East, leave hundreds of thousands dead, and nearly bankrupt the U.S. treasury. Likewise, the Russian war in Afghanistan, which lasted from December 1979 until February 1989, left the country ravaged, with one million dead

(including roughly one hundred thousand Russians), and played a role in the collapse of the Soviet Empire by December 31, 1991. The Russians, moreover, have fought two recent wars with the restive Chechen Republic, first in 1994, then in 1999. Hundreds of thousands died and huge swaths of Chechnya were totally destroyed, including the capitol, Grozny. The wars proved to be an embarrassment to the Russian government, both because of their difficulty in putting down the rebellion and also because of the brutal, indiscriminate methods they used, killing civilians and combatants alike. In each of these conflicts, the U.S. and Russian superpowers achieved little or nothing positive, inflamed entire regions in war, emptied their treasuries, and seemingly learned little or nothing from their various military adventures. Ignoring Havana as irrelevant, as did Washington and Moscow in the Cuban missile crisis, was consistent with this pattern of not taking seriously capacities and motives of small countries determined to assert their sovereignty, even in the face of what might look like tremendous odds against them.

15. The Sotheby's *Scream* video is at: https://www.youtube.com/watch?v=T5tkz1QOzas.

16. Sebastian Cosor's masterful short film is at: https://www.youtube.com/watch?v=qz6gT7S9_XI. Cosor's choice of soundtrack is brilliant: Pink Floyd's classic "The Great Gig in the Sky," from their 1973 album, *Dark Side of the Moon*. The vocals, by Claire Torry, were improvised in the studio by Torry over three takes. The spookiness of what meets the eye and the ear is perfect.

17. This short film by Cosor is spooky and also funny, due to the juxtaposition of the wailing, flailing Munchian screamer and the jolly Santa Claus hat worn by the screamer. The film is visually stunning. See the film at: https://vimeo.com/34830801.

18. The shorter video, with "Scream to Us" wailing on the soundtrack, is also effective. It is at: https://www.youtube.com/watch?v=bWlNVyFn4qA.

19. See Daniel Kahneman, *Thinking Fast and Slow* (New York: Doubleday, 2011), 264–65. Kahneman credits cognitive psychologist Gary Klein with the term *pre-mortem*. It was developed to help people resist what Kahneman calls "the planning fallacy": excessive optimism regarding our ability to identify and solve problems; our capacity to predict the future; and in general for assuming the world is more understandable and benign than it really is (255). The protocol is this, according to Kahneman: "Imagine that we are a year into the future. We implemented the plan, as it now exists. The outcome was a disaster. Please take five to ten minutes to write a brief history of that disaster" (265).

NOTES TO CHAPTER 2

1. Arthur M. Schlesinger Jr., *A Thousand Days: John F. Kennedy in the White House* (Boston: Houghton Mifflin, 1965), 841.

2. Harry G. Frankfurt, *On Bullshit* (Princeton: Princeton University Press, 2005), 61.

3. Ibid. The book is a follow-up to a 1986 article that, at the time of its publication, received relatively little attention: "On Bullshit." See: Harry G. Frankfurt, "On Bullshit," *Raritan Quarterly Review* 6, no. 2 (Fall 1986). Frankfurt's book brilliantly combines a dispassionate, even occasionally tedious, analysis, as if the author were discussing any other central concept in analytical philosophy, like "truth," or "reason," and others, on the one hand; while, on the other hand, the subject of his analysis is "bullshit," which requires him to discuss this kind of shit and that kind of shit, and in general to devote considerable space to the metaphorical significance of fecal material, human produced and otherwise. The publisher, Princeton University Press, has also played it straight—almost. On the tenth anniversary of the publication of Frankfurt's runaway best seller, the press took out a full-page

advertisement in *The New York Review of Books*. The ad has a photo of a stack of books of different colors, but all copies of *On Bullshit*. The caption at the top of the page, in red lettering, reads: "10 years later and it's still piled high," *New York Review of Books*, April 2, 2015, 13. And just before the 2016 presidential election, Princeton University Press placed another full-page advertisement for *On Bullshit* in which the header says, in a very large font: "Bullshit is a greater enemy of truth than lies are"—which has become perhaps the most quoted passage from the book. See: *New York Review of Books*, September 29, 2016, 15. The ad occupies the page immediately following the conclusion of an article on the presidential campaign that contains this sentence: "Trump's defeated Republican rivals can testify that it's horrendously difficult to oppose a candidate unconstrained by truth or facts." See: Jonathan Freedland, "U.S. Politics: As Low as It Gets," *New York Review of Books*, September 29, 2016, 13–15. As far back as May 2016, Frankfurt himself had weighed in on candidate Donald Trump as the epitome of a bullshitter. See: Harry G. Frankfurt, "Donald Trump Is BS, Says Expert in BS," *Time*, May 12, 2016.

4. Frankfurt, *On Bullshit*, 61.

5. The reason the previous paragraph is just so much bullshit, rather than a pack of lies, is that the entire exercise that produced this received pseudo-wisdom derives principally from the need to exclaim that "we won"—that the crisis was essentially a game in which Washington emerged the winner. Sentiments like these are meant to bring us to our feet and cheer for the good guys' victory over the bad guys. The views expressed are manifestly untrue, but they are bullshit because the assertions have nothing to do with the real Cuban missile crisis. The narrative is driven by a need that is totally irrelevant to the historical event.

6. Graham T. Allison, *Essence of Decision: Explaining the Cuban Missile Crisis* (Boston: Little Brown, 1971).

7. Ibid., 39.

8. The same statement appears in the second edition of Graham Allison's book: "During the crisis, the U.S. was firm but forbearing. The Soviet Union looked hard, blinked twice, and then withdrew." See: Graham Allison and Philip Zelikow, *Essence of Decision: Explaining the Cuban Missile Crisis*, 2nd ed. (New York: Longman's, 1999), 77.

9. Allison and Zelikow presented essentially the same view at a conference held at Harvard's Kennedy School of Government in September 2012, just before the fiftieth anniversary of the crisis. Despite the revelations of the prior quarter-century revealing the centrality of events in Cuba before and during the crisis, Cuba remained a black box of no great interest to Allison and Zelikow. In their view, Kennedy was still steely, Khrushchev still blinked (twice), and Castro watched from the sidelines. In the final section of their book, "'The Deal' Resolving the Cuban Problem," Castro is mentioned twice: first they note that Khrushchev was alarmed by Castro's contingent request to nuke the U.S. if the expected U.S. invasion of Cuba takes place; and second, that "there had been no time to consult with Castro." Ibid., 361–66, 363. For an alternative view, see James G. Blight and Philip Brenner, *Sad and Luminous Days: Cuba's Struggle with the Superpowers After the Missile Crisis* (Lanham, MD: Rowman & Littlefield, 2002), 1–31.

10. JFK's assassination in Dallas on November 22, 1963, is an essential ingredient in Kennedy's continuing celebrity status. Just as one can travel to Graceland in Memphis and visit the "Jungle Room" and try to imagine what Elvis (and others) did or did not do therein, one can take all manner of JFK assassination tours in Dallas. Here is one example, from the *Dallas Morning News*, in 2012: http://www.dallasnews.com/news/news/2012/10/11/jfk-trolley-tour-takes-passengers-on-historic-journey. The tour, called "The JFK Assassination Trolley Tour," was originally called "The 5.6 Seconds Tour," after the duration of time it took Lee Harvey Oswald to fire three shots at the president's head. It sounds weird; it *is* weird. But some reportedly emerge weeping from the trolley at the end of the tour.

11. McGeorge Bundy, covering note to the president on Henry Kissinger's memo regarding the Berlin crisis, July 7, 1961. Cited in Scott D. Sagan, "SIOP-62: The Nuclear War Plan Briefing to President Kennedy," in *International Security* 12, no. 1 (Summer 1987): 22–51, 23. Bundy refers in his note to the inflexibility of responses available to Kennedy in the event of war with the Soviet Union. Alas, he tells the president, the U.S. nuclear strategy comes down to two options: don't use the nuclear forces at all; or use all the nuclear forces, which are targeted at the Soviet Union, Communist China, and Soviet-dominated states in Eastern Europe. The system was, in essence, a doomsday machine. If JFK had authorized the use of U.S. nuclear forces, he probably would have initiated a series of steps at the end of which the world as it was then known would have turned into a smoking, radiating ruin. This was roughly the same system that was in place in October 1962. Kennedy believed, probably correctly, that during the Cuban missile crisis he would be forced to either do nothing or set in motion Armageddon. Do you still wonder why Kennedy and McNamara were deeply traumatized when they learned the facts of nuclear life in 1961 and 1962?

12. Schlesinger, *A Thousand Days*, 841.

13. Theodore C. Sorensen, *Kennedy* (New York: Harper & Row, 1965).

14. Ibid., 717.

15. Ibid., 718.

16. Robert F. Kennedy, *Thirteen Days: A Memoir of the Cuban Missile Crisis*, afterword by Richard E. Neustadt and Graham T. Allison (New York: Norton, 1969). Many years later, Theodore Sorensen disclosed that he had written large portions of the first draft of the book, working closely with Robert Kennedy, just as he had worked with President Kennedy. How much of the book is Robert Kennedy's and how much is Sorensen's is much less important than the book's brilliant depiction of a White House, and the entire world, on the edge of the unthinkable.

17. Ibid., 47–48.

18. *Thirteen Days* became the basis for a compelling made-for-TV movie in 1974, *The Missiles of October.* It was released by Viacom Pictures and starred William Devane as JFK, Martin Sheen as RFK, and Howard Da Silva as Nikita Khrushchev. All three are brilliant. Should you find yourself wondering who played Fidel Castro, the answer is that no one played Castro. He never appears in the film, just as he plays no role in *Thirteen Days*. One of our students once put the absence of a Cuban presence in the book and film this way: "They are about a bunch of white guys sitting around in conference rooms in Washington and Moscow." Had the Cuban context been included, the cast could not have all been white, nor all guys, nor about what happened in conference rooms. The entire island was mobilized, not just for war, but for what the Cubans believed would be the total destruction of their country.

19. Harvey J. Kaye and Keith McClelland, eds., *E. P. Thompson: Critical Perspectives* (Philadelphia: Temple University Press, 1990), 231.

20. E. P. Thompson, quoted in James G. Blight, in a multiple book review the *Los Angeles Times Book Review*, November 2, 1997.

21. Noam Chomsky, "The Cuban Missile Crisis: How the U.S. Played Russian Roulette with Nuclear War," *The Guardian*, October 15, 2012.

22. On JFK, Chomsky seems incapable of learning from history. He decided long ago that Kennedy was a war-mongering tool of the American imperialist establishment, and over the past half-century he has repeated his accusations, in varying ways. Chomsky is somehow immune from the facts, as they have evolved from the historical record over the past thirty years of our own involvement in the two episodes that exercise Chomsky: the Cuban missile crisis and the U.S. war in Vietnam. In the missile crisis, Kennedy courageously resisted escalating the conflict, which was recommended by all his military advisers

and many of his civilian advisers. He did likewise on proposals to Americanize the war in Vietnam. The evidence is by now overwhelming that had he lived, Kennedy would not have Americanized the war. On Vietnam, see James G. Blight, janet M. Lang, and David A. Welch, *Virtual JFK: Vietnam If Kennedy Had Lived* (Lanham, MD: Rowman & Littlefield, 2009).

23. Roger Hilsman, JFK's director of Intelligence and Research in the State Department, reported in 1967: "There was nothing to do but wait. As the meeting [late at night, Saturday, October 27th] broke up, President Kennedy remarked that now it could 'go either way.'" *To Move a Nation: The Politics of Foreign Policy in the Administration of John F. Kennedy* (New York, Doubleday, 1967), 224. Stanford historian Barton J. Bernstein used Hilsman as his source in an influential article on the crisis nine years later: "The Week We Almost Went to War," *Bulletin of the Atomic Scientists*, February 1976, 12–21, 14. There is no evidence in the transcripts of the taped recordings of the meeting in question that Kennedy ever said it could "go either way." JFK spends this meeting, which went late into the night on the most dangerous weekend in recorded history, trying to convince his advisers that a diplomatic way out of the crisis was still possible. (Many were clamoring for military action against Soviet positions in Cuba, following the news received by the group at around 4:30 p.m. that day, that an unarmed U-2 spy plane had been shot down over Cuba and the pilot killed.) Hilsman, however, strongly implies that JFK had made his final offer, and that either a peaceful solution or nuclear war was about to happen, that Kennedy felt he had done what he could and that was that. But there are reasons to believe that this implication was created by Hilsman in an effort to achieve increased dramatic effect. JFK was committed to a peaceful solution. Moreover, Hilsman was not a member of Kennedy's inner circle. He never attended any of their meetings. His information was secondhand.

24. "Anatomy of a Crisis," CBS News special report, October 28, 1962, narrated by Charles Collingwood. This half-hour program replaced the regularly scheduled offering *Ted Mack's Original Amateur Hour*, a black-and-white TV forerunner of *America's Got Talent* and similar competitions. One sponsor was a product called Sominex, an over-the-counter sleeping aid for, as Ted Mack put it, "simple nervous tension." We screened this video at one of our critical oral history meetings on the crisis. In the darkened room, several of JFK's former advisers could be heard chuckling at former Defense Secretary Robert McNamara's comment: "Oh yeah, we had a lot of nervous tension, but getting rid of it wasn't so simple."

25. The film was underwritten in part by Kevin O'Donnell, Kenneth O'Donnell's son. The Kenneth O'Donnell character is central to the action. He is played by the film's only high-profile actor (Kevin Costner).

26. In his memoirs, Rusk explains the game of "blink" and his use of it as a metaphor on October 24, 1962. See Dean Rusk, *As I Saw It*, with Richard Rusk and Daniel S. Papp (New York: Norton, 1990), 237.

27. The entire script, by screenwriter David Self, is available at: http://www.dailyscript.com/scripts/13_days.html. This scene is approximately two-thirds of the way into the script.

28. A 1974 television docu-drama, *The Missiles of October*, also portrayed the reaction of JFK and his advisers to the confrontation at the quarantine line as a kind of rah-rah cheerleading exercise. Dean Rusk commented: "The television program *The Missiles of October* misrepresented our reaction in the EXCOMM when the Soviet ships turned back. The filmmakers had people jumping around and clapping, as if their high school team had just scored a touchdown. That was not the mood at all. It remained very serious business. We knew that the missiles already in Cuba had to be taken out and that the Soviet buildup was continuing. We still had a most dangerous crisis on our hands." Rusk, *As I Saw It*, 237.

29. Our essential partner in re-visioning the Cuban missile crisis has been the National Security Archive at George Washington University. This non-governmental, non-profit

dynamo of an organization wields the Freedom of Information Act (FOIA) with precision and persistence on a dizzying array of recent historical events. The Cuban missile crisis was topic number one when former *Washington Post* reporter (and Watergate Committee investigator) Scott Armstrong founded the Archive in the early 1980s. He made the missile crisis a top priority for its document gathering. It has remained in the forefront of the Archive's interests ever since, under Director Thomas Blanton, Research Director Malcolm Byrne, ace Cubanologist Peter Kornbluh, and ace Sovietologist, Svetlana Savranskaya. A good place to begin to understand the Archive's documentary achievement is in Laurence Chang and Peter Kornbluh, eds., *The Cuban Missile Crisis, 1962*, revised ed. (New York: New Press, 1998). See also the Cuban missile crisis page of the Archive, at: http://nsarchive.gwu.edu/nsa/cuba_mis_cri/. On the subject matter of this chapter, see the insightful piece by Cuba specialist and longtime National Security Archive adviser Philip Brenner, "Turning History on Its Head": http://nsarchive.gwu.edu/nsa/cuba_mis_cri/brenner.htm.

30. This conference is the subject of James G. Blight, Bruce J. Allyn, and David A. Welch, *Cuba on the Brink: Castro, the Missile Crisis and the Soviet Collapse*, rev. ed. (Lanham, MD: Rowman & Littlefield, 2002).

NOTES TO CHAPTER 3

1. Felix Kovaliev, in James G. Blight, David Lewis, and David A. Welch, *Cuba Between the Superpowers: Antigua, January 3–7, 1991* (Unpublished), 97–98. Kovaliev, director of the Russian Foreign Ministry Archives, read the Russian copy of Alekseev's cable to Khrushchev into the record of our Antigua conference. Prior to this, the existence of the cable was unknown to Western scholars of the crisis.

2. Kurt Vonnegut, *A Man without a Country* (New York: Seven Stories Press, 2005), 20.

3. A telling example of American blindness to Cuba's role is in Robert Kennedy's influential memoir of the crisis, *Thirteen Days: A Memoir of the Cuban Missile Crisis*, afterword by Richard E. Neustadt and Graham T. Allison (New York: Norton, 1971). The final chapter is titled "The Importance of Placing Ourselves in the Other Country's Shoes." It begins this way: "The final lesson of the Cuban missile crisis is the importance of placing ourselves in the other country's shoes" (102). This is an important insight. But it is also the only time "Cuba" or "Cuban" appears in the chapter. As usual in U.S. accounts of the crisis, the phrase *Cuban missile crisis* refers to Cuba only in passing as the temporary location—like parking spots on city streets—of Soviet missiles deemed by Washington to be threatening to U.S. interests. Robert Kennedy continues: "During the crisis, President Kennedy spent more time trying to determine the effect of a particular course of action on Khrushchev or the Russians than on any other phase of what he was doing" (Ibid., 102). While this was an important step, leaving out Cuban "shoes" was a serious error of omission during the crisis, and it has been a serious error of omission in recalling the history of the crisis. Kennedy's successor, President Lyndon Johnson, liked to call Vietnam "that damn little pissant country." (The Wiki entry for "pissant" defines it as "an insignificant or contemptible person or thing.") Johnson's inability to put himself in the shoes of the Vietnamese communists cost him his presidency, and he declined to run for reelection in 1968 after it became clear that his reassurances that the U.S. was winning the war were false. JFK, his brother Robert, and in fact his entire administration treated Cuba in October 1962 as a "damn little pissant country," and it nearly brought about the end of civilization. LBJ is quoted in George Herring, *LBJ and Vietnam: A Different Kind of War* (Austin: University of Texas Press, 2010), 31.

4. Two of the most significant scholarly efforts to include points of view other than Washington's are: Aleksandr Fursenko and Timothy Naftali, *"One Hell of a Gamble": Khrushchev, Castro and Kennedy, 1958–1964* (New York: Norton, 1997); and Michael Dobbs, *One Minute to Midnight: Kennedy, Khrushchev, and Castro on the Brink of Nuclear War* (New York: Knopf, 2008). Among the problems with the Fursenko and Naftali book is the authors' reliance on Russian sources to make inferences about Cuban motivations and capabilities. The book was a milestone, however, in the use of Russian sources to frame an analysis of the Cuban missile crisis. Dobbs, who worked closely on his book with the talented and determined "docu-hounds" at the National Security Archive at George Washington University, is a fluent Russian and Spanish speaker, who unearthed a good deal of new material on the crisis in both Russia and Cuba.

5. Americans' inability to resonate with the Cuban pursuit of martyrdom in the Cuban missile crisis, of the noble sacrifice, is somewhat puzzling in light of similar mythic episodes in U.S. history. The most famous of these is probably the battle of the Alamo, in San Antonio, Texas, in February to March 1836. A couple of hundred "Texians" (as advocates of an independent Texas then called themselves) holed up in a Spanish mission for nearly two weeks before being slaughtered by Mexican forces, under the brutal General Antonio Lopez de Santa Ana. Everyone in the mission was killed. The leader of the Texas independence movement, Sam Houston, made good use of the cry "Remember the Alamo" in subsequent battles with Mexican forces. The Alamo itself, restored to its ruined, heroic splendor, has long been the most popular tourist site in Texas. And of course the lore of the American Civil War is full to overflowing with martyrs, especially (but not only) among the Confederates.

6. Just to give you a sense of how insular the Western understanding of the crisis had become, in the mid-1980s, when we began our investigation, many Western specialists on the Soviet Union actually told us that Nikita Khrushchev's memoirs were probably not written by Khrushchev, but instead had been drafted by the KGB and circulated as "disinformation," or propaganda. This belief was strong, in spite of the compelling detail in the memoirs, and also in spite of having been translated and annotated by several outstanding Western scholars. Fortunately, the full story of Nikita Khrushchev's memoirs came out after the end of the Cold War, written by his son and collaborator in producing the memoirs, Sergei N. Khrushchev. See Nikita Khrushchev, *Khrushchev Remembers*, 2 vols., trans. and ed. by Strobe Talbott, introductions, commentary, and notes by Edward Crankshaw and Jerrold Schecter (Boston: Little, Brown, 1970 and 1974). For the fascinating story of how the memoirs were produced and made their way to the West, see Sergei N. Khrushchev, ed. and trans. by William Taubman, *Khrushchev on Khrushchev: An Inside Account of the Man and His Era, by His Son Sergei Khrushchev* (Boston, Little, Brown, 1990). The punch line: the author of Khrushchev's memoirs is actually *Khrushchev.*

7. As mentioned, we first saw Fidel's "Armageddon letter" on November 23, 1990, when our assistant, David Lewis, translated it from Spanish. The official English version from the Cubans appeared one week later: "Letters Between Fidel and Khrushchev," *Granma*, International English edition, December 2, 1990. *Granma,* the Cuban Communist Party daily newspaper, is named for the yacht that Fidel Castro and eighty-one of his fellow exiles rode from Mexico to Cuba in November 1956 to begin an uprising against the U.S.-backed dictator, Fulgencio Batista, an uprising that would culminate in the triumph of the Cuban Revolution on January 1, 1959. The letters had been published a week before in the Spanish edition of the newspaper. Both editions contain a lengthy introduction that is unsigned but which was written under the close supervision of Fidel Castro. The official Cuban translation, including the introduction and the five letters between Castro and Khrushchev, is reprinted as Appendix 2 to James G. Blight, Bruce J. Allyn, and David A. Welch,

Cuba on the Brink: Castro, the Missile Crisis, and the Soviet Collapse (Lanham, MD: Rowman & Littlefield, 2002), 502–19.

8. The psychological literature on eidetic memory is filled with controversy. Some say such accurate (or "photographic") memory is impossible. Others say it is widespread, especially in children. See Ulric Neisser, *Memory Observed: Remembering in Natural Contexts* (San Francisco: Freeman, 1982), 377–424.

9. We were about to discover how brilliant David Lewis was. We already knew David was quadrilingual: in English, Spanish, French, and German. He had yet to accompany us to Cuba, and had not at this point participated in any of our conferences. When we showed his translation of Fidel's "Armageddon letter" to our colleague Jorge Dominguez of Harvard's Government Department and the leading American scholar of Cuban foreign policy, Jorge was amazed. In particular, according to Jorge, our young colleague had grasped the difference between a preemptive nuclear strike by the Russians, prior to a presumed U.S. attack on Cuba, and a retaliatory strike on the U.S., in response to an annihilating attack on the island that would have already begun. This distinction became very important as we began to try to grasp what Fidel thought he was doing and why what he thought he was doing was not—to use a word that was applied to his request to Khrushchev by Western commentators—"crazy," or "suicidal." As Jorge explained to us, rendering Fidel's state of mind at that pivotal point was both difficult and important, and David Lewis had nailed it. The Cubans, who can be very particular about the translations from Spanish of non-Cubans (David Lewis held Mexican citizenship), eventually agreed with Jorge. At the end of the January 1992 Havana conference on the crisis, Fidel Castro's personal interpreter, Juana ("Juanita") Vera, developed a sore throat, and David actually filled in for her in a private conversation several of us had with Fidel. This had no precedent, according to our Cuban colleagues. David was that good.

10. When we first visited Bejucal, in the spring of 1992, we were impressed by its proximity to both Mariel Harbor, where most of the nuclear-related Russian equipment was off loaded (thirty-seven miles), and to the various command centers in Havana (seventeen miles). It resembled an oversized mogul, or bump, such as one finds on Scottish golf courses, only much larger.

11. We discussed the circumstances regarding the drafting of the letter, at various times in the early 1990s, with both Fidel Castro and Aleksander Alekseev. In addition, another Russian official, Oleg Darusenkov, who was more fluent in Spanish than Alekseev, was periodically called in to help with the drafting and translating process. Darusenkov, who participated in several of our conferences, worked before and after the crisis as a personal aide to Ernesto ("Che") Guevara. In the 1980s, Darusenkov became head of the Cuba desk of the International Department of the Communist Party of the Soviet Union (CPSU). After the end of the Cold War and the collapse of the Soviet Union, Darusenkov made a successful new career for himself selling Mexican soap operas to Russian and East European television networks.

12. Kovaliev, cited in Blight, Lewis, and Welch, *Cuba Between the Superpowers*, 97–98.

13. Jorge Risquet, cited in Ibid., 102. When he made this statement, Risquet was the Politburo member in charge of Cuba's international affairs, a position much more powerful, in the Cuban system of 1991, than the foreign minister. In fact, Risquet became something of a stand-in for Fidel Castro, prior to the January 1992 conference in which Fidel himself participated. Here is Risquet, at the very end of the January 1991 Antigua conference, trying yet again to explain why Fidel Castro's Armageddon letter to Nikita Khrushchev was fully rational, not crazy:

> We did not know on the 26th and 27th that there had already been exchanges between Kennedy and Khrushchev, and that, practically at the same time, an

> agreement was almost at hand. While Fidel wrote his letter and saw an imminent invasion, the basis for an agreement between the U.S. and the Soviets was already taking shape. *We did not know!* Our perception was that there would be an invasion or air strike. . . . So it seems to me that our perception that an invasion or air strike was imminent was a fully rational perception. It was not the product of a feverish mind; it was a fully logical conclusion. (Ibid., 102)

14. The story of the planned nuclear attack on the U.S. naval base at Guantanamo is mainly due to Michael Dobbs. He has established that a joint Russian-Cuban force, led by Colonel Dmitry Yazov and Raul Castro, was set to attack the base with Soviet FKR, nuclear-tipped cruise missiles, once hostilities began. As Dobbs discovered in research in Cuba and Russia, the Americans knew about the FKR missiles in Mayari, where Raul Castro's headquarters were located, but they were convinced the missiles were equipped only with conventional warheads and had no nuclear capability. (This was true generally of U.S. officials. They did not believe Russian nuclear warheads had reached Cuba.) See Dobbs, *One Minute to Midnight*, 124–29. See also Dobbs's illustrated piece on the Guantanamo planning posted on the website of the National Security Archive at George Washington University: http://nsarchive.gwu.edu/nsa/cuba_mis_cri/dobbs/gitmo.htm. If hostilities had begun, and if the Russian FKRs had been equipped with nuclear warheads (which was the Russian-Cuban plan), the U.S. response would have been swift, nuclear, and totally devastating to eastern Cuba, including Cuba's second biggest city, Santiago de Cuba. Thousands would have been killed almost immediately, perhaps tens of thousands, mostly Cuban civilians, but also Russian and Cuban military personnel, including Yazov and Raul Castro. Escalation was virtually guaranteed. Armageddon was just over the horizon.

15. See the special issue of *Arms Control Today*, posted on November 1, 2002, devoted in part to the 2002 Havana conference on the 40th anniversary of the Cuban missile crisis. The quote from Nikolai Leonev (who was head of the KGB in Latin America during the crisis) is from a section called "A Conversation in Havana," edited by Thomas Blanton and James G. Blight, in which Leonev took part, during a lunch break at the conference. Svetlana Savranskaya, director of Russian Studies at the National Security Archive who acted as Leonev's interpreter during the conversation, translated Leonev's remarks.

16. Fidel Castro, letter to U Thant, acting secretary general of the United Nations, November 16, 1962. The entire letter is available in James G. Blight and Philip Brenner, *Sad and Luminous Days: Cuba's Struggle with the Superpowers After the Missile Crisis* (Lanham, MD: Rowman & Littlefield, 2002), 209–13, 213. Excerpts from the letter, and the context in which the letter was drafted and sent, is in James G. Blight and janet M. Lang, *The Armageddon Letters: Kennedy/Khrushchev/Castro in the Cuban Missile Crisis* (Lanham, MD: Rowman & Littlefield, 2012), 197–202.

17. We first heard about Che Guevara's suicidal plan from Oleg Darusenkov, Guevara's personal aide and liaison with the Russian political and intelligence operatives in Cuba. In the early 1990s, we asked a Cuban colleague to check on the story, and he confirmed that such a plan existed: in the event of a U.S. invasion, the Russians and Cubans in the western sector of Cuba planned to mount a nuclear attack against U.S. forces occupying the island, an attack in which they believed they would all be incinerated in a U.S. nuclear counterattack. It is of course unknown whether the plan would have been implemented because the U.S. never invaded the island. But it is known that Guevara was prepositioned with his field commanders in one of the huge caves of the easternmost Cuban province, Pinar del Rio. In addition, the extremity of such a planned martyrdom is completely consistent with Guevara's radical understanding of an inevitable, climactic clash between the forces of socialism and the forces of imperialism. The cave that served as Guevara's headquarters is

called Cueva de los Portales, which has become a Cuban national monument and a popular tourist attraction in western Cuba. See Dobbs, *One Minute to Midnight*, 244–46.

18. Fidel Castro, cited in Blight, Allyn, and Welch, *Cuba on the Brink*, 251.

19. Nikita Khrushchev, quoted in Sergei N. Khrushchev, *Nikita Khrushchev and the Creation of a Superpower* (University Park, PA: Penn State University Press, 2000), 625. In this valuable book, Sergei Khrushchev offers a candid, behind-the-scenes view of his father, Nikita, at the height of his power. In its way, the book is as essential to understanding Nikita Khrushchev as Theodore Sorensen's *Kennedy* and Arthur Schlesinger Jr.'s *A Thousand Days* are to understanding the atmosphere and day-to-day realities faced by the leaders of the superpowers during the dark days of the Cold War. See also Blight and Lang, *The Armageddon Letters*, 112–18 for the Cuban context in which the letter was drafted by Castro and sent by Alekseev. The aide who delivered the contents of Fidel's Armageddon letter orally to Khrushchev was Oleg Aleksandrovich Troyanovsky. At our 1992 Havana conference on the crisis, Troyanovsky reported that he still found it difficult to speak about his experience of receiving Fidel's letter and then summarizing its contents for Khrushchev. Sergei Khrushchev recalls a conversation in which several of us participated at the conference, including Troyanovsky:

> The sharpness of our perceptions is smoothed over with the passage of time. Events that took place many years before begin to be viewed differently, especially since we know the sequel. But even more than a quarter of a century later, Oleg Aleksandrovich [Troyanovsky] couldn't talk about it calmly. The apocalyptic sound of Castro's message, he said, made a shocking impression on him. (S. Khrushchev, *Creation of Superpower*, 626)

20. This is the point argued in our short, animated film, directed by Koji Masutani, "Was Castro Crazy?" available at www.armageddonletters.com and https://www.youtube.com/watch?v=q2Y4314xQ0Q.

21. Vonnegut, *A Man without A Country*, 20.

NOTE TO PART II

1. Leonard Cohen, "You Want It Darker." This is the title track on Cohen's fourteenth and final studio album. Columbia Records released it on October 21, 2016. Cohen, who was suffering from cancer and severe spinal pain when the album was being made, recorded his parts in his home in Los Angeles, and then emailed his material to his musical collaborators. Many acclaimed it as his masterpiece. Cohen died on November 7, 2016, at age eighty-two.

NOTES TO CHAPTER 4

1. The Oxford English Dictionary Online. The definition of *habitable* is at: https://en.oxforddictionaries.com/definition/habitable.

2. Hilary Mantel, interview with Jeffrey Brown, *PBS NewsHour*, April 3, 2015. The interview is available at: http://www.pbs.org/newshour/bb/bringing-tudors-television-wolf-hall/.

3. Peabody, aka Mr. Peabody, and his adopted human son, Sherman, were arguably the smartest and funniest creations of a bygone era of animation. In each show, the two used the WABAC (pronounced "Way Back") machine to time and space travel to meet up with historical figures, prevent disasters, and thus render history more or less what we thought it was all along. Peabody, the super-sophisticated beagle with geeky glasses, and his perpetually clueless though well-meaning accomplice, Sherman, were hugely entertaining and taught our generation of kids a little history to boot. Ninety-one episodes ran on network TV in 1959 and 1960. Lately the egghead duo has undergone a renaissance: a 2013 movie and a 2015 Netflix TV series. In our estimation, Peabody's puns were better (i.e., more ridiculous) in the original version. The 2013 movie does have some good ones, however, such as when Peabody and Sherman space/time travel to ancient Egypt to meet up with Sherman's classmate, Penny, and Peabody declares with arched eyebrow that she is "in de-Nile." Not bad. And the lip-synched animation in the more recent incarnations is certainly more sophisticated.

4. Hilary Mantel, *Wolf Hall* (New York: Henry Holt, 2009), and *Bring Up the Bodies* (New York: HarperCollins, 2012). Hilary Mantel had previously been fairly well known as a British writer of odd, often macabre, Hitchcock-like novels and short stories, and as a book reviewer for the British press, especially *The Guardian*. But her two historical novels about Thomas Cromwell veritably exploded onto the English-speaking literary world beginning in 2009, making her a figure of global renown. Once the author of books that sold very modestly, the first two installments of her Cromwell trilogy sold hundreds of thousands in hardback and millions more globally in more than two-dozen languages. There was a preexistent audience for the books: that group of readers for whom no detail about the Tudors is too trivial, no Tudor scandal less than lascivious. But the size of the Tudor-geek readership is fairly small.

As if by magic, Mantel's combination of magnificent storytelling and her well-publicized obsession with historical accuracy expanded her readership exponentially. We belong in this group of those with no previous interest in, or knowledge of, the English Tudors. Frankly, we were amazed at how vivid this previously unknown (to us) period and cast of characters became to us. We read each of the novels three times. Eventually, we wondered: How might we graft Mantel's method onto a retelling of the Cuban missile crisis, an event few people know anything about, and for whom those who think they know something about it tend to buy into the mythology rather than the reality of what happened in October 1962?

5. For us, the essential herald of Mantel's achievement, and her possible relevance to our enterprise, was a review of *Wolf Hall* by the well-known Harvard Shakespearean scholar Stephen Greenblatt, "How It Must Have Been," *New York Review of Books*, November 5, 2009, 22–25. From the moment we read the first sentence of this brilliant encomium to Mantel's historical fiction, we were hooked, intrigued, and on the lookout for ways to incorporate Mantel's combination of artistry and historical accuracy into our own work. Here is that first sentence, which has in our household achieved iconic status: "*Wolf Hall* is a startling achievement, a brilliant historical novel focused on the rise to power of a figure exceedingly unlikely, on the face of things, to arouse any sympathy at all" (Ibid., 22). Greenblatt refers to Thomas Cromwell, of course. But consider the two personalities who loom largest in the account of the Cuban missile crisis we present in this book: many consider JFK's Defense Secretary Robert McNamara to be a war criminal for his prosecution of the war in Vietnam under Kennedy's successor, Lyndon Johnson, while Fidel Castro, a hero to some, is to many others one of the 20th century's supreme villains, a dictator, a megalomaniac, a man who was obsessed with exerting one-man rule over the island of Cuba for more than half a century. Perhaps, we mused, encouraged by Greenblatt's comments, we could

pick up some pointers from this great novelist about how to bring McNamara and Castro to life, as they experienced it then and there, in the most dangerous crisis in recorded history. We make no claim to be anything like Mantel's equals as storytellers. But we do know the history of the Cuban missile crisis as well as anyone ever has. So, okay, we thought: let's give it a shot.

6. Yes, *of course*, we have seen the BBC's six-part series called simply *Wolf Hall*, even though it covers the period of Cromwell's life in both *Wolf Hall* and *Bring Up the Bodies*. We've seen it several times, and we never cease to be mesmerized by Mark Rylance as Cromwell, who is in every scene and who conveys as much in a furtive glance as many actors communicate in a long monologue. The Royal Shakespeare Company's play is also interesting (we saw it in New York in July 2015), although it has much less of the brooding, often sinister subtlety of the BBC series, with a Cromwell who, as critic James Wood put it, "is reticent, taut, controlled: a master of silences" (James Wood, "Invitation to a Beheading," *The New Yorker*, May 7, 2012, 71–74, 74). The difference is owing to the conventions of live theater, in which one is always at risk of losing the audience if the jokes and slapstick are not forthcoming at frequent intervals. For an insightful comparative analysis of the books, the series, and the play, see Fintan O'Toole, "The Explosions from Wolf Hall," *New York Review of Books*, May 21, 2015, 23–24.

7. Mantel, *Wolf Hall*, 3.

8. "Across the Narrow Sea" is the title of chapter 1 of *Wolf Hall*, 3–14.

9. Hilary Mantel, in "Hilary Mantel, Harriet Walter: The Lives of Others," a discussion moderated by Timberlake Wertenbaker, Union Chapel, London, September 11, 2015. Available at: http://rsliterature.org/library-article/hilary-mantel-harriet-walter-the-lives-of-others/. Unlike many video podcasts involving famous "talking heads," this conversation is well worth watching—more than once. Mantel's principal interlocutor is Harriet Walter, the eminent British actress, and one of Great Britain's greatest Shakespeareans. In this conversation, Mantel and Walter, with considerable assistance from their activist moderator, Timberlake Wertenbaker, compare notes on the possibilities and limitations of fully entering the point of view of another, whether an actual historical character, such as Thomas Cromwell, or many of the fictional characters Walter has played in her forty-year career on stage, in movies, and on television.

10. This is not only our view of Mantel's success in mastering the history of the Tudor age. In fact, our view wouldn't count for much anyway, since most of what we know or believe about the Tudors derives from Mantel's two Cromwell volumes. But you *should* believe the bevvy of Tudor-ists from all over the scholarly world who have expressed their astonishment at both Mantel's command of the facts and the plausibility of the exercise she calls "using the imagination when the facts run out." The indispensible collaborator with Mantel in her effort to "slide inside" Thomas Cromwell is Mary Robertson, who retired in 2013 as the William A. Moffett Curator of British Historical Manuscripts at the Huntington Library in Southern California. Robertson is believed by many scholars to know more about Thomas Cromwell and his world than any living human being. The encomia to Robertson by historians of the period are legendary. (A sample is available at: http://huntingtonblogs.org/2014/05/robertson/.) Hilary Mantel apprenticed herself to Mary Robertson for five years before ever committing a word to the page on Cromwell, and she has worked with her throughout the drafting of both *Wolf Hall* and *Bring Up the Bodies*. Both books are dedicated to Robertson. The dedication to her in *Bring Up the Bodies* is a particularly poignant expression of gratitude of the apprentice to her master, replete with the idiosyncratic spelling found in the documents provided to the student by the master: "Once again to Mary Robertson: after my right harty commendacions and with spede."

11. Mantel, *Bring Up the Bodies*, 406.

NOTES TO CHAPTER 5

1. Søren Kierkegaard, *The Concept of Anxiety: A Simple Psychological Orienting Deliberation on the Dogmatic Issue of Hereditary Sin*, ed. and trans. by Reidar Thomte and Albert B. Anderson (Princeton: Princeton University Press, 1980), 156.

2. Robert S. McNamara, remarks at Brown University, April 27, 2005. See James G. Blight and janet M. Lang, *The Armageddon Letters: Kennedy/Khrushchev/Castro in the Cuban Missile Crisis* (Lanham, MD: Rowman & Littlefield, 2012), 3–16, for the context in which McNamara made these remarks. The quotation itself is on 5, just as it appears in the notes of the event's note taker.

3. Elmore Leonard, *Maximum Bob* (New York: HarperCollins, 1991).

4. One of the central ideas that eventually drove the Cuban missile crisis project that Bob McNamara and we led is traceable to our first meeting with Bob, in July 1984, at a conference in Big Sky, Montana. It was the first major meeting of the Project on Avoiding Nuclear War, headquartered at our home institution, the Center for Science and International Affairs at Harvard's Kennedy School of Government. McNamara was one of the participants. Many of the others were specialists on nuclear strategy and arms control, including several who had worked for McNamara in the Kennedy Defense Department: Ted Warner, Jim Thompson, Tom Schelling, and Richard Zeckhauser, among others. Also participating were academics who had written widely on the nuclear threat. And then there was us, the note-takers, newbies who knew most of the people in the room only by reputation. The task was to examine the threat of nuclear war and then design policy-relevant strategies for reducing the risk.

For much of the first day or so, the conference was, frankly, pretty boring: talking heads taking turns talking and debating various estimates of nuclear risk, the speakers disagreeing politely and only marginally with each other. McNamara did not speak until the first day's discussion was drawing to a close. Finally, he asked to speak. What happened next was extraordinary, at least it seemed so at the time to us. As, however, we became familiar with "Maximum Bob," his performance at the Big Sky conference seemed in retrospect rather typical, at least for him.

We paraphrase Bob's intervention as follows:

> You people don't know what you're talking about. You are talking about some presumed level of risk, at this moment, in the comfort of this isolated conference center, while we all sip our coffee and eat our cookies. Some say the risk is high; most say it is low; everyone seems to think it is in any case manageable. But ladies and gentlemen, this conversation is insane, in light of what I know about the Cuban missile crisis. Together with the Russians, we came very close to destroying our societies and probably all of human civilization with it. What should be of interest is not some vague estimate of the risk of nuclear war at time X, or in situation Y, under conditions of Z. What we should be addressing is: "What brought us to the eve of total annihilation in October 1962?" We have got to be specific, and we have to begin with the missile crisis. But as I look around the room, I don't see anyone—and I include myself here—who knows enough about the missile crisis to put forth a plausible judgment about what happened, what didn't happen, and why, and what are the lessons we should draw from it. I will close with what some of you will think is a provocative proposition: whatever the estimated risk of nuclear war may be today or at some other hypothetical time, the risk in the missile crisis was dangerously high and, because of the possible consequences of such a war and the possibility of

> another such nuclear war–threatening crisis, I believe nuclear weapons must be abolished as soon and as safely as possible.

Beginning in that moment, our talismanic questions became: (1) what actually happened in the Cuban missile crisis; and (2) what are the lessons we need to learn in order never to put human civilization at risk again? More than thirty years later, we are still at it.

5. "Mary Don't You Weep" originated in the American South among slaves. It is a song of both hope and resistance. The most famous version of the song was by an African American gospel group called The Swan Silvertones. In that version, lead singer Claude Jeter inserted a riff about a bridge over deep water that, according to Paul Simon, inspired him to write the iconic 1970 hit song, "Bridge over Trouble Water."

6. Hoyt Axton, "Joy to the World." The most famous version of the song is by the California trio, Three Dog Night, which released it in November 1970 on their fourth studio album, on Dunhill Records.

7. It was an iconic "Maximum Bob" moment. It was April 1999. We were bringing out our new book on the U.S. war in Vietnam: Robert S. McNamara, James G. Blight, and Robert K. Brigham, with Thomas J. Biersteker and Col. Herbert Y. Schandler, *Argument Without End: In Search of Answers to the Vietnam Tragedy* (New York; PublicAffairs, 1999). We were launching the book tour at our home institution, Brown University. Bob was nervous, as he always was when the Vietnam War was to be discussed. He realized fully that people from all across the political spectrum assigned a good deal of the blame for the war to him personally, so he had to be prepared for tough questions, and even the occasional shouting match. Bob's principal strategy in such cases was just to keep talking, to put off the moment of truth when the Q&A portion of the program began. In a moment of cosmic illumination following this particular session at Brown, Bob turned to one of us (JGB) and said: "You're humorous. I'm not humorous. From now on, we need to build some humorous time into our presentation."

8. James G. Blight and David A. Welch, interview with Paul Nitze, at his office on the seventh floor of the U.S. State Department, May 6, 1987. (At the time, Nitze was U.S. Special Ambassador for the arms control negotiations with the Soviet Union.) Also present was Nitze's assistant, Anne Smith, who was assisting Nitze with his memoirs.

9. Roger Angell, "Late Review," *The New Yorker*, January 19, 2004, 31–32, 32.

10. The excerpt is from *The Fog of War* available at: https://www.youtube.com/watch?v=3lrH7RtiobQ.

11. The two books are: McNamara, Blight, and Brigham et al., *Argument Without End*; and Robert S. McNamara and James G. Blight, *Wilson's Ghost: Reducing the Risk of Conflict, Killing and Catastrophe in the 21st Century*, expanded post-9/11 paperback ed. (New York: Public Affairs, 2003).

12. McNamara first went on record with one of us (JGB) and David Welch with these three essential ingredients of his Cuban missile crisis stump speech in an interview on May 21, 1987, at his office in Washington, DC. The interview is in James G. Blight and David A. Welch, foreword by McGeorge Bundy, *On the Brink: Americans and Soviets Reexamine the Cuban Missile Crisis* (New York: Noonday Press of Farrar, Straus & Giroux, 1990), 186–200.

13. Robert S. McNamara, in the 2004 Academy Award-winning Errol Morris film *The Fog of War: Eleven Lessons from the Life of Robert S. McNamara*. The statement, along with other statements in the film by McNamara on the Cuban missile crisis, is available at: https://www.youtube.com/watch?v=3lrH7RtiobQ. The text of McNamara's comments on the missile crisis in the movie is in our book, based on the movie: James G. Blight and janet M. Lang, *The Fog of War: Lessons from the Life of Robert S. McNamara* (Lanham, MD: Rowman & Littlefield, 2005), 59, added.

14. The following sections appeared, in somewhat different order and context, in James G. Blight, Bruce J. Allyn, and David A. Welch, *Cuba on the Brink: Castro, the Missile Crisis and the Soviet Collapse*, expanded paperback ed. (Lanham, MD: Rowman & Littlefield, 2002). The first (hardback) edition appeared in 1993. The book contains the most comprehensive statement ever to appear in print of the Cuban perspective on the event known in Cuba as the "October crisis." The empirical core of the book is the edited, but complete, transcript of the January 1992 Havana conference on the crisis, augmented with nearly three-dozen short essays by the authors that provide historical, cultural, and personal context for the interventions at the conference table.

The original plan, which the two of us worked out with the Cubans on several visits to the island in 1991, was for Fidel to give some introductory remarks, leave the conference, and return three days later to answer questions from the participants. But in the run-up to the conference Fidel, having reviewed the extensive briefing materials received by all participants (mostly declassified documents whose release was obtained by the National Security Archive at George Washington University), was fascinated and angered all over again, as he read about the U.S.-Russian "betrayal" that resolved the crisis without Cuba being consulted or even properly informed about the terms of the agreement. His interest piqued, Fidel's deputy Jorge Risquet informed us in Cuba, the day before the conference was to begin, that Fidel would participate in the entire conference as "just another participant." Sure enough, as we entered the conference room, we scanned name cards identifying the participants and noticed one that said, "Fidel Castro Ruz," using the matronymic that Cubans treat more or less as optional.

The conference was distinguished by a degree of directness and civility that few of us expected, once we learned that Fidel would participate. Fidel's reputation for long, argumentative, rambling statements was already well known to us. The Cold War had ended less than two weeks before the conference began, when the Soviet Union broke up and became, temporarily, The Commonwealth of Independent States. Cubans were wary of their former Russian patron, and their traditional adversary, the U.S. Conference participants, described the experience as revelatory, breathtaking—as authentic a journey back in space and time to Havana, Washington, and Moscow in October 1962 as we are ever likely to achieve.

The conference was recorded in the "floor languages" of the three sets of participants using UN-level simultaneous interpreters. Our team translated the entire conference into English after we returned to Brown University following the meeting.

15. Blight, Allyn, and Welch, *Cuba on the Brink*, 26–28.

16. General Anatoly I. Gribkov, in Ibid., 60–62.

17. Robert S. McNamara, in Ibid., 250–51.

18. Fidel Castro, in Ibid., 251–52.

19. Robert McNamara, in Ibid., 378–79.

20. Sir Arthur Conan Doyle's *The Sign of Four* began its serialization in *Lippincott's Magazine* in February 1890. It is available at: https://www.gutenberg.org/files/2097/2097-h/2097-h.htm#chap06. Holmes's lecture to Watson about possibility and probability takes up most of chapter 6, "Sherlock Holmes Gives a Demonstration. "A postmodern version, with lots of special effects and contemporary touches, appeared in 2014 in the BBC's production, with Benedict Cumberbatch as Holmes and Martin Freeman as Watson. It is called "The Sign of the Three," rather than "Four," for reasons too complex to go into in an endnote.

21. Less than two weeks after the January 1992 Havana conference, we brought the historical highlights home to the U.S. in a briefing at the National Press Club in Washington, DC. Participants in the January 21, 1992, briefing included Robert McNamara; JFK aide and historian Arthur Schlesinger Jr.; Jose Antonio Arbesu, chief of the Cuban Interests

Section in Washington, DC (the top-ranking Cuban diplomat in the U.S.), and a key behind-the-scenes organizer of the Havana conference; and Sergei Khrushchev, son of the former Soviet leader Nikita Khrushchev and his father's biographer. This was the first time, nearly thirty years after the Cuban missile crisis, that knowledgeable Americans, Russians, and Cubans gathered in a public forum in the U.S. to discuss the most dangerous event in recorded history. In addition, several excellent published pieces soon appeared on the conference. See: J. Anthony Lukas, "Fidel Castro's Theater of Now," *New York Times*, January 20, 1992; See especially Arthur Schlesinger Jr., "Four Days with Fidel Castro," *New York Review of Books* 34, no. 6 (March 26, 1992): 22–29. In a rare but startling slip up, the editors of the *New York Review* inserted into Schlesinger's piece a line drawing of the Colombian writer Gabriel Garcia Marquez, who was a close friend of Fidel Castro's but had nothing to do with the Havana conference, and labeled it "Fidel Castro." Even more peculiar: the figure in the drawing (by staff artist David Levine) has him smoking an outsized *pipe* rather than his trademark Cuban cigar. The mystery recently deepened further when, after searching the web, we could find no evidence, either literary or photographic, that Garcia Marquez ever smoked a pipe. (He was in his youth addicted to cigarettes.)

NOTES TO CHAPTER 6

1. Townsend Hoopes, *The Limits of Intervention: An Inside Account of How the Johnson Policy of Escalation in Vietnam Was Reversed* (New York: Longman, 1969), 128–29. This book is an insufficiently appreciated classic, a cautionary tale of what can happen if great powers ignore the mindsets of smaller powers bent on asserting their sovereignty and independence. Hoopes served in the McNamara Pentagon during the years when the war in Vietnam was escalating out of control. The Johnson administration claimed it was in Vietnam to prevent another communist takeover, this time of South Vietnam by North Vietnam. But in Hoopes's persuasive argument, devotion to world communism could not have motivated the forces of Ho Chi Minh to throw themselves at the American meat-grinder year after year, eventually piling up casualties in the millions. Instead, according to Hoopes, "What motivated Hanoi and enabled its leadership to hold 19 million primitive people to endless struggle and sacrifice against odds that were statistically ludicrous was the goal of national independence" (Ibid., 127). This is an example of a phenomenon identified by British philosopher Isaiah Berlin as "the inflamed desire of the insufficiently regarded to count for something among the cultures of the world" (Isaiah Berlin, "The Bent Twig: On the Rise of Nationalism," in *The Crooked Timber of Humanity: Chapters in the History of Ideas* [New York: Knopf, 1959], 238–61, 261.) See also: Robert S. McNamara and James G. Blight, *Wilson's Ghost: Reducing the Risk of Conflict, Killing and Catastrophe in the 21st Century*, expanded post-9/11 paperback ed. (New York: Public Affairs, 2003), 221–23. No leader of modern times, in our view, exceeds Fidel Castro in (to cite Berlin) his passion to make his country "count for something among the cultures of the world." His dedication to this principle was, alas, matched by the incapacity or unwillingness of U.S. and Russian leaders to correctly identify what drove Fidel and the Cuban Revolution to what Washington regarded as excessively emotional and erratic behavior.

2. Fidel Castro, speech on Cuban television, October 23, 1962. Available in an English translation on the website of the University of Texas' Latin American Network Information Center, at: http://lanic.utexas.edu/project/castro/db/1962/19621024.html. This speech of Castro's, like the others on this website, is reprinted from the CIA's translation over its

Foreign Broadcast Information Service (FBIS, pronounced "Fibbus" by Cold War aficionados). On the context in which the speech was given, see James G. Blight and janet M. Lang, *The Armageddon Letters: Kennedy/Khrushchev/Castro in the Cuban Missile Crisis* (Lanham, MD: Rowman & Littlefield, 2012), 76–78. Reading this excerpt now, it almost defies credibility that neither Moscow nor Washington picked up anything worrisome from the speech. When Fidel concludes with "there are no ambiguities of any kind," we now know that this is what he meant: The Yankees are about to attack; the Yankees will nuke Cuba into total oblivion; the Yankees will provide Moscow with the justification they need to nuke the U.S. and destroy it.

3. Readers previously familiar with the vast literature of the Cuban missile crisis may find the emphasis in this chapter strange, even bizarre. Our focus is not on Kennedy or Khrushchev, not on their aides and other subordinates carrying out their orders in a fog of crisis, nor do we frame our perspective as a game, like chess, in which there is a winner and a loser or else the game ends in a tie. It is also not about the weapons themselves—the Russian nukes that Khrushchev ordered installed in Cuba under a cloak of deception and secrecy. All these factors were obviously involved and important in the causation of the crisis, the escalation of the crisis, why the crisis was so dangerous, and why, on the last weekend of October 1962, it appeared to be careening out of the control of leaders in Washington and Moscow, and why the crisis was ultimately resolved short of war.

Throughout this book and in this chapter, we focus on the sources and evolution of the *Cuban* understanding of these events, with special attention to the way Fidel Castro and his Cuban colleagues attempted to transform what they believed was their imminent doom into martyrdom in the cause of world socialism. For the Cubans, and for their forty-three thousand Russian allies manning the missile sites in Cuba, the key to the Cuban missile crisis had nothing to do with avoiding a nuclear war. *Repeat: their objective was not to avoid a nuclear war, the outcome that obsessed leaders in Washington and Moscow.* Rather, in Cuba the issue quickly became: how to derive honor and purpose from a nuclear attack by the U.S. that was inevitable, an attack that would completely destroy Cuba. How might they transform their nascent victimhood into nascent martyrdom? Cuba's quest for martyrdom is blatantly obvious in retrospect if one but takes seriously what the Cubans were actually saying and doing during the year and a half between the failed U.S.-backed invasion at the Bay of Pigs and the Cuban missile crisis. In the event, neither Moscow nor Washington evinced the slightest interest in the Cuban view. The U.S. perspective might be summarized as: "Who gives a damn about the Cubans, who are after all just pawns of the Russians?"

The unholy marriage of martyrdom and weapons of mass destruction is much discussed these days, often in the context of conflict in the Middle East, or South Asia or Northeast Asia. But tiny Cuba was the original laboratory in which was mixed total dedication to a cause requiring the complete liquidation of a much more powerful enemy, combined with proximity (albeit mediated by their Russian ally) to enormous nuclear firepower. Cuba was the original, fast-forward, hyperproliferated state. In June 1962, Cuba had zero nuclear weapons on its territory. By late October, five months later, 162 nukes were present, as were their launch vehicles and Russian specialists capable of firing them.

4. The full text of JFK's speech is available on a very useful website built and maintained by Prof. Vincent Ferraro of Mt. Holyoke College. It is available at: https://www.mtholyoke.edu/acad/intrel/kencuba.htm. A video of the roughly eighteen-minute speech may be found at: https://www.youtube.com/watch?v=rmA9CZqAWO4. For the context in which the speech was written and delivered, see Blight and Lang, *Armageddon Letters*, 70–73. Interestingly, Stephen King, the king of horror novelists, has offered an account of what it was like to watch Kennedy's speech on TV. In King's account, a time and space traveler

from the present (Maine, 2009-ish) finds himself in Dallas, Texas, in October 1962. The protagonist, Jake Epping, is in a bar where he and the waitress are chatting about Cuba. The waitress waves at the TV and says, " 'That stuff . . . Cuba. Like I give a shit.' But on the night of October 22nd, less than a week later, President Kennedy was also talking about Cuba. And then everybody gave a shit" (Stephen King, *9/22/63* [New York: Scribner's, 2011], 504). See 504–7 for the reactions to the speech of the patrons of the Dallas bar, which are compelling.

5. For a fascinating virtual tour of the relevant parts of the U.S. Civil Defense Museum, see: https://www.civildefensemuseum.com/cdmuseum2/supply/water.html. There is a certain weirdness to all the Civil Defense relics of the bygone Cold War era: so much preparation; so many supplies in storage; so much confidence that a nuclear war between the Russians and the Americans could be survived in a bomb shelter; and, when the nuclear war was over (anywhere from thirty minutes to a few hours after it began), you could return to the surface and pick up wherever you left off. It is hard to know how much of this baloney people actually believed, but the fact is: an all-out nuclear war between Russia and the U.S. would have killed hundreds of millions of people in short order and made earth uninhabitable thereafter. *The Road* scenario would have provided the concluding chapter of the saga of life on planet earth. The 17.5 gallons of water, or 17.5 *million* gallons of water in storage, would have meant nothing.

6. Readers seeking a deeper immersion in the literature of the Cuban perspective on the Cuban missile crisis than we provide in *Dark Beyond Darkness* might begin by perusing three previous books deriving from our Cuban missile crisis project, along with their endnotes and references: James G. Blight, Bruce J. Allyn, and David A. Welch, *Cuba on the Brink: Castro, the Missile Crisis and the Soviet Collapse*, expanded paperback ed. (Lanham, MD: Rowman & Littlefield, 2002); James G. Blight and Philip Brenner, *Sad and Luminous Days: Cuba's Struggle with the Superpowers after the Missile Crisis* (Lanham, MD: Rowman & Littlefield, 2002); and Blight and Lang, *Armageddon Letters*.

This chapter on Fidel at the brink of Armageddon draws on all three books, but it leans most heavily on our *Armageddon Letters*. Most of that book deals with Kennedy and Khrushchev. That material, focused on Washington and Moscow, is relevant to this discussion principally for negative reasons: neither the Russians nor the Americans understood the Cuban attitudes we describe in this chapter; neither predicted Cuban behavior and the Cuban-inspired attitudes of Russians in Cuba manning the missile sites; and neither Kennedy nor Khrushchev believed, until it was almost too late, that Cuban attitudes *mattered*.

In this chapter, we use endnotes to highlight those pages of *Armageddon Letters* that are relevant to Fidel's psychological and physical journey to, as he and most Cubans believed in late October 1962, annihilation and martyrdom. The story has emerged from a wide variety of sources in Cuba, to which we have had access over the past thirty years. If you want to follow up on aspects of Fidel's narrative by digging into our primary and secondary sources, we encourage you to do so, as follows: (1) begin with the endnotes to this chapter, and follow them to the relevant section they identify in *Armageddon Letters*. (2) Go to the endnotes in *Armageddon Letters* and explore the scholarly terrain of the crisis. (Suggestion: begin with the two appendices and the endnotes to them; both are focused on our sources.) (3) Head to *Cuba on the Brink* and *Sad and Luminous Days*—both the body of the texts and their endnotes—in addition to many other works (by us and others) that make up what scholars like to call "the literature" of our subject.

Here is the path we recommend: first, you vicariously follow Fidel in his Jeep as he prepares for Armageddon; next, you consult the American and Russian contexts for understanding why Fidel is in his Jeep in the first place; and finally, you get a glimpse of our nerdy world of Cuban missile crisis scholarship. The path looks like this:

Fidel's Narrative →	Enhanced Narrative →	Primary & Secondary Sources
Dark Beyond Darkness →	*Armageddon Letters* →	*Cuba on the Brink* & *Sad & Luminous Days*

For those of you who burrow into the deep scholarship of October 1962, we say, as one of our Harvard mentors, Graham Allison, once said to us: "Welcome to the Cuban Missile Crisis Chowder and Marching Society."

7. Blight and Lang, *Armageddon Letters*, 52–54. This section of *Armageddon Letters* is in the section of the book called "Sleepwalk," which we believe is an apt metaphor for the mutual ignorance with which the leaders of the U.S., Cuba, and Russia confronted each other.

8. Ibid., 54.

9. Ibid., 55–56.

10. Ibid., 55.

11. Ibid., 56. This defiant statement underlies the main title for a path-breaking work on revolutionary Cuba's place in the world of the latter 20th century: Jorge I. Dominguez, *To Make a World Safe for Revolution: Cuba's Foreign Policy* (Cambridge, MA: Harvard University Press, 1989). Dominguez attempts, with notable success and erudition, to understand the central anomaly of Cuban foreign policy after the revolution: this small, poor Caribbean country, so long under the sway of Washington, chose to ally itself with Washington's arch enemy and, in addition, to "go global," as we might now say. Cuban foreign policy, in fact and somewhat shockingly, at times resembled that of a much larger power. In the course of a single decade, 1975 to 1985, Cuban hard power and soft power was projected in such far-flung countries as Angola, Namibia, Zaire/Congo, Ethiopia, and Algeria, in addition to virtually every country in Central America and several in South America as well. The responsibility felt by the Fidelistas in Cuba to "make the Revolution" is also the major theme of Lee Lockwood's remarkable, several-month-long "interview" with Castro, conducted at intervals all over the island in the summer of 1965. The book begins with a handwritten inscription from Fidel: "El deter de todo revolucionario es hacer la Revolución." See Lee Lockwood, *Castro's Cuba, Cuba's Fidel* (New York: MacMillan, 1967). Lockwood's epigraph from Machiavelli's *The Prince* points to the tremendously disruptive nature of the Revolution, especially in its early years: "There is nothing more difficult to carry out, more perilous to conduct, or more uncertain of success, than the initiation of a new order of things" (i).

12. Blight and Lang, *Armageddon Letters*, 56–58.

13. Ibid., 76–78.

14. Ibid., 77.

15. Ibid., 78.

16. Ibid., 112–18.

17. Fidel Castro to Acting Secretary-General of the United Nations, U Thant, hand-delivered to the secretary general by Cuban ambassador to the UN Carlos M. Lechuga, November 15, 1962. Reprinted in full in Blight and Brenner, *Sad and Luminous Days*, 210–13, 213.

18. Keeping Fidel Castro and the Cubans in the dark regarding the Washington-Moscow diplomatic channel had dire consequences. On the last weekend of October 1962, two of the

three participants, the U.S. and Russia, are desperate to end the crisis, head for the exit ramp, and in the process compromise with each other in a way that is face-saving for both Washington and Moscow. The third participant, Cuba, has no idea that there is a deal in the making; Havana still believes that war is inevitable, imminent, and that Armageddon will follow. In fact, just as Kennedy and Khrushchev are becoming truly frightened of losing control of the crisis and thus in a mood to compromise, the Cuban view becomes ever more belligerent, the Cubans feeling they have nothing to lose and posthumous honor to gain by trying to shoot down U.S. reconnaissance planes.

Kennedy had no communication with Castro. But Khrushchev did. Khrushchev seems to have believed that his young ally had lost his mind and become suicidal when he discovered that the Cubans were shooting at U.S. planes. But Khrushchev had only himself to blame. After a year and a half of preparation for catastrophic war with the U.S.; after the deployment of nuclear missiles on the island to buttress Cuban security; and after receiving dozens of confirmations from the Russians that they would go to war on Cuba's behalf—now, in late October 1962, the Cubans are held to be certifiably crazy by both superpowers for trying to implement war plans developed over the past year and a half that they believe are still operative. Bottom line: if one, or possibly two, unarmed U.S. low-flying reconnaissance planes had been shot down (the Cubans failed to shoot down *any*), the U.S. would likely have retaliated by bombing the site responsible for the shoot down. This, in turn, might well have triggered the Russian-Cuban nuking of Guantanamo, and possibly the use of nuclear-tipped FKR cruise missiles (range: roughly forty miles) against the U.S. invasion force just outside Cuban territorial waters. And that would have been the beginning of the end of the world, as it was formerly known.

19. The video of the Mirage F1 low pass is available at the following URL: https://www.youtube.com/watch?v=VYa0bI98kWA.

20. This Armageddon letter of Fidel Castro—its full text and the context in which it was written—is in chapter 3 of *Dark Beyond Darkness.*

21. Blight and Lang, *Armageddon Letters*, 144–48.

22. *Butch Cassidy and the Sundance Kid*, a 1969 film directed by George Roy Hill and written by William Goldman. Paul Newman stars as Robert LeRoy Parker, alias "Butch Cassidy," and Robert Redford as Harry Longabaugh, alias "The Sundance Kid." The film won several Academy Awards and was the largest-grossing film in the year following its release.

23. See a short animated film, *Was Castro Crazy?* (directed by Koji Masutani) that dramatizes the issue of Fidel's mental health, using the *Butch Cassidy and the Sundance Kid* analogy at www.armageddonletters.com (in the short films section) and at https://www.youtube.com/watch?v=q2Y4314xQ0Q.

NOTE TO PART III

1. "Darkness" is widely available in many anthologies and on the Internet. The posting at poetryfoundation.org is also linked to a substantial biographical essay on Byron. A powerful reading of the poem, together with visuals of apocalyptic devastation, can be found at: https://www.youtube.com/watch?v=5uN5btgxsfI.

NOTES TO CHAPTER 7

1. Harry G. Frankfurt, *On Truth* (New York: Knopf, 2006), 101. *On Truth* is Frankfurt's follow-up book to his unexpectedly best-selling *On Bullshit* (Princeton: Princeton University Press, 2005). Frankfurt says throughout *On Truth* that this book was more difficult to

write than its predecessor because so many in academia and elsewhere (but especially in academia) subscribe to a postmodern view: that "truth" contains such a large personal component that, in effect, the term should be dropped, except when it is placed in quotation marks, and thus used in an ironical fashion. Frankfurt acknowledges the obvious: that personal perspectives and biases inevitably mix with objective reality, rendering our understanding a hybrid made of various portions of each. But he is vehement, as we are, about retaining a strong emphasis on the existence of an objective reality, our understanding of which may only be approximated, but, in effect, there really is a *there* there. Frankfurt writes that he refers to truth in "the spirit of [French Prime Minister] Georges Clemenceau's famous response, when he was asked to speculate as to what future historians would say about the First World War: 'They will not say that Belgium invaded Germany' " (Frankfurt, *On Truth*, 27). In our context: historians cannot say—in fact, no one can say truthfully—that nuclear war is impossible, because on the last weekend of October 1962 it was not only possible, it was probable. That's the truth!

2. Leonard Cohen, "Take This Waltz," from Cohen's 1988 album *I'm Your Man*, backup vocals by Jennifer Warnes (CBS Records, 1986).

3. *Shakespeare in Love*, a 1998 film directed by John Madden, produced by Harvey Weinstein, and written by Marc Norman and Tom Stoppard. The film garnered seven Academy Awards, including Best Picture, Best Actress (Gwyneth Paltrow), and Best Supporting Actress (Judi Dench).

4. Nonspecialists, consider yourself alerted: Kenneth Waltz is a revered figure in the field of international relations. Thus, by referring to Waltz as the "bullshitter-in-chief" of the nuclear theory crowd, we are prepared to receive a good deal of abuse in print, none of it, we predict, relevant to our proposition that Waltz's so-called "realist" view of the nuclear threat is, in the sense of the term as used by Princeton's Harry G. Frankfurt, *bullshit.* Even those who totally disagree with his views on nuclear weapons seem, for some reason, almost to worship him. Since he died in 2013, Waltz-mania has only increased.

The deification of Kenneth Waltz began a long time ago. In our era as students at Harvard's Kennedy School of Government (the mid-1980s), one of the first readings assigned in several courses touching on nukes was a 1981 paper by Waltz whose conclusions were rejected by nearly every one of our professors. That paper was: Kenneth N. Waltz, "The Spread of Nuclear Weapons: More May Be Better." It was an *Adelphi Paper* #171, one of a series published by London's International Institute for Strategic Studies, in 1981. Waltz's concluding section begins: "The slow spread of nuclear weapons will promote peace and reinforce international stability." The paper is available online, in its entirety at: https://www.mtholyoke.edu/acad/intrel/waltz1.htm. Virtually all of the ideas on nukes Waltz went on to promote over the next thirty years are already present in his 1981 Adelphi paper. The one teacher of ours who agreed with Waltz was Thomas C. Schelling, who would go on to win the 2005 Nobel Prize in Economics. Tom said he would summarize Waltz's view as espousing "a nuke in every shopping mall," an outcome that would have been consistent with Waltz's zeal for spreading nuclear weapons.

To use an expression that became popular among nuke nerds in the 1990s, Waltz was "a nuclear proliferation optimist." More is better. A lot more is a lot better. Why? Because, to use a metaphor people often used when discussing Waltz's views: in a world full of nukes, leaders and nations behave the way porcupines copulate, which is *very carefully.* Waltz's nemesis over the past quarter-century has been Scott D. Sagan of Stanford. Sagan's book, *The Limits of Safety: Organizations, Accidents and Nuclear Weapons* (Princeton: Princeton University Press, 1993), is a tour de force and, from our perspective, a decisive refutation of Waltz, based on a sophisticated and deeply sourced variant of Murphy's Law called Organization Theory. In his book, and in subsequent writing, Sagan can also be pretty scary, as he catalogues the accidents that, with a slightly different script, could have led to nuclear war. Unsurprisingly, Scott Sagan has always been interested in the Cuban missile crisis and was actually instrumental in arousing our own interest when the three of us were in residence together at Harvard. On the debate between proliferation optimists and pessimists, see also: James G. Blight and David A. Welch, "Risking 'the Destruction of Nations': Lessons of the Cuban Missile Crisis for New and Aspiring Nuclear States," in *Security Studies* 4, no. 4 (June 1995): 811–50.

A final reference to the risk of nuclear accidents deserves its own brief paragraph. Please see British comedian John Oliver's scary, hilarious, informed, and irresistible presentation of the threat of nuclear annihilation at: https://www.youtube.com/watch?v=1Y1ya-yF35g. Our students love it for its entertainment value and also find it appropriately disturbing. If Scott Sagan were a British comedian, he would be the John Oliver who produced that show. And vice versa.

5. Our Harvard teacher Thomas Schelling told us that Stanley Kubrick came to visit him when Kubrick was in the early stages of making a film about the nuclear threat. In effect, it was to be Kubrick's response to the Cuban missile crisis, which had just concluded. Kubrick told Tom he wanted to make a serious film in which nuclear war began via some means that people like Tom—experts on nuclear strategy and arms control—believed were plausible. Tom told Kubrick that he didn't believe a nuclear war could start by any plausible path he could think of. Kubrick said later that because people like Tom Schelling actually believed that nuclear war had a vanishingly small likelihood, he believed he had entered a real-life version of the theater of the absurd and, for this reason, *Dr. Strangelove* became a satire—a very dark satire, certainly, but a film drenched in the absurdities of the assumptions of those who were sometimes called, in those days, the "nuclear priesthood."

6. Sigmund Freud, ed. by Angela Richards, *New Introductory Lectures on Psychoanalysis* (New York: Penguin, 1987), Vol. 2 of the Penguin Freud Library, 105–6. (Originally published in 1933.) Whatever one may think of Freud these days—his reputation seems lately to be shakier than it has in a long time—Freud's influence has been vast. As the poet W. H. Auden wrote about Freud: "To us he is no more a person now, but a whole a climate of opinion" (W. S. Auden, "In Memory of Sigmund Freud," in *W. H. Auden, Collected Poems,* edited by Edward Mendelson (New York: Random House, 1976], 215–18, 217 for quote; also available at: https://www.poemhunter.com/best-poems/wh-auden/in-memory-of-sigmund-freud/.)

7. Joan Didion, *The Year of Magical Thinking* (New York: Knopf, 2005).

8. Mickey Baker and Sylvia Vanderpool (aka "Mickey and Sylvia"), "Love Is Strange," issued on Groove Records, 1956. Watch and listen at: https://www.youtube.com/watch?v=3DbyAdxp4DQ.

9. Dave Barry, *Dave Barry Is Not Making This Up* (New York: Random House, 1994). Barry has said that when he uses this expression he wishes "to distinguish between fact and hyperbole." It is in this context that the "Barry Rule" seems to apply to an analysis of Kenneth Waltz's view on nuclear weapons. We have discovered from our students, the vast majority of whom have never heard of Kenneth Waltz—there is some suspicion that we are making him up. How, the skeptics ask, could someone possibly believe what we attribute to him? If you are inclined to be skeptical, we do solemnly swear: Jim Blight and janet Lang are not making Kenneth Waltz up.

10. Scott D. Sagan and Kenneth N. Waltz, *The Spread of Nuclear Weapons: A Debate* (New York, Norton, 1995), 44. This is a fascinating book by two leading, amiable, but deeply opposed specialists on nuclear danger. A subsequent 2nd edition appeared in 2003: *The Spread of Nuclear Weapons: A Debate Renewed* (New York: Norton, 2003), with new sections on India, Pakistan, terrorism, and missile defense. The main body of the book remains the same, as neither author was able to convince the other of, basically, anything.

11. Sagan and Waltz, *Spread of Nuclear Weapons*, 44–45.
12. Ibid., 45.
13. Ibid., 45.
14. Ibid., 5.
15. In his decade and a half of intermittent debate with Kenneth Waltz over the risk of nuclear war, Scott Sagan must have occasionally been on the verge of tearing his hair out from pure frustration. Waltz's "nuclear optimism" is anti-intellectual, which is a serious charge to level against an individual regarded as nothing if not an intellectual. Here is Waltz, responding to Sagan's litany of nuclear accidents, including several occurring at the height of the Cuban missile crisis:

> "Love is like war," the chaplain says in Bertolt Brecht's *Mother Courage*, "it always finds a way." For half a century [as of 1995], *nuclear* war has not found a way. The old saying, "accidents will happen," is translated as Murphy's Law holding that anything that can go wrong will go wrong. Enough has gone wrong, and Scott Sagan has recorded many of the nuclear accidents that have, or nearly have, taken place. Yet none of them has caused anybody to blow anybody else up. (Waltz and Sagan, *Spread of Nuclear Weapons*, 93)

In other words, according to Waltz, Sagan's examples of near misses to nuclear detonations and, in some cases, to nuclear war, actually prove that the optimist Waltz, not the pessimist Sagan, is correct. We fallible human beings have inadvertently "tried" to blow up the world, so to speak, but we just haven't succeeded. Waltz's conclusion: "Deterrence has worked 100 percent of the time. We can deter small nuclear powers. After all, we have deterred big nuclear powers like the Soviet Union and China. So sleep well" (Emily Langer, "Kenneth N. Waltz, Scholar of International Relations, Dies at 88," *Washington Post*, May 21, 2013).

But this is precisely the sort of comment that Harry G. Frankfurt calls "bullshit," in the following sense: "Bullshit is unavoidable whenever circumstances require someone to talk without knowing what he is talking about. Thus the production of bullshit is stimulated whenever a person's obligation or opportunities to speak about some topic exceed his knowledge of the facts that are relevant to the topic" (Frankfurt, *On Bullshit*, 63). What is it, specifically, that Waltz cannot possibly know? The short answer is: *the past and the future.* He can't possibly know enough about the proximity to nuclear war in past events to conclude that, for all time, we are safer with nukes than without them. And he knows nothing whatever about the future, and the extent to which, in the felicitous phrasing of the poet Elizabeth Barrett Browning, "the future will [or will not] copy fair my past" (Elizabeth Barrett Browning, "Sonnets from the Portuguese," Sonnet #42, in *Robert and Elizabeth Barrett Browning: Poems and Letters,* selection by Peter Washington (New York: Knopf, 2003], 197–98, quote on page 197, works in brackets added.) Waltz is bullshitting us when he tells us we can "sleep well" because the peace is protected by thousands of nukes.

So we must ask ourselves: Should we bet on Waltz or Sagan? Does nuclear optimism or nuclear pessimism make more sense? It's a no-brainer. Waltz's complacency is unsupported by anything other than his arrogant claim to know what he cannot know, whereas Sagan's skepticism is documented by the historical facts as they are currently revealed to us, including virtually everything about the Cuban missile crisis we have discovered over the past thirty years.

16. It is generally claimed that Waltz's greatest contribution to the study of international relations is his *Theory of International Politics* (New York: Addison-Wesley, 1979). Some claim that it is the most influential book written by an international relations scholar since World War II. It is a deceptive book, in our view. It is filled to overflowing with symbolic logic,

hair-splitting distinctions between different types of "isms," and, in general, Waltz's book puts on the airs of a scientific treatise. The problem is that there is no science to underpin Waltz's superstructure. He talks the talk of a science of international relations, but he cannot walk the walk, because international politics is an art form—a high-stakes art form, but still an art form. The behavior of sovereign states, Waltz's subject matter, cannot be studied in a laboratory, the variables cannot be manipulated in blinded studies, and all retrospective attempts to do so are delusional. There may be patterns, or there may not be patterns. But there are no laws. There is no reason to think we know nearly enough to feel comfortable that reasonable leaders will find ways to avoid Armageddon in perpetuity. There is only "a woven web of guesses," as the philosopher Sir Karl Popper once put it, channeling the Greek philosopher Xenophanes of Colophon (Karl R. Popper, *Conjectures and Refutations: The Growth of Scientific Knowledge* (New York: Routledge, 1963), 34.

17. Kenneth Waltz, "Why Iran Should Get the Bomb: Nuclear Balancing Would Mean Stability," *Foreign Affairs*, July/August 2012, 1–5, available online at: https://www.acsu.buffalo.edu/~fczagare/PSC%20504/Waltz.pdf. See also Waltz's follow-up interview with Zachary Keck of *The Diplomat*, posted July 8, 2012, at: http://thediplomat.com/2012/07/kenneth-waltz-on-why-iran-should-get-the-bomb/.

18. See Bruce Riedel, "Farewell, Sandy Berger, the Clinton Man Who Stopped Armageddon," posted on *The Daily Beast*, December 2, 2015. Riedel, who worked for Berger at the time on the National Security Council, credits Berger, and his boss President Bill Clinton, with preventing a South Asian nuclear catastrophe that seemed very close to igniting.

19. Waltz, interview with Zachary Keck.

20. *Shakespeare in Love* (see endnote 3, above, this chapter).

21. On October 19, 1962, in a meeting with the Joint Chiefs of Staff at the White House, Gen. Curtis LeMay urged Kennedy to attack Cuba immediately and massively with U.S. air power. Getting nowhere with Kennedy, LeMay became frustrated and told the president that in refusing to attack Cuba, Kennedy's behavior was "worse than the appeasement at Munich" (in reference to Britain's September 1938 capitulation to Hitler's designs on Czechoslovakia). You can listen to LeMay's rant, and Kennedy's only partially successful attempt to mask his anger with humor, at: http://www.history.com/speeches/lemay-and-kennedy-argue-over-cuban-missile-crisis. Even the agreement between Kennedy and Khrushchev on October 28th left LeMay completely unmoved. Believing that the agreement was a "hoax" perpetrated by Khrushchev, and that the Russians had no intention of removing their missiles from Cuba, LeMay said that the agreement to end the crisis and the threat of nuclear war was "the greatest defeat in our history." See Robert Dallek, "JFK vs. the Military," *The Atlantic*, September 2013 commemorative issue on the fiftieth anniversary of the assassination of President John F. Kennedy in Dallas. Bob McNamara recalls these moments in Errol Morris's 2014 Academy Award-winning film *The Fog of War: Eleven Lessons from the Life of Robert S. McNamara*.

> In a sense, we'd won. We got the missiles out without war. My deputy and I brought the five Chiefs over and we sat down with Kennedy. And he said, "Gentlemen, we won. I don't want you ever to say it, but you know we won, I know we won." And LeMay said, "Won? Hell, we lost. We should go in and wipe 'em out today." LeMay believed that ultimately we're going to confront these people in a conflict with nuclear weapons. And, by God, we better do it when we have greater superiority than we will have in the future. (From the script of *The Fog of War*, available at: http://www.errolmorris.com/film/fow_transcript.html.)

McNamara's crazed cackle while telling this tale suggests how absurd he thought LeMay's position was and adds depth to McNamara's view that if someone other than Kennedy had been president in October 1962, events could easily have led to Armageddon.

22. Alan Robock, "An Open Letter to President-Elect Trump About Nuclear Weapons and Nuclear Winter," *Bulletin of the Atomic Scientists*, posted November 11, 2016. See also Robock's much more detailed, but still lucid and quite readable, review of the emerging science of nuclear winter, in *Climate Change* 1 (May/June 2010): 418–27. A pdf of this illuminating article is available online on Alan Robock's website at Rutgers: http://climate.envsci.rutgers.edu/pdf/WiresClimateChangeNW.pdf.

23. A useful portal through which to enter the findings of contemporary climate science and nuclear winter is Alan Robock's 2013 TED talk in Hoboken, New Jersey, posted on August 31, 2013, "Nuclear Winter: Still Possible But Preventable," available at: https://www.youtube.com/watch?v=qsrEk1oZ-54. Robock is particularly good, just as in a previous generation Carl Sagan was very good, at assisting nonspecialists to connect the dots of climate science, computer modeling of nuclear weapons blast and atmospheric effects, disrupted weather patterns across the globe, agronomy under the deprivations of nuclear winter, and many other factors that have led to a resurgence of interest in nuclear winter to a level not seen since the scary days of the first Reagan administration in the early 1980s. Robock's use of graphics, screwball humor, and a nerdy but knowing demeanor together make him an ideal purveyor of news to nonscientists that is both disturbing and exceedingly complicated. The TED talk, in the standard eighteen-minute format, gives the big picture of the "forest" of contemporary climate science and the ways it bears on the potential consequences of even a so-called small nuclear war.

If, however, you seek a more detailed view of the "trees" of climate science, with an eye toward understanding why the concept of a "small" nuclear war should be dropped from our vocabulary, see Michael J. Mills, Owen B. Toon, Julia Lee-Taylor, and Alan Roback, "Multidecadal Global Cooling and Unprecedented Ozone Loss Following a Regional Nuclear Conflict," posted at *Earth's Future*, April 1, 2014. You will understand from the first word of the title to this piece—*multidecadal*, a word that is second nature to Robock et al. but which we had never before encountered—that you have entered (to slightly alter the metaphor of green things from trees to weeds) the deep weeds of a very multidisciplinary science.

24. For a powerful exhibit of photos of Hiroshima, pre- and post-bombing, see the collection of Alan Taylor, "Hiroshima Bombing Before and After the Atomic Bombing: 25 Photos," posted on May 12, 2016, at: https://www.theatlantic.com/photo/2016/05/hiroshima-before-and-after-the-atomic-bombing/482526/. The occasion was the visit, a few days later, of President Barack Obama to Hiroshima, the first U.S. president ever to do so.

25. Carl Sagan was probably the most controversial and influential anti-nuclear activist-intellectual of the nuclear age. In addition to his undoubted brilliance as a climate scientist, he was a driven and talented promoter of his ideas and himself with the public via his best-selling books for lay people and his spectacularly successful TV series (and book) *Cosmos*. A brief and admiring account of Sagan's life and work may be found in Joel Achenbach's piece in *Smithsonian Magazine*, March 2014, available online at: http://www.smithsonianmag.com/science-nature/why-carl-sagan-truly-irreplaceable-180949818/?all. For a more critical, yet still appreciative view of Sagan's impact on science and science policy, see Jill Lepore, "The Atomic Origins of Climate Science," *New Yorker*, January 30, 2017. Lepore quotes the conservative pundit William F. Buckley on some testimony Sagan had given before a Congressional committee investigating nuclear winter. Buckley said Sagan was so arrogant "that he reminded me of, well, me." When it aired in 1980, *Cosmos* became the most watched program in the history of PBS. Sagan's charisma was conveyed by the combination of his scientific knowledge, a killer stare at the camera, and a deep, rolling baritone that dwelled on the consonants, thereby seeming to actually speak in the oral equivalent of italics, with almost everything getting special emphasis. Carl Sagan was equal parts Ivy League professor and Old Testament prophet. Here is a three-minute clip from

Cosmos dealing with the nuclear threat: https://www.youtube.com/watch?v=kdTmAQksc54.

26. See Robock, "Nuclear Winter"; Robock, "TED Talk"; and Robock, in a 2014 TV interview explaining why the climatic consequences of a nuclear war have become his preoccupation: https://www.youtube.com/watch?v=-clx85iTvrE.

27. Our analysis in this section is indebted to the pioneering work of Alan Robock, climatologist of Rutgers University (and a member of the Intergovernmental Panel on Climate Change, which shared the 2007 Nobel Peace Prize with Al Gore, former U.S. vice president and a global leader of the campaign to stop and reverse climate change); and also Ira Helfand, of the International Physicians for the Prevention of Nuclear War (IPPNW), a group that won the 1986 Nobel Peace Prize for its work in promoting our understanding of the medical consequences of a global nuclear war.

Two sources—one by Robock and one by Helfand—are key to understanding the global consequences of a nuclear war between India and Pakistan, and thus why it must never occur. See: (1) Alan Robock, "Nuclear Famine and Nuclear Winter: Climatic Effects of Nuclear War, and Catastrophic Threats to the Global Food Supply." Given at a symposium on The Dynamics of Possible Nuclear Extinction, at the New York Academy of Medicine, March 1, 2015. It is accessible at: https://ratical.org/radiation/NuclearExtinction/AlanRobock022815.html. Robock reports the results of recent computer modeling studies carried out with collaborators Michael Mills, Brian Toon, and Lily Xia. (2) Ira Helfand, *Nuclear Famine: Two Billion People at Risk?* (Global Impacts of Limited Nuclear War on Agriculture, Food Supplies and Human Nutrition), 2nd ed., November 2013. See the full report at: http://www.psr.org/assets/pdfs/two-billion-at-risk.pdf.

There are three separable issues in any analysis of the global impact of war in South Asia: (1) the risk of war between India and Pakistan; (2) the risk that any war between India and Pakistan will go nuclear; and (3) the risk that a nuclear war in South Asia will lead to nuclear winter and extinction of the human species. There is reason to worry on all three counts: (1) is always too high, and sometimes it is very high; and because (2) is estimated by most specialists to be progressively higher, as Delhi and Islamabad depend increasingly on their nukes to underwrite their efforts to get their way in the region. (Pakistan has the fastest-growing nuclear arsenal in the world.) For an insider's account of how dicey the South Asian nuclear situation can get, see: Bruce Riedel, *Deadly Embrace: Pakistan, America, and the Future of Global Jihad* (Washington, DC: Brookings, 2011), especially 38–59.

It is on (3) that the work of Robock, Helfand, and their colleagues is of the greatest importance. They believe the international community, led by the great powers, especially the U.S., must begin to view the prevention of nuclear conflict in South Asia as having a direct impact on the security of peoples and countries all over the world—as a possibility that can be ignored only by ignoring *one's own* national interests. In other words, avoiding nuclear war in South Asia, viewed in the light of the new research on nuclear winter and nuclear famine, is as important to U.S. security interests as preventing nuclear war in Missouri, California, et al.

28. In some accounts, Stalin said this to British Prime Minister Winston Churchill at the 1943 Tehran Conference, after Churchill objected to Stalin's suggestion that the Allies open a second front in France.

29. Cormac McCarthy, *The Road* (New York: Random House, 2006), 278–81.

NOTES TO CHAPTER 8

1. An earlier version of this chapter appeared in a piece for *Truthdig*: "The Goldsboro Incident" at http://www.truthdig.com/report/item/the_goldsboro_incident_how_the_world_might_have_ended_20150623 (posted June 23, 2015).

2. The Macmillan entry for *dumb luck* is at: http://www.macmillandictionary.com/dictionary/american/dumb-luck.

3. On April 15, 1912, the *Titanic* sank, after a collision with an iceberg. More than 1,500 people perished, including Captain E. J. Smith. E. J. Smith, quote in Nassim Nicholas Taleb, *The Black Swan: The Impact of the Highly Improbable*, 2nd ed. (New York: Random House, 2010), 42.

4. Our former colleague and collaborator, Robert McNamara, took considerable flak from foreign policy and defense intellectuals for his absolute insistence on the total abolition of nuclear weapons. Bob's critics argued roughly as follows: U.S. and Russian nuclear weapons, and the ever-present, moment-to-moment threat of a civilization-ending Armageddon, have probably contributed greatly to the absence of World War III—despite the tremendous tensions, ideological disparities, and incompatible ambitions of the two superpowers. That's the critics' first point: nukes do a lot of the heavy lifting in preventing global war. They also made a second point: trying to abolish nukes in a world in which thousands already exist could be very dangerous, and it might actually increase the risk of Armageddon. Thomas Schelling, our teacher and a strategist who once advised McNamara while he was secretary of defense, emphasized the potential danger inherent in a world without nukes but in which many countries and even some subnational groups know how to build nukes and to deliver them. The problem, according to Tom Schelling, would be "hair-trigger mobilization plans to rebuild nuclear weapons and mobilize or commandeer delivery systems. Every crisis would be a nuclear crisis. Any war could become a nuclear war" (quoted in "The Unkicked Addiction," *The Economist*, March 7, 2015).

McNamara never claimed that a world with zero nukes would be paradise. But underlying his nuclear abolitionism was this implicit ethical principle: anything that can be done to (in his phrase) "lengthen the fuse" between the onset of a crisis and igniting a nuclear Armageddon should be done. This elapsed time is so precious, he believed, that it is worth paying a high price in resources and in political compromise with those who may not share our values to the degree we might wish. In holding this view, McNamara was in sophisticated company. Noted British philosopher Derek Parfit put the matter this way in the conclusion to his influential 1984 book, *Reasons and Persons* (Oxford, UK: Oxford University Press, 1984):

> I believe that if we destroy mankind, as we now could, this outcome would be much *worse* than most people think. Compare three outcomes:
>
> (1) Peace.
> (2) A nuclear war that kills 99% of the world's existing population.
> (3) A nuclear war that kills 100%.
>
> (2) would be worse than (1), and (3) would be worse than (2). Which is the greater of the two differences? Most people believe that the greater difference is between (1) and (2). I believe the difference between (2) and (3) is *very much* greater. (453; emphases in the original)

What most disturbed Bob McNamara, and what concerned Derek Parfit, was the prospect of terminating the human experiment (3), after only a few thousand years of what we now regard as civilization, versus an outcome—while hideous, regrettable, filled with horror beyond description—that provides for the possible rebuilding of human civilization on the only planet we are sure is suitable for us. In this sense, for McNamara and Parfit, those involved in a nuclear war would be committing an act that is immoral beyond the usual dimensions of morality and immorality. It would be actualizing the unthinkable. Parfit tells why this is so: "If we do not destroy mankind, these few thousand years may be only a tiny fraction of the whole of civilized human history. The difference between (2) and (3) may thus be the difference between this tiny fraction and all of the rest of human history. If we compare this possible history to a day, what has occurred so far is only a fraction of a second" (453–54).

Is it any wonder that in the last quarter-century of his life, Bob McNamara roamed the earth like an ethics-obsessed Diogenes, searching for a way to make the ultimately immoral act—one that he and his colleagues and adversaries nearly committed in October 1962—impossible, or as close to impossible, as fallible human beings can make it?

5. Kenneth Waltz, the bullshitter-in-chief of nuclear strategy and arms control, rejected all of this as irrelevant because the psychology of leaders, he believed, was irrelevant to state behavior. Waltz was in love not only with nukes but also with his so-called "realist" theory: states are like billiard balls (or can be seen to act like billiard balls); they move in directions they are pushed or pulled; leaders—those who think they are in charge of the foreign and domestic policy of states—don't really matter, for purposes of predicting and explaining state behavior; and the psychological reality of those in charge—their thoughts, motives, feelings, state of mind—is irrelevant to state behavior. We repeat, as we wrote in the previous chapter: we are not making this up. We wish we were. We wish Waltz were a figment of our imaginations. But he was real, and really well regarded, and really influential. He still is.

Waltz's love affair with his theory, and with nukes, drives his view of the triviality of the kinds of accidents that are the empirical core of the analysis of Waltz's nemesis, Scott Sagan. In our view, psychological factors, what leaders believe in a crisis in which the possibility is real that it may go nuclear, are the least predictable "accidents" of all. Who knows what leaders might think in a situation for which there can be no realistic preparation, when they seem to be on the brink of nuclear war?

What follows is, we believe, the essence of Kenneth Waltz's view of why accidents in general, and the psychological aspects of leaders on whose decisions nukes may be detonated or not, are all fluff, inventions, of nervous Nellies like Scott Sagan and other nuclear fussbudgets. As you read it, try to call to mind what we now know—what you now know—about the Cuban missile crisis. Here is Waltz:

> Who cares about the "cognitive" abilities of leaders when nobody but an idiot can fail to comprehend their destructive force? How can leaders miscalculate? For a country to strike first without certainty of success, all of those who control a nation's nuclear weapons would have to go mad at the same time. Nuclear reality transcends political rhetoric. (Scott D. Sagan and Kenneth N. Waltz, *The Spread of Nuclear Weapons: A Debate* [New York: Norton, 1995], 98.)

By Waltz's reckoning, Kennedy, Khrushchev, and Castro were all "idiots" because all miscalculated. But were they idiots? Or did they have good reasons for believing what they believed and acting as they did? And was Fidel Castro "mad" when he urged Khrushchev on the final weekend of October 1962 to nuke the U.S. after the U.S. invasion of Cuba had begun? Or was Fidel sane, as we believe, but trapped in a crazy situation? Was the Cuban missile crisis so dangerous, and so relevant to our world, because Fidel was crazy, or because he was sane?

6. The scary details of the Goldsboro incident are in Eric Schlosser, *Command and Control: Nuclear Weapons, The Damascus Accident, and the Illusion of Safety* (New York: Penguin, 2013), 245–53. This prize-winning book is a marvel of investigative reporting. As usual, the devil is in the details, and Schlosser's book serves up thousands of details in his history of nuclear-related accidents.
7. Our subtitle is inspired by Ron Rosenbaum's fascinating account of how specialists think about the nuclear threat: *How the End Begins: The Road to Nuclear World War III* (New York: Simon & Schuster, 2011).
8. On virtual history, see James G. Blight, janet M. Lang, and David A. Welch, *Virtual JFK: Vietnam If Kennedy Had Lived*, paperback edition with a new preface on the war in Afghanistan (Lanham, MD: Rowman & Littlefield, 2010), especially chapter 6, 198–249. We address the question: If Kennedy had not been assassinated, and had been reelected president in 1964, would he have "Americanized" the war in Vietnam, as did his successor, Lyndon B. Johnson? Our answer is "no," though not everyone agrees with us. See also the companion film to the book, by Koji Masutani, also called "Virtual JFK: Vietnam If Kennedy Had Lived." Information on the film is available at: http://virtualjfk.com.
9. Schlosser, *Command and Control*, 485.

10. This is the concluding line in "Who Cares About the Cuban Missile Crisis?" a short, partially animated film by Koji Masutani available at www.armageddonletters.com (in the short films section) and at https://www.youtube.com/watch?v=zObCklM5LPw. We have tried, in the space of just over four minutes, to convey the essence of what we have learned in thirty years of research on the crisis.

11. In addition to a chaotic conflict at the moment of independence from Great Britain in the late 1940s, the wars between India and Pakistan usually categorized as "major" occurred in 1965 (over the disputed territory of Jammu/Kashmir, along the northwest borderlands); in 1971 (over who would rule the former East Pakistan—which became the independent state of Bangladesh); and in 1999 (again, over jurisdiction in Jammu/Kashmir). There have been hundreds of incidents, however, often involving Islamic terrorists, underwritten and encouraged by Pakistan, attacking Indian positions in Jammu/Kashmir, or carrying out terrorist operations in other parts of India. The Indians, for their part, often react with overwhelming military force to Pakistani-inspired incidents. These have become especially worrisome since May 1998, when both Pakistan and India conducted open testing of their nuclear weapons. Both sides now know that the other side could go nuclear, if it so chose. Western analysts believe that the Pakistani nuclear forces have a shorter "fuse" than the Indian forces: the Pakistanis must, in other words, be prepared to go nuclear earlier than the Indian forces due to the disparity in the size of the military forces of both countries. Pakistan, being much smaller than India, would not be able to hold out for long, it is believed, in the face of a full-scale Indian onslaught; India, on the other hand, with its massive conventional military forces, could take a "wait and see" attitude.

12. The episode was very believable, based on our own understanding of past crises involving India, Pakistan, and the U.S. The summary of the relevant parts of the plot is our own. (Sorry: we omitted the scene in which we learn that the U.S. secretary of state broke her washing machine, which her hubby, NSC staffer Henry McCord, fixes, of course.) The complete script is available online at: http://www.springfieldspringfield.co.uk/view_episode_scripts.php?tv-show=madam-secretary-2014&episode=s02e18. (The header in the document seems to indicate that the show aired in 2014. Actually, it first aired on March 27, 2016.)

NOTES TO CHAPTER 9

1. Cormac McCarthy, *The Road* (New York: Random House, 2006), 160–61.
2. George Gordon, Lord Byron, letter of late July 1816, from the Villa Diodati, Geneva, Switzerland. Quoted in Gillen D'Arcy Wood, *Tambora: The Eruption That Changed*

the World (Princeton, NJ: Princeton University Press, 2014), 66. Wood does not give the date of the letter or to whom it was addressed. But see William K. Klingaman and Nicholas P. Klingaman, *The Year without Summer: 1816, and the Volcano That Darkened the World and Changed History* (New York: St. Martins, 2013), 135, on which we are told that the letter was addressed to Byron's British publisher, and written on July 22, 1816. Byron's publisher was John Murray, son of the founder of the legendary British publishing house, also called "John Murray, Publishers"; and Byron did indeed write to Murray on July 22, 1816. But we cannot find the passages in question—the "stupid mists," etc. In that letter, which is full of gossip, Byron says he supposes he ought to apologize for his egotism, "but it's not entirely my fault"—a thoroughly Byronesque statement. The letter is available online at: https://petercochran.files.wordpress.com/2011/01/byron-and-murray-1816-18192.pdf. We will leave further exploration of this tidbit of Byroniana to the Byronologists.

3. Gillen D'Arcy Wood, "1816, The Year without a Summer," in BRANCH (Britain, Representation and Nineteenth Century History), no date (but probably 2014, the year Wood's *Tambora* was published). The article is available online at: http://www.branchcollective.org/?ps_articles=gillen-darcy-wood-1816-the-year-without-a-summer. The piece contains a concise summary of the contents of Wood's *Tambora.* See also Wood, *Tambora,* "Introduction: Frankenstein's Weather," 1–11.

4. Wood, "1816, The Year without a Summer."

5. The 1815 eruption of Mt. Tambora in what is now Indonesia, and the subsequent "year without a summer" of 1816, were until recently little known or appreciated outside the small community of scientists who study volcanoes. But with the 2015 two hundredth anniversary of the eruption approaching, two new books appeared that were written for lay people, both historically well informed but very accessible. The first to appear was W. K. Klingaman and N. P. Klingman (father and son, historian and meteorological scientist, respectively), *The Year without Summer: 1816* (2013). It is really two books in one: mainly a straightforwardly historical account, drawing on a plethora of sources from many regions of the world, interspliced with a scientific counterpoint in which the historical accounts are placed in the context of current knowledge: regarding floods, famines, temperature reductions, and the probable effects of all of the above on social disintegration. The book is especially strong, and quite moving, on how the calamitous weather resulted in vast flooding in the lower regions of Ireland, especially the north; the onset of epidemics; and the beginnings of the Great Migration of the Irish to other parts of the English-speaking world, notably the U.S. but also Canada, Australia, and New Zealand.

Although the Klingamans' book is solid and readable, Gillen D'Arcy Wood's *Tambora* is a much rarer creature: a brilliantly uncategorizable book—part scientific treatise, part memoir of a globe-trotting adventurer, part exegesis of some of the great works of English literature influenced by Tambora's eruption, and part Jeremiad about the climate crisis on our horizon of the 21st century, unless the human race finds within itself the gumption to turn global weather patterns around by consuming less, much less, atmosphere-polluting fossil fuel. Wood, who is descended from a long line of Australian Protestant clergymen, has written books on romantic poetry and a historical novel about a plague (which actually occurred) in New York City in the early 19th century.

What comes across indelibly in *Tambora* is Wood's insatiable curiosity and his willingness to follow clues to the history of Tambora wherever they may lead, by whatever means is necessary. Just to give one example: early in the book, Wood discusses the various characteristics of the mountain in Indonesia, Mt. Tambora, the eruption of which has become his obsession. Suddenly, almost without warning, the reader becomes aware that Wood is describing his own climb of this isolated, treacherous mountain, lugging his cameras and notebooks with him. In so doing, Wood distinguishes himself as an excellent travel writer, in addition to his obvious comfort and familiarity in the various scientific literatures that bear on the argument he makes in support of the claim in his subtitle, that the event was "the eruption that changed the world."

Wood is also a skilled advocate for his cause. Here is a lecture given at Brigham Young University in 2015, just after his book was published: https://www.youtube.com/watch?v=naB-QTUNHfk. In addition, his "trailer" for his book should be taken as a kind of model for the way academics speak across the knowledge gulf to citizens who may share interests with authors. The "trailer" gives the impression of Wood speaking off the cuff, but in fact, the presentation is very well organized, perhaps he is even reading from cue cards. No matter. He is interesting and convincing: https://www.youtube.com/watch?v=xbDZVMnXUWI. Academics take note of the smashing coordination of the author's deep lavender polo shirt with the similarly hued flowers just over his right shoulder.

6. Wood, "1816, The Year without a Summer."

7. Mt. Tambora's eruption, leading to "the year without a summer," produced a refugee crisis of 21st century-sounding proportions. In 1816, hundreds of thousands of people died of starvation and famine-friendly diseases like cholera. Tens of thousands were driven from their homes, towns, and villages in search of food and shelter. As with contemporary refugee crises in Africa and the Middle East, the extreme conditions, chiefly scarcity of one kind or another, led to ethnically related violence and great cruelty toward people regarded as "others" rather than as "us." Switzerland was especially vulnerable not only because of the vast flooding and crop failure but also because the Swiss were organized into relatively self-sufficient cantons whose officials zealously guarded their own resources and often used violence to keep "other" Swiss from neighboring cantons from gaining access to their stores of food. See Klingaman and Klingaman, *The Year without Summer*, 263–66, for a graphic depiction of the human disaster in Switzerland. More predictably, due to their suppression and exploitation by the England, the Irish suffered horribly as tens of thousands died of starvation and disease. Many decided to sail to America, but often the trip was in vain. Klingaman and Klingaman quote a newspaper report of a boat of Irish refugees landing in Philadelphia, where locals soon discovered that many of the Irish had died on the difficult journey of starvation and that of the small number who could actually *walk* off the boat, many soon died, then and there, in the streets of Philadelphia (191–93).

8. See endnote 2, above, regarding this particular letter from Byron to his publisher, John Murray Jr. in London. One may reasonably ask why Byron chose Geneva in the summer of 1816 as his base of operations: for his writing, his rigorous exercise routines, his hiking and traveling while his poetical ideas simmered in his fertile brain. The short answer is that Byron was trying to keep a step ahead of those who sought to call him to account: for his role in destroying his marriage; and particularly his creditors, to whom he was head over heels in debt, a situation that would worsen with every passing year. Byron was twenty-eight. He would never see England again. David Ellis suggests that Byron may have felt some affinity for the Calvinist milieu of Geneva (Geneva having been John Calvin's city of residence). Byron was born in Calvinist-Presbyterian Scotland and spent part of his youth in Aberdeen, a Calvinist stronghold. See David Ellis, *Byron in Geneva* (Oxford: Oxford University Press, 2011), 1–2. Whatever the reasons Byron wound up in Geneva, the weather would not be among them.

9. A different interpretation of Byron's "Darkness" is offered by one of his recent biographers, Fiona MacCarthy, in her massive *Byron: Life and Legend* (London: John Murray, 2002). MacCarthy connects the poem only to Byron's personal history; namely, to the "bleakness and despair that followed his banishment [from England] winding in and out of his past amatory history . . . which Matthew Arnold called 'the pageant of his bleeding heart'" (304). To MacCarthy, it seems, the weather had nothing to do with it. Neither did the starving Swiss who had taken to the roads in search of food, or who had already begun

to sell their children for food; nor did the poem call to mind wave after wave of famine-induced epidemics that were already wiping out substantial portions of the populations of England, even before Byron departed for Geneva. According to MacCarthy, the only connection the poem has to Switzerland at all is that "Darkness" shows how conscious Byron was of the landscape around him: "the uncompromising scenery of Switzerland itself" (Ibid., 305). Scenery? Do mass starvation, social upheaval, and widespread violence constitute "scenery"? We wonder if the biographer fell so completely under the spell of her subject that she forgot that the great poet in the summer of 1816 was also a human being in a particular place at a very particular moment of the history of Europe, and much of the rest of the world as well. This does not mean that Byron's poetry can be "reduced" to his surroundings, only that the poem had some very immediate sources very close at hand.

10. On Turgenev's translation of Byron's "Darkness," see Anthony Rudolf, "Byron's 'Darkness': Lost Summer and Nuclear Winter." This fifteen-page piece was published by Rudolf's own publishing house (London: Menard Press, 1984) and is now available in pdf format on the web at: http://www.ilankelman.org/menard/Rudolf1984a.pdf. The article contains the original English version, by Byron, and also Turgenev's Russian translation, which Rudolf says was slightly altered by the tsarist censors.

11. Alan Robock is quoted to this effect in Fred Pearce, "Boom," *New Scientist*, August 7, 1999. Robock also mentions it near the end of his 2013 TED talk. See Alan Robock, "Nuclear Winter: Still Possible But Preventable": https://www.youtube.com/watch?v=qsrEk1oZ-54.

12. We enthusiastically recommend the reading given the poem by an individual who goes by the pseudonym "Tom O'Bedlam." His voice is equal parts molasses and rolling thunder, which seems to us just about perfect for reading "Darkness." In addition, this particular reading is accompanied by post-apocalyptic graphics that are stark reminders of what is at stake in trying to prevent the onset in our own time of a post-nuclear "darkness." Watch and listen at: https://www.youtube.com/watch?v=5uN5btgxsfI.

13. The indispensible Poetry Foundation, which publishes *Poetry Magazine*, is underwritten by a $200 million gift from Ruth Lilly, heir to the Lilly Pharmaceutical fortune. "Darkness" is available at: https://www.poetryfoundation.org/poems-and-poets/poems/detail/43825.

14. Mary Oliver, "The Uses of Sorrow," in *Thirst* (Boston: Beacon Press, 2006), 52.

NOTE TO PART IV

1. We say "attributed to Anne Frank" because while the web buzzes with thumbnails, blog entries, and other postings giving Anne Frank as the author of this passage, we can find no proof that she ever wrote this. We also encountered several postings in chat rooms from frustrated people looking, as we were, for evidence that this actually comes from Anne Frank. In any case, it is a lovely passage, and we are grateful to whomever may be its author.

NOTES TO CHAPTER 10

1. *Caddyshack*, a 1980 film directed and written by Harold Ramis, distributed by Warner Brothers Pictures. The golfer Ty Webb (played by Chevy Chase) instructs the caddy Danny Noonan (played by Michael O'Keefe) on a Zen approach to golf. The idea is to

become one with the golf ball. Ty Webb puts on a blindfold and hits a ball over a pond, with the ball coming to rest next to the hole. Danny the caddy is amazed. Ty then puts the blindfold on Danny, who tries to "be the ball," thus in no need of actually seeing the hole, the pond, and the usual array of items that constitute a golfer's pre-shot checklist. Danny, alas, chunks the ball into the pond, apparently not having quite mastered the art of "being the ball."

2. Stephen Batchelor, *Buddhism without Beliefs: A Contemporary Guide to Awakening* (New York: Riverhead Books, 1997), 46. This sparkling little book is ostensibly about the theory and practice of Buddhism, by an author who speaks and reads Tibetan and Korean and has lived in monasteries in India and South Korea. You might expect therein to encounter some indecipherable interpretations of (say) Tibetan prayer flags, or perhaps some riffs on versions of the Zen Buddhist koans like "What is the sound of one hand clapping?" But the book is a thoroughly humanistic, refreshingly modest, and penetrating essay on some practices and principles associated with (among other traditions) Buddhism, at the core of which is Batchelor's belief that all spiritual traditions that are truly relevant and useful for us in the modern age must regard *empathy* as their core concept and concern. His short chapter on what he calls "Integrity" (45–48) is, in our estimation, one of the finest summaries we have ever read of the need to focus on what unites us as human beings, and to find ways to successfully resist the unfortunate tendency we all have to focus instead on what divides us: our religions, languages, forms of government, skin color, and so on. We hardly need add that in the present global climate of opinion, empathy is in too short a supply. Moreover, in the nuclear age, the absence of empathy is not *just* unfortunate. It can be lethal. The close call to Armageddon in the Cuban missile crisis—the danger of which was due almost entirely to the absence of empathy between leaders in Washington, Moscow, and Havana—demonstrates that in situations of crisis that involve countries with nukes, the absence of empathy can lead to catastrophe.

3. Clifford Geertz, *Local Knowledge: Further Essays in Interpretive Anthropology* (New York: Basic Books, 1983), 58 (emphasis in original). Geertz's proposition—empathy consists in trying to figure out what the devil some other individual or group (with whom one does not necessarily share a language, history, or culture) is up to—this seems to us more profound every time we consider it. Our task in seeking to empathize, it seems to us, is both simple to describe but often extraordinarily difficult to actually achieve. Geertz nails it, as he often did, with a single turn of phrase: we have to be willing and able to state what "the other" believes is going on—but that is only the first part. Next, we have to state *to the other* what we think he or she believes is going on. Sorry, but you are not finished. Next, we must listen to "the other's" reaction to our effort to state what the devil he or she thinks is happening. Finally, we have to be willing to revise our estimate of "the other's" viewpoint, in line with what we are told, and we have to be willing to do this as many times as it takes until we get it right. Try doing this next time you have an argument with someone. We think you'll find it takes a lot of effort, and often what seems like an almost oceanic quantity of patience.

For all that, you could still be wrong because, like it or not, you are an outsider to the thoughts, feelings, and dreams of "the other," just as "the other" is an outsider to your inner life. There is no way to fix this problem absolutely. You will never *be* someone else. You must accept this, which is why it is necessary to regard anything you believe about another's inner life as a *question*, as a *hypothesis*, as something that might be true, or might not be true.

We have written at length about empathy elsewhere, and about its centrality (either due to its presence or its absence) in leaders' decisions when war and peace is on the line. See James G. Blight and janet M. Lang, "When Empathy Failed: Using Critical Oral History to Reassess the Collapse of U.S.-Soviet Détente in the Carter-Brezhnev Years," *Journal of Cold*

War Studies 12, no. 2 (Spring 2010): 29–74. This piece, along with responses by six scholars and former high-level U.S. decision-makers, is available free and online on the website of the National Security Archive at: http://nsarchive.gwu.edu/carterbrezhnev/C-B%20-%20When%20Empathy%20Failed%20-%20Blight%20&%20Lang%20-%20jcws.2010.12.2.29.pdf. See also the brilliant and provocative book by Zachary Shore, *A Sense of the Enemy: The High Stakes History of Reading Your Rival's Mind* (New York: Oxford, 2014); and also our essay on the implications of Shore's effort to retell the history of 20th century decision-making on war and peace in a way that places empathy (and its absence) at the core of the analysis: James G. Blight and janet M. Lang, "The Empath: Can Historical Narratives + Cognitive Psychology = Foreign Policy Relevance?" The piece will be posted on *H-Diplo*, the official discussion website of the Society of Historians of American Foreign Relations (SHAFR), in late 2017.

4. It is useful to keep in mind the critical difference between *describing* and *explaining*. Note the subtitle of Graham Allison's classic political science treatise on the Cuban missile crisis (second ed., with Philip Zelikow), *Essence of Decision: Explaining the Cuban Missile Crisis* (Boston: Addison Wesley Longman, 1999). The book is framed by three "models" through which the authors endeavor to figure out why Kennedy or Khrushchev did or didn't do this or that. Our view is that explanation has a place in historical studies, but first, we need to describe as completely as we can what the experience of the crisis was like for whomever is the decision-maker we are trying to understand. Otherwise, your explanation may be based mostly on your theoretical concepts rather than the actual, real-time, moment-to-moment reality—we call it the "psychological reality"—of a decision-maker. This is the sort of thing we attempt in this book, chapter 6, when we invite you to vicariously jump into Fidel Castro's jeep and ride along with him on the most dangerous weekend in recorded history. An effort to do something similar with Kennedy and Khrushchev is in James G. Blight, *The Shattered Crystal Ball: Fear and Learning in the Cuban Missile Crisis,* foreword by Joseph S. Nye Jr. (Lanham, MD: Rowman & Littlefield, 1992), especially 55–83.

5. "I Second That Emotion," written by William ("Smokey") Robinson and Al Cleveland, performed by Smokey Robinson and the Miracles, released by Motown Records, 1967.

6. The importance of *crisis* cannot be emphasized enough. We all have an intuitive grasp of what it means to be in a crisis—not enough time, confusing signals, frustration, and stakes high enough to make you worry about losing something valuable. But it is still a huge problem for those of us concerned about the risk of nuclear war. The problem is this: all the planning, the generation of possible scenarios to which it may be necessary to respond, how to deter adversaries without provoking them beyond some point of no return, and even identifying such points of no return—all of this is done in a non-crisis mode. It has to be, of course. But when you try to build into your planning process the awareness that the devil will be in the details, as seen by leaders in a deep *crisis*, you have no idea how to do it. Why? Because the essence of a crisis is its weirdness, its unexpectedness, the confusion you feel, as your expectations are wrong time after time, until you feel almost as if you are going crazy with uncertainty and worry. If you are a senior decision-maker in charge of some aspect of the nuclear planning process, you remember thinking something like "Do we really have to spend all this time on the threat of nuclear war, when everybody knows that a decision to go to nuclear war would probably be the costliest, most regrettable decision a human being could make?" In other words: only an idiot or otherwise insane person would ever go down that road.

But suddenly, like JFK, or Khrushchev or Castro, the thing that seemed so wildly improbable is beginning to look disconcertingly real. Not only is a nuclear war possible, it looks like it is becoming more likely by the hour. None of these guys predicted the behavior of the others accurately. This is why we often refer to the context in which the Cuban missile crisis occurred as "an empathy free zone." Kennedy thought: Khrushchev won't lie to me about something as important and dangerous as nuclear weapons, but Khrushchev did lie to him. Khrushchev thought: Kennedy won't discover our deployment until it is too late and, even then, he won't object, because we will only have achieved what the Americans have long had, which is nukes close to the adversary's territory. (NATO had nukes in Turkey, very near the Soviet Union, which greatly irritated Khrushchev.) But Kennedy and his advisers did discover them before they were fully installed, and Kennedy did thoroughly object to Russian missiles ninety miles from the coast of Florida. Castro thought: because we now have Russian missiles in Cuba, an American move against us is a move against the Russians, who will defend Cuba's interests as if they were Russia's. But at crunch time, the Russians cut and ran, as the Cubans saw it, their betrayal embodied in their removal of their missiles, leaving Cuba to fend for itself. If these leaders had understood one another, had empathized with one another, there would have been no Cuban missile crisis. But there's the rub: none of them was wise enough to foresee ahead of time the reactions of the others. And once the crisis was underway, all asked themselves a dangerous question: If I could be wrong about something as fundamental as that, what else have I been wrong about? On the role of *crisis*, see Blight, *Shattered Crystal Ball*, 41–43, and 142–43.

7. Niall Ferguson, ed., *Virtual History: Alternatives and Counterfactuals* (New York Basic Books, 1997), 438–39.

8. The third volume of the Cromwell trilogy will be called *The Mirror and the Light*, and it will cover the final four years of Cromwell's life: from the execution of Anne Boleyn to Cromwell's own beheading four years later on July 28, 1540, in the Tower of London. That is all we know about the third volume of the trilogy. As Mantel has explained, the key reason why her history is what we call "habitable" is that she—the author—first inhabits the people about whom she is writing as fully as can be imagined.

> I don't write in sequence. I may have a dozen versions of a single scene. I might spend a week threading an image through a story, but moving the narrative not an inch. A book grows according to a subtle and deep-laid plan. At the end, I see what the plan was. (Hilary Mantel, "My Writing Day," *The Guardian*, April 16, 2016).

As she describes the process, although she is the undoubted author, it often feels to her as if she is taking dictation from a moody, sometimes uncooperative, and usually cryptic boss—at her computer, scribbling with her pen, waking in the middle of the night to record a dream or nightmare—her boss being somewhere, or someone outside of her. And that is only the beginning. Between Hilary Mantel's habitation of her characters, and our own, is that dark realm we usually refer to, blankly, as literary "art."

9. Geertz, *Local Knowledge*, 58.

10. Estimates vary concerning how many people Henry VIII put to death in the thirty-seven years of his reign in England. One scholar puts the number somewhere between fifty-seven thousand and seventy-two thousand (Emma Mason, "How Many Executions Was Henry VIII Responsible For?" *BBC History Magazine*, December 28, 2014). Numerical precision in all Tudor matters is spurious. Let's take a number of executions of various kinds (and there were many kinds, ranging from brutal to cruel to whatever is beyond cruel) in the middle range of that estimate—say sixty-five thousand total executions under Henry VIII. Let's say, therefore, that approximately two thousand people were executed per year during Henry's reign. Thomas Cromwell would have been the executive officer on most that occurred during Cromwell's time as the king's Chief Minister, roughly 1532–1540.

That's eight years, during which something in the neighborhood of sixteen thousand people were put to death by the English Crown, most of which Cromwell would have overseen, sometimes up very close and personal, as when he engineered, at Henry's order, the execution of Anne Boleyn, Henry's second wife; and many others for which Cromwell was at a much further remove. In any case, you doubtless get the picture: in that time and place, torture and execution were two of the most important instruments of state with which the king and his faction achieved and retained control of the government, public monies, control of the population, and so on. It was that way while Cromwell had Henry's ear. But it was also that way long before, and long after, the reign of Henry the VIII.

11. See Jorge I. Dominguez, "Pipsqueak Power: The Centrality and Anomaly of Cuba," in *The Suffering Grass: Superpowers and Regional Conflict in Southern Africa and the Caribbean*, eds. James G. Blight and Thomas G. Weiss (Boulder: Lynne Rienner, 1992), 57–78. This brilliant piece, by the top American scholar of Cuban foreign relations, should be required reading for all foreign policy-makers of big powers. Its message: Hey, big guy, what you don't know can hurt you, even if what you don't know is the mindset of your smaller, recalcitrant adversary or ally that insists on its own way of doing things.

NOTES TO CHAPTER 11

1. John Milton, *Paradise Lost*, Book 1, lines 63–64. First published in 1667, the work is widely available online. See, for example, Dartmouth College's John Milton Reading Room at: https://www.dartmouth.edu/~milton/reading_room/pl/book_1/text.shtml.

2. Robert Lowell, quoted in Kay Redfield Jamison, *Robert Lowell, Setting the River on Fire: A Study of Genius, Mania, and Character* (New York: Knopf, 2017), 3. This is the first biographical study of the great New England poet to focus on his bipolar disease, which is distinguished by alternating bouts of mania and depression. Jamison, a clinical psychologist and specialist on mood disorders, is an admirer of Lowell and a fellow manic-depressive sufferer. Lowell's view, which Jamison shares, is that Lowell's greatest poems—with their path-breaking flights of metaphor and brutal self-examination—derive in large part from his illness. During manic episodes, Lowell's mind generated cascades of extravagantly dissonant metaphors, symbols, and allegories, which he was able to slowly work through, step by step, in the deep depressions that inevitably followed the flights of mania. In both phases of his illness, according to Jamison, Lowell showed great strength of character: while manic, Lowell was somehow able to retain useful material for his poetry amid all the shouting and wildly inappropriate behavior of which he was capable; and while depressed, he did not give in to thoughts of suicide that accompanied the depressions, and even somehow began during those periods to form his manic visions and voices into the more linear requirements of written poetry. One gets the impression, from Lowell's poetry and now from Jamison's study of him, that the title of this book, *Dark Beyond Darkness*, describes not only Cormac McCarthy's *The Road* but also the interior life of America's greatest post-war poet.

3. Sigmund Freud, "Remembering, Repeating and Working-Through," in *The Complete Psychological Works of Sigmund Freud*, 24 vols., vol. 12, ed. James Strachey (London: Hogarth, 1974), 147–56. Available online at: http://www.history.ucsb.edu/faculty/marcuse/classes/201/articles/1914FreudRemembering.pdf. Whatever one may think about the scientific underpinnings of Freud's theories and clinical techniques—which range from worshipful to dismissive—it seems undeniable that he got some things right. We would include Freud's notion of the compulsion to repeat among the propositions that seem obvious and everywhere, once you begin to look for them.

We cannot think about this Freudian concept without thinking about the adventures of George, a close friend of ours, in New York City many years ago. George was raised on a farm in rural North Dakota and spent much of his adult life teaching in semirural New Hampshire. One year, George decided, against the wisdom of his wife, to head to New York City for a conference, one that we were also attending. On George's first attempt to ride the subway, he was perhaps seen by the wrong pair of eyes for what he was: a country guy, naïve about city ways, and unused to being on the lookout for trouble, or at least the kind of trouble that can occur on a half-deserted New York City subway platform, while waiting for a train.

George was mugged, kicked around, and told to shut up until his assailant was out of sight. In telling us about this the following day, we asked George if he was going to take taxis from now on in the city. "Nah," he replied, "I'm on my way back down into the subway." When asked about it, George said, "I gotta prove to myself that I can take subways when I want to or need to." When we asked him what the assailant stole from him, he said: "Not a damn thing. My pockets were dead empty, by design." Then he gave us a wink, which implied something along the lines of "you gotta get up pretty early in the morning to get the best of a country boy from rural North Dakota," even in New York City.

4. Elizabeth Barrett Browning, Sonnet 43 (the final sonnet), of her *Sonnets from the Portuguese*, written in the mid-1840s, and finally published, at the insistence of the poet's husband, Robert Browning, in 1850. (In *Robert and Elizabeth Barrett Browning: Poems and Letters*, selection by Peter Washington [New York: Knopf, 2003], 198–99, quote on page 198.)

5. See chapter 2 of this book, "The Bullshit," for specific instances, over the years, when former officials and scholars begin with the peaceful outcome of the crisis and work their way backward to a retrospective explanation of the event. The principal problem for those of us living more than a half-century after the crisis is that we are too often lulled by the mountains of documents and scholarship and academic theories into believing that the experience of the crisis was something like the exercise of trying to explain it after the fact. Scholars who do this are not necessarily committing any epistemological "sins." But a warning label should accompany retrospective efforts to explain the crisis, more or less as follows: *"What follows is a rational reconstruction of an event that was experienced as chaotic and horrifying by the involved leaders. We provide a theory of the Cuban missile crisis, which probably bears little or no relation to the way it was experienced, in the interest of advancing our theories of decision-making."* Of course, there are no such warning labels preceding statements on the crisis by eminent scholars such as Kenneth Waltz and Graham Allison and dozens of others who theorize about the crisis. If they did so, they would be admitting, at least tacitly, that their views contain no insight into what the next deep nuclear crisis will look like and feel like, moving forward, in a fog of crisis—which is another way of saying that their theories should be taken as irrelevant to both the Cuban missile crisis and to the prevention of nuclear war in the 21st century.

Think about it this way: Robert McNamara says in Errol Morris's movie *The Fog of War* that "We *lucked out*! It was *luck* that prevented nuclear war in the Cuban missile crisis!" (See chapter 5, this book, Endnote #13.) If the driving force leading to the avoidance of nuclear war in October 1962 was plain dumb luck, what is there to theorize about? The answer is clear: nothing at all. But such is the love of theories in academia that the theorists prefer to abandon the actual Cuban missile crisis, rather than abandon their theories of some imagined crisis that fits with their theories.

6. "There But for Fortune," written by Phil Ochs in 1963 and released the following year. The song became an unexpected hit for Joan Baez in 1965, when she released it on *Joan Baez/5*.

7. As of 2017:

Nations with nuclear weapons (9): Russia (7,000), United States (6,800), France (300), China (260), Britain (215), Pakistan (120–130), India (110–120), Israel (80), North Korea (<10). Total: ~14,900.

Nations hosting nuclear weapons (5): Belgium, Germany, Italy, Netherlands, Turkey.

Nations in nuclear alliances with the U.S. and/or NATO (23): Albania, Australia, Bulgaria, Canada, Croatia, Czech, Denmark, Estonia, Greece, Hungary, Iceland, Japan, Latvia, Lithuania, Luxembourg, Norway, Poland, Portugal, Romania, Slovakia, Slovenia, South Korea, Spain.

Sources: The Federation of American Scientists (FAS), https://fas.org/issues/nuclear-weapons/status-world-nuclear-forces/ and The International Committee to Abolish Nuclear Weapons (ICAN), http://www.icanw.org/the-facts/nuclear-arsenals/.

8. Scott D. Sagan and Kenneth N. Waltz, *The Spread of Nuclear Weapons: A Debate* (New York: Norton, 1995), 5.

9. Nassim Nicholas Taleb, *Fooled By Randomness: The Hidden Role of Chance in Life and in the Markets*, 2nd ed. (New York: Random House, 2005), 18.

10. Carl Richards, "Avoiding the "Lucky Fool Syndrome,'" *New York Times*, 10 March 2014.

11. Ibid.

12. See Lee Ross, "The Intuitive Psychologist and His Shortcomings: Distortions in the Attribution Process," in *Advances in Experimental Social Psychology*, Vol. 10, ed. Leonard Berkowitz (New York: Academic Press, 1977), 173–220. The Fundamental Attribution Error has recently been brilliantly applied to decision-making when war and peace is on the line. The Nobel Laureate Daniel Kahneman, of Princeton, and political psychologist Jonathan Renshon, at the University of Wisconsin, have addressed the problem of why hawkish advice to decision-makers usually wins out. They trace the reasons for this back to the biased way we are wired. See especially their "Why Hawks Win," *Foreign Policy*, October 13, 2009; and the longer and more technical, but still accessible, "Hawkish Biases." In Trevor Thrall and Jane Cramer, eds., *American Foreign Policy and the Politics of Fear: Threat Inflation Since 9/11* (New York: Routledge, 2009), 79–96.

13. We have previously found the Fundamental Attribution Error a useful idea within which to understand three decisions by three recent U.S. presidents: (1) the decision of President John F. Kennedy *not* to escalate the conflict in Vietnam, in spite of recommendations by many senior advisers that he do so; (2) President Lyndon Johnson's decision in 1965 to send hundreds of thousands of American troops to Vietnam in a vain attempt to stem the tide of the communist campaign to dislodge the U.S.-backed government in Saigon; and (3) the disastrous March 2003 decision of President George W. Bush to attack Saddam Hussein's Iraq in the wake of the terrorist attacks of September 11, 2001. See James G. Blight, janet M. Lang, and David A. Welch, *Virtual JFK: Vietnam If Kennedy Had Lived* (Lanham, MD: Rowman & Littlefield, 2009), 250–73, especially 269–73, where we discuss five major biases evident in decisions taken by leaders to go to war.

Johnson veritably oozed fear and loathing of communism and communists, as he understood them (which was imperfect, to say the least). Thus, when after much theatrical agonizing about whether to commit U.S. troops, he finally authorized a full land, sea, and air effort involving U.S. troops in the hundreds of thousands, his logic was: you can't reason with these communists, who keep attacking our ally in Saigon. So we will have to bomb them to the conference table, if that is what it takes. Likewise with Bush: portraying Saddam Hussein as incontrovertibly evil, and (lacking any evidence, then or since) behind the attacks of 9/11, he ordered the invasion of Iraq, in what became the costliest and longest war in American history, with still no end in sight to the violence in the region that has followed the overthrow of Saddam. If Johnson had tried to empathize with the Vietnamese communists, and Bush had made an effort to empathize with Saddam's Ba'ath Party in Iraq, both would have seen that U.S. hostility, aggression, and overbearing arrogance all were instrumental in leading to the resistance to U.S. efforts in Southeast Asia in the 1960s and the Middle East in the 2000s. Both decisions were overflowing with examples of the Fundamental Attribution Error: they act from evil impulses, not in response to us; we must therefore destroy them. This anti-empathetic logic led to the two most disastrous American wars so far.

Kennedy was the outlier, principally because he knew the history of Vietnam's relations with the West, and he realized that in the eyes of the world, the U.S. did not have the right, let alone the obligation, to try to destroy the Vietnamese communists; and he also understood that the U.S. did not have the means to destroy them other than by committing genocide, something he was unwilling to countenance. Kennedy's view of the adversary was nuanced, more or less as follows: yes, they have committed terrible crimes against our ally; but yes, they have their reasons for not trusting us; and they are utterly committed to achieving victory, and they will do so, because they live there, and we don't, and thus at some point we will leave, and they know it; so I am not going to get the U.S. in a war we cannot win by any means other than committing acts that betray what our nation stands for.

14. *Mission Impossible 2*, a 2000 movie directed by John Woo, written by Bruce Geller and Ronald D. Moore, distributed by Paramount Pictures. The quotation in the text can be accessed here: https://en.wikiquote.org/wiki/Mission:_Impossible_II.

NOTES TO CHAPTER 12

1. Michael Dobbs, "Lost in Enemy Airspace," *Vanity Fair*, posted on June 1, 2008, 12:00 a.m. (The quotation is in the introduction to the article.) The story of the U-2 lost over Siberia during the Cuban missile crisis is also in Michael Dobbs, *One Minute to Midnight: Kennedy, Khrushchev and Castro on the Brink of Nuclear War* (New York: Knopf, 2008), 269–75.

2. http://www.cooperkatz.com/comments/Anniversary-Campaigns-Worth-Celebrating (posted on the firm's 17th anniversary).

3. The phrase *Black Saturday* was used in many American memoirs of the Cuban missile crisis and was quickly picked up by western scholars as a catchphrase signifying, mainly, the peak of nuclear danger, before JFK and his associates snatched peace and victory from the jaws of Armageddon. But to us, one of the most interesting applications of "Black Saturday" was by the Russian journalist Fyodor Burlatsky, who had as a young man been part of Nikita Khrushchev's speechwriting team. In 1983, two years before Mikhail Gorbachev came to power in the Soviet Union, Burlatsky published the script of a short play, called "Black Saturday," *Literaturnaya Gazeta*, November 23, 1983. The *LG* was roughly equivalent to the *New York Review of Books* in that it published a wide range of intellectuals: philosophers, historians, political scientists, poets, and so on. Burlatsky was editor-in-chief of *LG* and, when Gorbachev became general secretary of the USSR in 1985, Burlatsky and the *LG* became a forum for pro-Gorbachev writers. Burlatsky's play was produced in Moscow in the mid-1980s. All the "action" takes place in the White House in interactions between JFK and RFK. We presented a film of the play at our second critical oral history conference, at Harvard, in Cambridge, Massachusetts, in October 1987, with Burlatsky participating. The signature feature of the play is that both Kennedy brothers become, in

effect, Russians: extremely emotional, sometimes in tears, given to heart-wrenching monologues to the audience about the gloom and doom of the nuclear age. When we asked Burlatsky about the way he had portrayed the Kennedy brothers, he told us that he had always heard that the Irish were emotional people, like the Russians. Fyodor Burlatsky's play is also in F. Burlatsky, *New Thinking*, trans. by Lev Bobrov (Moscow: Progress Publishers, 1988), 86–116.

4. As of 2017:

Nations with nuclear weapons (9): Russia (7,000), United States (6,800), France (300), China (260), Britain (215), Pakistan (120–130), India (110–120), Israel (80), North Korea (<10). Total: ~14,900.

Nations hosting nuclear weapons (5): Belgium, Germany, Italy, Netherlands, Turkey.

Nations in nuclear alliances with the U.S. and/or NATO (23): Albania, Australia, Bulgaria, Canada, Croatia, Czech, Denmark, Estonia, Greece, Hungary, Iceland, Japan, Latvia, Lithuania, Luxembourg, Norway, Poland, Portugal, Romania, Slovakia, Slovenia, South Korea, Spain.

Sources: The Federation of American Scientists (FAS), https://fas.org/issues/nuclear-weapons/status-world-nuclear-forces/ and The International Committee to Abolish Nuclear Weapons (ICAN), http://www.icanw.org/the-facts/nuclear-arsenals/.

5. Of course, the .95 probability estimate is only an educated guess. But we use it here because so many commentators on the Cuban missile crisis like to cite various estimates of the probability of nuclear war, both by participants in the crisis and by scholars, after the fact. During our critical oral history of the Cuban missile crisis, however, Robert McNamara became convinced that the probability of nuclear war by Black Saturday was very high. Bob liked to spike his conversation with probabilities. It was Bob who first used the .95 probability; at least he was the first person we heard use it. One of us (JGB) wrote a paper with Bob in 2001 that made this point: Robert S. McNamara and James G. Blight, "The Miracle of October: Lessons from the Cuban Missile Crisis." The paper was written as a backgrounder for a BBC film team with whom were consulting what became a fine effort to tell the Cuban and Russian story of the crisis, *The Other Side of Armageddon*, produced for BBC 4 by Wark Clements productions. *The Miracle of October* is available online at: http://the-puzzle-palace.com/files/OctMiracle.pdf.

6. Gilbert Ryle, *The Concept of Mind* (Oxford: Oxford University Press, 1949), 16–21. For our money, physicist-philosopher Michael Polanyi delivered the coup de grace to any notion that knowing *that* leads seamlessly to knowing *how*. Polanyi says he interviewed "physicists, engineers and bicycle manufacturers" and came up with "instructions" as to what needs to be done for a cyclist to maintain proper balance. The tongue-in-cheek "instructions" are too long to be quoted in full here, but the conclusion will give you some idea of his argument. According to Polanyi, "A simple analysis shows that for a given angle of unbalance the curvature of each winding is inversely proportional to the square of the speed at which the cyclist is proceeding. But does this tell you how to ride a bicycle? No." See Michael Polanyi, *Personal Knowledge: Towards a Post-Critical Philosophy* (Chicago: University of Chicago Press, 1958), 50. For a recent update of Ryle and Polanyi's distinction between *that* and *how*, see Siddhartha Mukherjee, "The Algorithm Will See You Now: When It Comes to Diagnosis, Will A.I. replace the M.D.?" *The New Yorker*, April 3, 2017, 46–53. Mukherjee even reinvokes the famous bicycle example, applying it to his seven-year-old daughter learning to ride her bike up a steep incline. When she gets it, he concludes, "I had not taught her rules to ride a bike up that hill. When her daughter learns to negotiate the same hill, I imagine, she won't teach her the rules either" (47).

7. By far the best, and possibly the only serious initiative for abolishing nuclear weapons, occurred at the conclusion of World War II. The U.S., which was the only nuclear

nation at the time, agreed in 1946 to give up its nukes and its nuclear program (except for so-called peaceful uses of splitting the atom, such as to generate power). Britain, France, and Canada agreed, but the Russians did not. Stalin believed that Western interests dominated the UN and that the Soviet Union would be treated unfairly. The U.S. plan, drafted by financier Bernard Baruch (the "Baruch Plan"), did not allow for a veto by any of the major powers, which worried the Soviets, who expected to be isolated and essentially powerless in such an arrangement. The Baruch Plan went aground on its inability to find a way to placate the Russians, while at the same time sticking to its no-nonsense, no-nukes thrust. Baruch wrote, in a statement that is (alas) as relevant today as it was seventy years ago:

> We are here to make a choice between the quick and the dead. That is our business. Behind the black portent of the new atomic age lies a hope which, seized upon with faith, can work our salvation. If we fail, then we have damned every man to be the slave of fear. Let us not deceive ourselves; we must elect world peace or (elect) world destruction.

Quoted in Joshua Williams, "The Quick and the Dead," Carnegie International Non-Proliferation Conference, June 16, 2005, available at: http://carnegieendowment.org/publications/index.cfm?fa=view&id=17078&prog=zgp&proj=znpp.

8. In 1982, during the last eruption of anti-nuclear sentiment in the West—when President Ronald Reagan promised to beat the Russians in the nuclear competition, whatever it took—Jonathan Schell in *The Fate of the Earth* urged us to "reinvent politics" in order to abolish nuclear weapons (New York: Knopf, 226). Since then, a dizzying variety of concrete schemes have been created over the years that their authors believe will, or might under certain conditions, lead to the abolition of nuclear weapons. This is sometimes known as "scenario building." Some are long on rhetoric and short on details; for example, *The Canberra Commission Report on the Elimination of Nuclear Weapons*, published in 1996: http://www.ccnr.org/canberra.html. It might be summarized in this way: nukes must be eliminated; mutual verification is necessary; and if only the U.S. and Russia, which together possess about 90 percent of the world's nukes, would agree to reduce their arsenals down to roughly what the others possess (say, five hundred or less), then serious negotiations could take place. Other scenarios are so complex, and the issues to be resolved so seemingly difficult, that it is difficult to muster much enthusiasm for even getting involved. See, for example, some of the models of disarmament presented by the many contributors to George Perkovich and James M. Acton, eds., *Abolishing Nuclear Weapons: A Debate* (Washington, DC: Carnegie Endowment for International Peace, 2009), available at: http://carnegieendowment.org/files/abolishing_nuclear_weapons_debate.pdf. Michael O'Hanlon of the Brookings Institution has developed another recent scenario. O'Hanlon argues for "dismantling," not "abolishing," nuclear weapons because, as he notes, the knowledge of how to build the weapons is here to stay. We can send missiles to the junkyard to be used for scrap metal, but they can be reconstituted, like lemon juice, if the need and opportunity arises. But even dismantling gives O'Hanlon the willies because "the act of disarmament is an inherently disruptive process . . . at a minimum, most remaining serious regional problems should be resolved before a treaty is negotiated." See: Michael O'Hanlon, *A Skeptic's Case for Nuclear Disarmament* (Washington, DC: Brookings, 2010), 90–91. The problem with all these complex schemes is, as we see it, that the authors invariably try to figure out everything ahead of time, so that the process of nuclear abolition might unfold in some super-smooth fashion, almost without assistance from its human originators. To do this, a lot of stuff, mainly political and psychological stuff, must be left out, because who knows, for example, whether Israel and the Palestinians will ever find a solution to their problems; or who knows whether Iran will resume trying to achieve a nuclear weapon capability despite

its 2015 agreement in which it promised the international community it would not; and so on. Of course, leaving out all the stuff that will not yield to scenario-building to any meaningful degree means the scenarios are rendered empty of content.

9. Peter Baker, "A Camelot Nostalgia Tour for Those Who Remember, and Those Who Don't," *New York Times*, August 31, 2013. Baker notes one of the unusual features of the 50th anniversary of Kennedy's assassination: it really didn't matter how old you were, or whether or not you had any memories of Kennedy and his murder. Everyone seemed to be interested, regardless of age. What this shows is what can happen over a period of years during which an anniversary is commemorated once a year, each year following the event it commemorates: a lot of momentum is established, and what follows is a dogfight for media time as everyone tries to get into the act. According to Baker:

> Fifty years later, the assassination of America's 35th president will once again captivate the nation—or so hope museum curators, book publishers, filmmakers, documentary producers, magazine editors and conspiracy theorists. Not content to wait until November, the marketplace is already brimming with all things Kennedy, the start of a "deluge," as the producer of one coming documentary put it. (Ibid.)

In principle, creating a "deluge" of this sort for Black Saturday should be even easier than the one that occurred in 2013 regarding Kennedy's assassination. First, Kennedy is obviously centrally involved. Second, so are Fidel Castro and Nikita Khrushchev, two of the most interesting figures of the 20th century. Third, the crisis is uber-dramatic: a paper-thin escape from the instant deaths of millions, followed by the end of the world as it was known to Kennedy, Khrushchev, and Castro, their constituents, and indeed to the entire world. The problem, we believe, is this: whereas principal features of the narrative of Kennedy's assassination have remained constant over the years—one guy, one gunman (or more), one murder, and so on—the narrative of the Cuban missile crisis, with Black Saturday at its core, has seemed with each passing year to dissolve into thin air. The exceptions have been the four anniversaries we hooked our project to 25th, 30th, 40th, and 50th). What might be done, for starters, is to model Black Saturday Remembrance Day after the anniversaries of Kennedy's assassination. Anniversaries work to get out the word, but they must be annual if they are to build the kind of irrational, somewhat sentimental attachment to them that transcends the generations and sustains it over the years.

10. Jonathan Deaton, "Joining the Conversation About Nuclear Weapons," a four-minute documentary film, winner of the 2015 Nukebusters Film Competition, sponsored by the Physicians for Social Responsibility (PSR). First prize, awarded to Deaton, was $5,000. Like the films of Errol Morris, Academy Award winner in 2004 for *The Fog of War*, the filmmaker is off screen posing questions for those on screen, and commenting on what they say. Also like Errol Morris, Deaton's set is disarmingly simple: two stools and a plain, off-white background. Deaton also shares with Morris a sharp eye and ear for cutting into, and out of, the various conversations he films, giving a powerful impression that what we are really seeing is one integrated conversation, rather than several.

11. NSquare is a $2.4 million investment by five foundations known for their interest in reducing the nuclear threat, led by the MacArthur Foundation, and its program officer, Emma Belcher. Eric Schlosser's comment is in the opening frames of NSquare's "Wondros Film," made for the TED organization: https://vimeo.com/wondrosglobal/review/184784643/31cac69751.

12. Chapin Boyer, "Why Young People Think Nuclear Weapons Are History," *Bulletin of the Atomic Scientists*, March 11, 2016, available at: http://thebulletin.org/why-young-people-think-nuclear-weapons-are-history9229. If Chapin Boyer is correct: the missing

element is visceral fear of nuclear weapons—like, this terrible thing really could happen right now, and we can't live under this mushroom cloud forever. With fear in very short supply among millennials, most of the efforts currently being made (at least that we are aware of) have little chance of recruiting millennials to the cause of nuclear abolition. Kids in Miami might worry about how long before their city is underwater. Kids in Flint, Michigan, might be afraid of drinking the city water. Kids in New Orleans may worry about the next big storm. And kids in many high schools in America may be afraid of gun violence inside their schools. But fear of nuclear war? No. It's too abstract, too far out in the periphery of their interests and concerns. Boyer's brilliant insight is to nail the reason why his entreaties to his fellow millennials fell on deaf ears. What needs to happen is to invert a message seen on many T-shirts a decade or two ago: "NO FEAR!" What is needed is good old-fashioned, reality-based, behavior-shaping, long-term-sustaining, intense *fear* of Armageddon on a regular basis, say once a year, every October 27th.

Annual Black Saturday remembrance has the potential to produce exactly this commodity because, in the event, fear and anxiety veritably oozed out of the pores of people all over the world, from the three most involved heads of state, to foot soldiers, to people watching the crisis unfold on black-and-white TVs with big wooden cabinets and tiny, fuzzy screens. The fear doesn't need to be invented; it needs to be *restored!* We don't need to feel invented fear, we need to feel some significant portion of the fear that our fellow human beings actually felt, in real time, when they feared the gig was up and it was curtains for the human race. Fear wasn't hypothetical; fear was uncomfortably real.

13. Arthur M. Schlesinger Jr., "Foreword" to Robert F. Kennedy, *Thirteen Days: A Memoir of the Cuban Missile Crisis* (New York: Norton, 1999), 10. (1969).

14. Although many of Kahneman and Tversky's examples come from everyday life, their own writing is often opaque. In fact, we think the very best place to break into their way of thinking is in a brilliant evocation of their decades-long intellectual partnership, by Michael Lewis, *The Undoing Project: A Friendship That Changed Our Minds* (New York: Norton, 2017). Lewis embeds the revolution Kahneman and Tversky created in a joint biography of these two fascinating people: two Israeli-American psychologists, both veterans of several stints in the Israeli Defense Forces, including twice during combat operations, in the 1967 Six Day War and the 1973 Yom Kippur War. They set out to prove that the fundamental assumption underlying the so-called science of economics—that human behavior can be understood as basically rational, no matter how irrational it sometimes seems—is upside down by showing that we are not rational, but our irrationality occurs in patterns that can be discovered via empirical research. We are, they discovered, reliably irrational. That could be your phase-one entry into the universe of Kahneman and Tversky.

Phase two—if you get that far, but don't worry if you don't—should be Kahneman's marvelous 2011 *magnum opus, Thinking Fast and Slow* (New York: Random House, 2011). The book is chock full of insights and is written for a general audience. If the idea of a "heuristic" is new to you, Kahneman's book can help. "The technical definition of *heuristic*," he writes, "is a simple procedure that helps find adequate, though often imperfect, answers to difficult questions. The word comes from the same root as *eureka*" (98). In one of Kahneman's examples, if I am presented with the question, "How much would you contribute to save an endangered species?" I may actually (though unconsciously) choose to answer a heuristic question that has more meaning for me, such as, "How much emotion do I feel when I think of dying dolphins?" (Ibid., 98).

15. Daniel Kahneman, "Bias, Blindness and How We Truly Think (Part 4)," *Bloomberg View*, October 27, 2011, available at: https://www.bloomberg.com/view/articles/2011-10-27/bias-blindness-and-how-we-truly-think-part-4-daniel-kahneman.

16. Daniel Kahneman, "Personal Stories Have More Impact." Interview with Eric Schurenberg, on Inc.com, available at: https://www.inc.com/daniel-kahneman/idea-lab-personal-stories-more-impact.html.

17. On the method of critical oral history, see James G. Blight and janet M. Lang, *The Fog of War: Lessons from the Life of Robert S. McNamara* (Lanham, MD: Rowman & Littlefield, 2005), 2–25. See especially 8–13 for critical oral history's FAQ.

18. T. E. Lawrence, *The Seven Pillars of Wisdom*, was published privately by Lawrence in 1922. This is Lawrence's personal account of his participation with Arab insurgents' efforts to separate themselves from the Ottoman Turkish Empire during World War I. The book is controversial: many have noted that is written in the form of a memoir but should be taken as a work of fiction. However that may be, the book has an almost hypnotic charm, so allusive is the language and so vivid are the characters. The book is available online at: http://www.limpidsoft.com/small/sevenpillars.pdf.

19. The phrase *theater of the real* comes from John Le Carre's novel *The Little Drummer Girl* (New York: Knopf, 1983), 95–108. Israeli intelligence operatives are seeking to recruit a British actress as a means of finding and executing a Palestinian, Khalil, who has been blowing up Israeli diplomats in Europe. The woman, Charlotte, is called "Charlie," and she must learn everything possible about Khalil's brother, Michel. Charlie is to contact Khalil after Michel's death, via Khalil's organization, claiming that she was Michel's lover. When the contact is made, the Israelis (who will be following Charlie) plan to kill Khalil. Charlie is reluctant, but in an intervention by the Israeli team's chief, Marty Kurtz, she is told that she has an unprecedented opportunity to step into "the theater of the real." But he warns: "Do not confuse our play with entertainment, Charlie. . . . There's no squeamish pulling back from the harsher scenes, no days off sick. It's peak performance all the way down the line" (107–8).

20. Public Papers of the Presidents of the United States. John F. Kennedy, *Containing the Public Messages, Speeches, and Statements of the President*, January 1 to November 22, 1963. United States Government Printing Office, Washington: 1964, 316. See also https://www.jfklibrary.org/Research/Research-Aids/JFK-Speeches/Nuclear-Test-Ban-Treaty_19630726.aspx.

21. Yes, even Castro became an abolitionist by the end of his long life. See James G. Blight and janet M. Lang, *Armageddon Letters*, 233–38, and endnotes 7 and 8 on page 274, for the story and documentation of Castro's embrace of nuclear abolition.

22. Thomas S. Kuhn, *The Structure of Scientific Revolutions* (Chicago: University of Chicago Press, 1962), 111.

23. Kuhn made liberal use of optical illusions from gestalt psychology as metaphors for paradigm shifts, resulting in scientific revolutions. One favorite was the rabbit-duck illusion: whether you begin, so to speak, on "Planet Duck" or "Planet Rabbit," once you see both for the first time you cannot *not* see it that way again, each time you look at it (Wikimedia Commons, public domain, https://commons.wikimedia.org/wiki/File:Duck-Rabbit_illusion.jpg).

24. Kuhn, *Structure*, 111.

25. Laura Prudom, "Showtime Developing Cuban Missile Crisis Limited Series from 'Godfather' Producer," *Variety*, April 5, 2016. Read the full story about the series inspired by our book, *The Armageddon Letters*: http://variety.com/2016/tv/news/armageddon-letters-showtime-limited-series-cuban-missile-crisis-1201746508/.

26. Emily St. John Mandel, *Station Eleven* (New York: Harper, 2014).

NOTES TO EPILOGUE

1. R. Queen, *Darkchylde: The Ariel Chylde Saga* (Curiosity Quills Press, October 2016). The author began this series in 1996 as a comic book, which was wildly successful, even

outselling many of the Marvel Comics at the time. This book is the first young adult novel to derive from the comic series. (The author is listed as "R. Queen" on the comics and books but as "Randy Queen" in interviews with the media.) The basic plot line concerns a girl whose nightmares become real, requiring a plethora of close calls, last-minute rescues, and victories achieved against the odds—the usual Marvel Comic–like fare, but with a female heroine who, it must be said, is not dressed for winter weather. Marvel Comics meets Victoria's Secret. We take our epigraphs where we find them.

2. Cormac McCarthy, *The Road* (New York: Vintage, 2006), 3.

3. Ibid., 6.

4. The film version of *The Road,* based on Cormac McCarthy's Pulitzer Prize-winning novel, appeared in November 2009, directed by John Hillcoat and written by Joe Penhall and starring Viggo Mortensen as Papa and Kodi Smit-McPhee as The Boy. The score is by Australian alt-rocker Nick Cave and Warren Ellis, and it perfectly complements the raw bleakness of the post-apocalyptic landscape inhabited by Papa & The Boy. Dimension Films distributed the movie. In a film review, Joe Morgenstern of the *Wall Street Journal* wrote that the film requires you to "hang on to yourself for dear life, resisting belief as best you can in the face of powerful acting, persuasive filmmaking and the perversely compelling certainty that nothing will turn out all right" ("'Road' Is Paved with Bleak Inventions," *Wall Street Journal,* November 27, 2009).

5. See endnote 1 above.

INDEX

ABOUT THE AUTHORS

James G. Blight and janet M. Lang were trained as cognitive psychologists. But in the mid-1980s, provoked by the nuclear war scare arising between the U.S. and Russia, they became involed in the Avoiding Nuclear War Project at Harvard's Kennedy School of Government. They have written or co-written fourteen books on the history of U.S. recent foreign policy, seven of them on the Cuban missile crisis.

Their work highlights the views of "the other side," and documents the risks that ignorance of "the other side" poses for U.S. foreign and defense policy. They served as principal advisers on Errol Morris' 2004 Academy Award-winning documentary, *The Fog of War.* Their short films on the Cuban missile crisis, live action and animated, are on their YouTube channel: https://www.youtube.com/user/armageddonletters.

In *Dark Beyond Darkness,* they take their readers to Cuba (*the history*) to experience the dread that is as applicable now as then (*the warning*), before suggesting a paradigm-shifting path to long-term action toward nuclear abolition (*the catalyst*).

Jim and janet are professors in the Department of History and the Balsillie School of International affairs at the University of Waterloo. (Note: the lower case "j" in janet's name is not a misprint. That is how she spells her name. The upper case "J" in Jim's name is also not a misprint. That is how he spells his name.)

The authors have been married for forty-one years.